Yashodhara

Princess Who Loved The Buddha

Yashodhara

Princess Who Loved The Buddha

Kusum Kapoor

GenNext Publication

Published by

GenNext Publication
5, Ansari Road
Daryaganj, New Delhi-110002
Phone: 011-47034999, 9811692060
E-mail: gennextpublication@hotmail.com

Distribution Network
gyanbooks.com
India, USA, Canada, UK, Australia, France

ISBN: 978-93-5663-513-5 (HB)

First Published, 2023

Printed at: Gyan Press, Delhi.

YASHODHARA: PRINCESS WHO LOVED THE BUDDHA
Author: KUSUM KAPOOR

In Memory of

SURAJ KAPOOR

My loving husband

Contents

Foreword

This is a fiction based on facts. A story about Yashodhara, Prince Siddhartha Gautama's chief queen. In this book neither the Buddha is a God as the Mahayanists and some Hindus (as Vishnu's incornation) make him out to be nor is his wife, a shadow. They both have been transformed to humans of flesh and blood, capable of having all kind of emotional frailties, felt by the suburban elites of seventh century BC, of north India.

Yashodhara comes out of obscurity full of glory but suffers the fate of queen Sita, wife of Kaushal king Rama, of the past.

Yashodhara and Siddhartha, both had to sacrifice their deep bond of love for the sake of their near and dear ones. Women are unique. For them, separation from their beloved is like dying before their death. Her husband left his parents and four* or more loyal wives for the benefit of the entire Shakya community.

Ancient women of India, fought, hunted, and led nomadic lives, shoulder to shoulder with their men. Who were, the worshippers of the black mother; Ma Kali, and they were capable to fend for themselves against all kind of evils. Great archers, who bore children, living in the dangerous world of the past. Slowly and gradually, as the nomads settled, their women got domesticated. Manu's Law started being rigidly followed till after the formation of guilds, when it got converted into fixed caste system where the Brahmans dominated.

Yashodhara comes from the Koliaya clan, a sub branch of the Kaushal Shakyas who were the precursors of the Mauryas. They were followers of primitive culture, where the goddesses were worshipped instead of gods. The proud tribe didn't much care for the superiority of the Brahman class yet tolerated them for the sake of the masses.

Bold, intelligent, well-read, beautiful yet assertive, Yashodhara won Siddhartha's heart and then lost it. When she realised that he carried a broader picture in mind for his future; of evoking wisdom in the misled masses carrying the weight of centuries old erroneous beliefs, she painfully let him go.

Prince Siddhartha, the heir apparent to the throne of Kapilvastu was prophesied to become a world famous religious leader. His father never let him receive any formal religious education yet he could recite the Rg Veda shlokas on his own, by listening to them here and there. He was shielded from all miseries of life. Yet King Shuddhodan could not defeat his destiny.

Prince left home at the age of twenty nine and matured into a great thinker, philosopher and social reformer. Which makes it a probability that he was sent to Taxila for higher studies, like most of the elite children of that period. I have taken the liberty of using the many hypothetical assumptions by famous scholars into the story. My sources are mostly secondary; translations of ancient texts; mostly Sanskrit, and other books by English or Hindi authors. Most words are spelled according to Sanskrit pronunciation and not Pali language. Other spellings used are from the Queen's English and not American.

The story about Siddhartha leaving the palace without his family's prior knowledge has been proven wrong by the ancient texts, but why he did leave at all has many versions. Here I came up with my original idea. According to my assumption he did so; along with other factors, for two reasons. One that it would be against the interests of Shakya Republic and second, if he did not agree with the oligarchical cabinet on every self destructive decision, his father might get expelled from his throne.

An authentic historical background is used to create the right milieu. Yashodhara's story runs on the borderline of realistic assumptions. Because there is hardly much written in the ancient texts, about her. Gautama couldn't have achieved his greatness without the thoughtful upbringing of Mahaprajapati, his mother and support of Yashodhara, his Chief Queen.

I have tried to sketch her life after studying social, cultural and religious conditions of her period. The same goes for other characters. The basic plot is based on the translations of ancient texts. But sincere effort is made to infuse life into it to make it a living legend.

Her one achievement seems to me that by gathering of women in their garden in a circle to discuss Buddha's ideas, she sowed the seeds of Mahayana Buddhism.

There is nothing in the story which is far fetched or unimaginable in regard to the data available.

Characters

Yashodhara – The Koliyan Princess – also known as Bhadrakanchan

Siddhartha Gautama – The Buddha, The Enlightened One or Tathagat

Rahul – Yashodhara's son

King Shuddhodan – Siddhartha's father

Queen Maya – Biological mother of Siddhartha

Queen Mahaprajapati – Maya's sister; Siddhartha's mother who brought him up

King Suprabuddha – Yashodhara's father

Queen Amita – Yashodhara's mother and Shuddhodan's sister

Yashodhara's childhood friends – Renu, Rohini, Surma, Ganga

Malti – Yashodhara's wet nurse and carer

Bhanumati – Yashodhara maid-in-waiting at Kapilvastu

Mrigi, Gopa and Utpalvarna – Junior wives of Siddhartha

Asitadev – The Royal Chaplain at Shuddhodan's court

Kaludayin – Asita's son and Buddha's friend

Mahanaam – Nephew and Prime Minister of Shuddhodan

Aniruddh – Mahanaam's brother

Shuddhodan's other brothers – Dhrotodan (wife – Mangala), Amritodan (wife – Vibhawari), and Ghanitodan.

Nand and Sundarinanda – Prajapati's son and daughter

Anand – Mrigi and Siddhartha's son and his disciple.

Sihahanu and Canchan – Siddhartha's grandparents.

Prasenjit – Kaushal King; Mahakaushal: his father, Vrudhabha: Prasenjit's son

Manudev and Chandrasen – Chiefs of Vaishali.

Bimbisar, Ajatshatru and Udayabhadra – three generations of Magadhan kings.

Bandhul – Prasenjit's friend and Senapati General.

Sage Kashyap, Acharya Kaundinya, Maudgalyana and Shariputra– Gautama's steadfast disciples.

Devdatta – Gautama's cousin, disciple and adversary.

Angulimal – a serial killer and disciple.

Sujata and Swasti – Uruvilva villagers. Sujata offered him 'kheer'.

Hieun Tsiang and Shi Banto – Chinese Pilgrims.

Chapter - 1

Seventh Century Nalanda

A THIRSTY SOUL IN SEARCH OF LIGHT,
PLUNGED INTO THE DESERT, EAST TO WEST
WHERE BUDDHA HAD DWELT HE CAME TO SEE,
KAPILVASTU AND THE BODHI TREE

The sun had risen up in the sky above the massive Nalanda university. Kokilas[1] were cooing in the shady mango groves nearby where once the Sramana[2] Buddha preached his following while his wife Yashodhara lived at the Kapilvastu Palace, hoping that her husband might still return to her.

The two guards at the gigantic main gates, were fiddling with a jangling bunch of keys to deal with an antique iron lock. Their long-faded robes swayed in the early morning breeze as their venture was complete. Their shaved heads were shining in the sun when they let in the team of sweepers waiting outside with their brooms, pails, and mops. They soon got busy sweeping the eight extensive compounds surrounded by high red-brick-walls, over which red clusters of perennials hung on heady vines. Manicured lawns were dotted with blossoming beds of different hewed flowers. Which were being watered by the gardeners. The green grassy patches were intercepted by various water bodies where white, pink, or blue lotuses were blooming and snowy swans sailed majestically emitting blithe sounds, as the dark ducks dawdled away circling the fanned-out lotus leaves, pecking!

The sweepers finished their business by noon and walked back towards the Nalanda village in vicinity. Herds of cattle were grazing in the

1. Cuckoos
2. Wandering ascetics. The Sramanas had their origin traced to the Indus valley. Sramanas later had rejected the authority of the Vedas and Brahamanas and complicated rituals for genuine investigations and logic, like the Buddha.

meadows mowing and nibbling at the grass, attended by poor boys. One of them was taking five water-buffaloes for a bath in one of the four rivers[1] flowing through the district singing a song in Bhojpuri, the local language. One such fellow by the name Swastik had inspired the Buddha to write his sutra on "Tending water buffaloes." The youth when twenty was given ordination.[2]

A lad with only a cloth wrapped around his waist was playing a flute sitting under a tree. The sound permeated through the serene, sunny ambience.

The north - eastern village of Nalanda was on the main trade route[3], which always use to be busy due to travellers, students, pilgrims, businessmen and foreigners from Japan, China, Indonesia, Myanmar and other eastern countries who wore strange clothes and spoke in unfamiliar tongues. A group of Buddhist monks in ocher loose clothes was treading the path quietly and calmly.

The highway was punctuated by water-huts and fresh farm fruit-vendors on the two sides. A bullock cart rattled by and the sound of folk songs sung at the weddings was heard in coarse female voices. Their colourful saris puffed up in the air like, sales. Traders rode in chariots while children played in the fields. The long procession of Bhikshus from Bodh Gaya, a city nearby, was following the two Chinese on the horsebacks, who were musing about their journey so far.

The elder Chinese recalled reaching the kingdom of Agni or Yanqi, in the Central Asia, at the base of Flaming Mountains, which was a Buddhist stronghold. He told his companion, "The benevolent king of Yanqi was so impressed by my divine knowledge that he provided me with all kind of help for my onward journey. On the condition that when I get back I'll teach him and his people, Buddhism for three years." He reminisced further, "It was actually the idea of his uncle Gyanchander and his precept Mokshagupta! The country had more than ten monasteries following Hinayana Buddhism and their scriptures were in a script somewhat similar to that of Hindus. But, do you know the most valued gift he gave?"

"No Master. What?"

"He commissioned an officer well versed in Mandarin and other Central Asian Languages to accompany me till the Iron Gate."

"You are so right. It was most useful to have him with us. As far as the monasteries are concerned I am familiar with the place since I use to keep

1. Phalgu, Mohane, Jirayan, Kumbhari.
2 Kulgopalaka Sutra, Mahagopalaka Sutra and Tripitaka 123.
3. Uttarpath, the northern highway.

coming on trips as a middleman to deliver silk to merchants on behalf of my master, but when I heard your talk at King Qu Wentai's court I forgot everything else. I transferred my responsibilities to a friend and decided to follow you till my last breath," informed the youth.

The good looking Mentor looked at the jumpy little fellow with a round face and even rounder eyes, full of fire, along with a bifurcated upper lip. However, loyalty and a thirst for knowledge were oozing out of every pore of his strong physique. He found him adorable. But said nothing.

*****

The two had ridden their horses followed by the mules laden with useful gifts from the king of Yanki, and his troops for their protection. They were using the masks and gloves to ward off sand and cold. Another present from the benevolent ruler.

After a hectic and tediously long journey they had reached the Turkic Khanate before the famous Iron Gate. The powerful ruler after receiving the letter of introduction from the Yanki king, Qu Wen tai, had given them a warm welcome. The tough Khan also returned the troops sent by the king, and let his own men follow the famous monk Hiuen Tsiang in his journey onwards.

After crossing the Iron Gates, the group reached 'Roof of the world', known as 'Bam-i-Dunya' by the Persians. These Pamir Mountains of central Asia are one of the highest ranges of our world. Where the cold wind blows with a piercing vehemence.'[1]

They had crossed the Amu Daria River on a huge raft with their horses and troops, arriving at Termez, where they had encountered a locality of more than a thousand Bhikshus. Exhausted and starving, they were welcomed at one of the monasteries and given shelter.

Well-rested after their arduous journey the Guru and the disciple had proceeded towards east through Kunduz to go to Balkh (Modern Afghanistan) to see the Buddhist sights and relics. Then, moved further to see the rock carved Bamiyan[2] Buddha statues which were a sight to behold.

From the capital of Kapisi[3] they moved to Adinapur. That is when their companions of the Khan's cavalry left them and went back.

1. Trans. -Li Rongxi
2. Bamiyan in Central Afghanistan
3. Regional capital, North of Kabul. * Pamir range (1), Situated in Gorno-Badakhshan was a significant center of Buddhism. It was at the border of India (now Pakistan) and Afghanistan. It is the region of Bamiyan Buddhas where the Taliban and Al Quaeda grew.

The 33 years old, famous Chinese scholar from China was followed by the local monks to visit Nalanda Temple. The younger Chinese was named Shi Banto and known as Monkey King, back home. He was short and stout with round eyes embedded deep in his puffy cheeks. His upper lip gave him a distinctive appearance.

After trotting quietly on the north road of Hind, the mentor spoke to his companion, again.

"Well Monkey, look at those distant, dim, spires; we are about to reach our destination."

Shi Banto looked at his master dressed in a fawn silken robe, another gift from the King of Yanqi,[1] and answered – "Yes Sir, after near death experiences of the four years of formidable journey. Including 'The Land of Pashtuns,' where everything had become blurry during the snowstorms and menacing robbers appeared from behind the tall rocks from nowhere."

"But the Turk guards fought them off. Didn't they?"

"No doubt they did! But prior to that, there was nobody to fight the deserts of shifting sands, scorching heat and ferocious winds which were as bad as the snow storms and land-slides of the treacherous mountains. Weren't they? Besides it is such a long land-route[2] from *Changan, the capital of Tang Dynasty* to Hind."

"Yes! And dicier for me because travelling outside the country of Tang (China) was forbidden by Emperor Gaozong, without a permit. It is only during the famine when the crops withered and died that people were allowed to leave, but banned from going towards the west, the enemy area.

I was risking arrest at every step. I walked by night and hid myself during the day. My two companions left me but help came from unexpected quarters. A Tartar from Steppes assisted me after I reached the western end of the great wall to cross the first master toll-gate. I was captured by the guards but The Commander, a Buddhist supported me. He warned me though, "Beware of the short cut you are planning to take to avoid the other four Beacon Towers. It goes through the Gobi Desert, an unforgiving land; illusions are caused due to thirst if you lose your way or water."

"I was given a chestnut horse who knew the Gobi desert well, and a goat skin bag full of clean water along with food. In fact, my horse saved my life."

"You survived because your cause was noble Master."

"The purpose of my pilgrimage is not to obtain personal offerings. It

1. Modern name, Turpan – town on the Silk Road (old name Yanki or Agni)
2. The Silk Road. By: Zuanzang (Translator: Li Yung-shi).

is that, I regretted my country was following imperfect Buddhist doctrine and the scriptures were incomplete. Having many doubts, I wished to go and find out the truth, and so I decided to travel to Hind in the west, at the risk of my life in order to seek the Buddhist teachings of which I have only heard. So that the Dew of Mahayana sutras would not have been sprinkled only at Kapilvastu but the sublime truth may also be known in the eastern country."

"You took on your hands a great mission. But wasn't the desert, real threat?"

"Yes. There were no birds, animals or grass visible in the barren land. With the horizon stretching forever; swirling hot winds in the day and deathly cold at night."

"I can imagine your appalling experiences but after crossing the famous Sindhu River, you felt that you have literally dived into the 'Land of the Hindu,' I mean 'Yindu', as you like to call it!"

"I sure do because that to me, seems the right pronunciation." "Remember, at Takshakshila, the capital of Gandhara[1] you told me that it was the first University of the world founded, by King Rama's brother Bharat, for his son, Takshak."

"Yes, According to the history of the place, Prince Bharat had moved from Ayodhya to Gandhara. Unfortunately at the valley of Purushpura (Modern Peshawar in Pakistan now), Buddhism and Hindu Shahis were declining in influence and Islam was gaining strength. It made me feel so sad ?"

"It sure is terrible for the followers of Buddhism and Hinduism! How far was King Rama's kingdom from Takshakshila?"

"I believe Ayodhya the capital of Saket or Kaushal kingdom at that time was 100-200 Li* from there."

"Why the stone statues of Buddha at Gandhara have only one style of curly hair and flowing garments with folds?"

"Due to the Greek and Roman influence left by Alexander The Great and the Kushans who came later and also believed in Buddhism.[2] King Kanishka administered the fourth Buddhist Council in Kashmira."

"You know it all Master!"

"Not really son. I didn't know that human sacrifice was still prevalent in some places of Yindu Land. And I would never forget the appalling

1. Taxila state had become a colony of Kashmir by seventh century (631 – AD). * A modern Li is half a km. (500 m.) * From chronicles, coins and stone inscriptions.
2. Style of Greco/Roman origin flourished during Kushan period.

experience we went through after being abducted by robbers who were also Ma Kali's worshippers."

Hiuen Tsiang then kept quiet for a long time. Banto did not disturb his reverie.

*****

After crossing the Ganga River the two pilgrims had been planning to move towards Kingdom of Udayana (Kashmir). On the way they stopped under a tree and unloaded the mules to let them graze on the vast grassland. The mentor settled himself against a thick tree trunk with closed eyes, in relief. 'At last I am sitting on the Buddha-Land.' What he didn't realise that it was also the country of myriad Hindu gods and goddesses. The main being 'Shakti' or the cosmic power of energy, intelligence and fertility. The dark mother demands blood, according to its practitioners, only then she becomes powerful enough to fructify the desires of devotees.

At the Kingdom of Udayana, Hiuen Tsiang was received by the king and important Buddhist monks. He found the valley, cold but with calm winds. A contrast after whisking winds around the Silk Road. They were on the move again, after two years, crossing the Great Palasha forest.

Trotting on their mules they were admiring the beautiful flame coloured 'Tesu' flowers and discussing their medicinal properties when some voices were heard from behind. They looked back and saw a group of dark skinned tribals passing by. The tourists were about to relax again when in a flash they found themselves surrounded by them. The robbers bound them up and took charge of their belongings. Their chief looked them over to decide if one of them was a good specimen, to thank the goddess for the loot! They jabbered among themselves excitedly and after tying the master's hands with a rope, they turned left and pushed him forward on a dirt road. Shi Banto tried to fight them off but he was outnumbered. There was a temple gong clanging faintly, at a distance. As the group moved towards the sound, ignored disciple tagged behind them ever alert for an opportunity to free his Master.

They were entering a cluster of trees. Hidden by those, near a dry pond was an ancient temple made of stone blocks with a curvilinear shaped Shikhara or roof- tower. A red triangular flag was fluttering at the tip. After the Antarala, the foyer there was The Garbhagriha or the sanctum where a Black, glossy Goddess with eight arms, holding various weapons, stood on a pedestal. Looking ferocious, with her bloody tongue hanging out. Under her one foot was the demon Raktabija whom she had killed by licking his blood. Her wide open eyes were threaded red, expressing her wrath. Her dark tresses were lose and flowing. In the ante-chamber was a black stone on the floor, with a grove in the centre, splattered with dried up blood. Banto shivered in his skin.

The senior priest started chanting mantras circumambulating around the idol. Sacred Ganga water was poured over the older Chinese from a pitcher while helpless Banto watched with horror. And soon a marigold garland adorned his pale neck. A hefty man came with a machete at the tip of which a lemon was stuck beforehand. The priest with a shaved head and a central tuft of long string of hair, plucked the lemon off and cut it with the machete to sprinkle its juice around. Orange vermilion and yellow turmeric powders were dusted on the blade. While this was going on, a humming chant was permeating the chilling ambience. The priest kneeled in front of the Deity and marked his own forehead with 'bhaboot', ash from a crematorium.

Some vermillion was smeared on the blazing forehead of the man to be sacrificed like a goat.

"Kneel in front of the Warrior Mother and place your neck on the sacrificial alter." The sacrificing priest thundered to Hieun Tsiang. "You are lucky to be chosen by her. You shall straight go to heaven."

Horrified Shi Banto was rooted to the ground just like the statue, as the demons of fear squeezed his heart. Calm Hiuen Tsiang was focused on praying.

As the stout priest raised his machete to sever the head from the body in one blow, there was thunder and lightning in the sky. Strong winds started blowing and whooshing. A dust storm rose heavily. The sandy dust blew in and blinded everyone. Banto jumped forward and grabbed his master. Freeing his hands he pulled him against the wind and started running, loosing his sense of direction.

Exhausted they stopped and found themselves at a village. The storm had abated. A Brahman was tilling his farm. Hiuen Tsiang asked for help.

'The farmer goes to the village-center and beats a drum and blows a conch. Loud and long. About eighty men gather and start their search for the robbers,'* who had disappeared in fright, thinking that Hiuen Tsiang was a holy man so the Goddess was angry. The mules were found grazing nearby along with their belongings. While the pilgrims wondered at the miraculous escape. They were fed by the locals, when the dense clouds above, split opened and the benign sun smiled at them.

*****

* From English trans. Of Hieun Tsiang's travelogue.

Hiuen Tsiang's mind came back to the highway going towards Nalanda. They needed to make a turn. He looked at his disciple who was smiling, "Were you thinking about…the episode where I was spared due to my cleft upper lip."

The Master chortled, "Sometimes it's good to be a defective piece."

A gust of warm wind took their attention. The two, stopped chatting as they could see the tips of the ten temples of Mahavihara, where Shilabhadra, the elderly abbot who belonged to a royal family, eagerly awaited their arrival. He was hundred years old and had been suffering from a long illness. Dejected, he wanted to die but since he received the news that the famous Chinese scholar of Mahayana Yogachar Buddhism was coming to Nalanda for studies, his spirits revived. Nalanda, since fourth century had started declining in its brilliance and he was concerned.

It was summer-time and he did not want the visitors to get caught in the afternoon heat with blazing sun overhead.

As soon as Hiuen Tsiang and retinue entered the gates, some senior students and teachers came out as a welcoming comity and stood, flanking the path leading to the main hall. The scholars dismounted their horses, and removed their Chinese backpacks. The Master's was, embellished with a bell hanging in the front and a straw hat at the back. He wiped his sweaty forehead and bowed reverently in front of the abbot with folded hands, uttering, 'Namaskaram,' with a peculiar accent.

Shilabhadra was over-whelmed with tears of joy because he realised that this young scholar would further disperse the Holy law of Buddhist ideals outside Bharat (India). As the guests moved towards the entrance they were all showered with fragrant Jasmine flowers. The Chinese took off their footwear outside the ornate door where their feet were washed; and same way of the bare-footed bhikshus who had callouses on their soles. Some were bleeding and a salve was applied to their wounds. After freshening up they were offered seats and a sweet and salted lemon drink to take care of the dehydration, if any, before the meal.

After some formal conversations and a simple meal the tired travellers were led to their quarters amongst the dormitory meant for ten thousand students and two thousand teachers.

Those who still had the energy, were taken for a guided tour of the establishment by a student.

The visitors were told, "The original Buddhist temple was founded by King Ashoka the great, in the third century. Even at that time the institution was financially strong. Now since King Harshavardhan of Kanyakubja has donated the revenue of more than a hundred villages for its upkeep, there is no dearth of anything. The daily supply of rice, milk and butter is provided for the monks at his orders." And the young bhikshu guide became quiet since the visitors were busy looking at the four gigantic corner-towers piercing the skies, with awe.

As the dusk began to merge into the night, evening prayers were chanted by one and all in a spacious compound. The humming of positive energy was flowing in the ten directions of the monastery.

On the meadows outside, last of the cowherds were hastily returning home. The baby monkeys in the nearby mango grove clung to their mothers, chirruping and the twittering birds were returning and feeding their hungry chicks in their nests.

*****

Abbot Shilabhadra became Hiuen Tsiang's teacher for the next five years. And Banto along with his mentor learnt to read and write Sanskrit so that he could help him in translations of ancient Buddhist literature in Chinese. They were told that the famous Buddhist scholar Nagarjuna had started his studies at the same Vihara. He was the founder of 'Shunyawad,' philosophy of the void.

While his Master got busy in his study of the Buddhist ideals, Banto started his research on his chosen topic of Princess Yashodhara the wife of Bodhisattva[1] Siddhartha. There is a woman behind the success of a man, but Pali Canon undermined the importance of women in the prince's life. His mother, four queens and his dancing girls were all ignored. However, as Banto came to know that ancient Sanskrit literature had some validated stories to tell he went after those. Thus, while learning Sanskrit and Pali languages he also started writing about Yashodhara's life in his spare time. He would spend hours in the library on the ninth floor of the sprawled out building of staircases and courtyards and go through the palm-leaf manuscripts. His eyes would fill with tears when he read the princess wailing for her beloved, in pain.

Sometimes Banto liked to walk around the numerous temples of Nalanda Mahavihara, up and down the steps. The eighty feet tall Buddha at the 'Sarai Temple' was so fascinating that he could never get enough of it. He would often stop to observe and also, feel with his fingers the artistic figures of the Gupta period engraved on the sides of the stone-staircases. There were scenes depicted from the Jataka Tales.[2]

---

1 A person, in Mahayana Buddhism who is able to reach nirvana but delays doing so through compassion for suffering beings.

2. Stories about the Bodhisattva's previous life time.

He would see Yashodhara, sitting in a chariot holding on to her husband Siddhartha and Chandak, driving it. Her curvaceous body draped at the waist in a beautifully embroidered lower garment and her bosom covered with a soft material tied at the back. A stole was thrown on her upper body to save her modesty. The Prince was bare chested but wore a cloth covering his waist and legs and a diadem over head. His neck and chest were adorned by pearls, gold chains and necklaces. Chandak, the charioteer was a short muscular man of the same age as Siddhartha. He had grown up step by step with the prince until he was mature enough to replace his father as the prince's man servant. The horse pulling the chariot was the prince's favourite, named Kanthak. All four were co-natal. The driver being his half-brother whose mother was a concubine[1] in King Shuddhodan's 'ranivas'.[2]

'They all looked so happy together. When did everything turn upside down? And how?' thought Banto. His heart ached for Yashodhara who was an accomplished rider, wonderful archer, played the Veena and served the poor with compassion. She was tenacious and strong willed and yet…

One morning at dawn, Hiuen Tsiang stood next to the window of his cell. His disciple Shi Banto had been talking to him late the previous night and had fallen asleep on the floor, covered with a sheet by his mentor. Master's forehead were being caressed by the gentle breeze. The soaring tips of the temples outside were 'above the mists in the sky, witnessing the birth of the winds and the clouds,'[3] thought poetic Hiuen Tsiang.

He stood spellbound till the chirping of some sparrows broke his reverie. He turned around and looked at the sleeping youth effectionatly, and spoke in a raised voice, "Wake up O' sleeping beauty! Did you come all the way in knee-deep snow of the highest Pamir mountains to slumber in comfort?"

Banto sprang up with a start.

"Sorry master, I was having a lucid dream."

"About girls?"

"Sort of! I mean I was witnessing a beautiful dance performance by Amrapali, the most accomplished 'nagarvadu'[4] of Vaishali[5], fourteen hundred years ago."

---

1 Since that was the age for polygamy by the affluent to have more faithful sons.

2 According to the map of the excavated remains of Nalanda Mahavihara.

3 In Hiuen Tsiang's words.

4. Courtesan.

5. Capital of Vrjji towards east of Aryavrat (North India under the Aryans).

"Oh, I am so sorry to have woken you up and dragged you out of her 'swapna kakshika'."

"No! No! Master I wasn't in her bedroom, my focus was on Siddhartha and his new bride Yashodhara at their newly constructed 'Vishram Bhawan'.[1] There were royal guests being entertained by the famous dancer and looked after by Shuddhodan's chief queen, Maha Prajapati Gautami."

"How is your research going on?"

"There isn't much available about the women in Prince Siddhartha's life in the Buddhist Canons."

Hiuen Tsiang was thoughtful as the nascent sun cast its brilliance on his creased forehead.

"That's a poignant point son. Our societies hardly ever give credit to our women, whether it is Prajapati, Yashodhara or some Chinese lady of royal descent. Forget about the common women's fate! However, do not forget that after getting ready we need to join the morning prayer assembly."

"Yes master!" He said, getting up and folding his blanket. "But, I am determined to write her biography in Sanskrit and Chinese to bring her to life."

"Do that but don't fall in love with her. Or else you'll loose sight of how you want to flesh out her character realistically."

"I'll keep that in mind, sir."

*****

The Black Buddha[2]

Banto entered the small, secluded garden, surrounded by tall walls, adorned by clump's of red flowers on its two sides. A statue of Buddha in black stone was lending the spot a peaceful ambience. Placed on a platform the enlightened one sat in a 'Bhoomisparsha-Mudra'.[3] The red Kakaiya bricks[4] on the walls were making the black statue stand out in contrast. He sat on the stone covered floor in front of the Buddha, cross-legged and was thoughtful.

He closed his eyes and visualised his visit to Kapilvastu with his mentor, before reaching the eastern part of the country. He could imagine the vast expanse of the desolate city in crumbling ruins. Dust clouds

1. The Palace of Tranquility and repose.
2. The statue of Black Buddha was called 'Telia Bherava', by the locals. 'Tel' is oil, used as a protective coating.
3. A sitting posture touching the ground. *Description by Archeological Excavator —T.N. Mishra.
4. Clay bricks kilned in small size. 4/2\1 inch. The uni had their own kiln.

swirling around the remnants of the royal precinct of King Shuddhodan, Siddhartha's father. The strong foundations still held the brick-laid eroding walls, even after 1500 years, just like the Buddha's philosophy. However, the marble statue on the top floor of Queen Mayadevi, Buddha's mother was still there, though chipped, soiled and uncared for.

His mind then, flitted to a small town, Ramgram where they had seen a most amazing spectacle. Near a monastery they saw a special stupa. They took some flowers in a basket to pay tribute to it. As they were praying adjacent to it, a three feet long water snake slithered out of a nearby pond and without being bothered by their presence started circumambulating around it. Finishing its errand, it moved back to the pool.

Dumbfounded Banto had looked at Hiuen Tsiang. Who returned his glance saying, "Miracles never cease to happen. Do they!"

The disciple was too stunned to say anything. Besides their attention was drawn by a gigantic shadow approaching them. It was a white elephant devoid of any accouterments. Both men stepped backwards and wondered whether to run away, since it appeared to be a wild one! The mammoth drank some water from the pond and sprayed it out of his trunk on the stupa. Nonchalantly he picked up their basket and upturned it on the stupa sprinkling the blossoms as an offering and went his way.

Hiuen Tsiang had sat down on a boulder flabbergasted, to jot that incident down immediately in his travelogue.

Both pilgrims anon had crossed a forest to reach the temple of the reclining Buddha. The place of his Mahaparinirvana at the town of Kushavati (Kushinagara). It was drab, dull and dead. 'Human memory!' Banto thought with grief.

He once again tried to recall the tedious-sounding names of the cities ruled by the Shakyans, the rice-growing tribe. The names Kotihava and Niglhawa however were stuck in his mind because of the magnificent Ashoka pillars they had witnessed there. With Buddhist tenets engraved on the red sand stone in Brahmi Script. The pillars were presumably embedded eight feet underground.*

Next the image of the Eastern Gate of Siddhartha's home floated in front of his mind's eye. The ruins had a large square building next to the gate known as the 'Mahavinishkramana Dwar' or the auspicious doorway.** Probably used for the guards and ammunitions. When Prince Siddhartha

---

* Ashoka Pillars were seen by Hiuen Tsiang.

** According to Hindu belief if you go towards east you find spirituality; towards north, wealth; towards west, knowledge and towards south, death. 'Vastu Shastra.'

had walked past this doorway all the guards posted at the gate had fallen asleep. 'Did someone on Prince's secret command, add a sleeping potion to their food?'

Towards the north-western gate, they had witnessed the 'Samai Mai' or 'the Goddess of the Woods,' temple. Fragments of many sculptures were strewn about. This was near the northern wing of King Shuddhodan's palace. Banto was visualising his queens Mahamaya and Prajapati dressed in brocaded saris and stoles, followed by young lady attendants walking down the pathway bordered by Merigold flowers, to pray at the temple. Their anklets jingling and the large earrings jangling as the cool breeze played with their front-locks. The slanting rays of the morning sun brightening up their faces, while the birds chirped and cheeped in a welcoming melody.

The palace was going to be Princess Yashodhara's home after her marriage.

*****

Hieun Tsiang and Shi Banto had treaded the paved and broad roads adjacent to the Hamsavati palace of king Shuddhodan, his father. Some of these made from bricks and brickbats had edgings on both sides, and one hand thick embankment made from iron slag.

'Who drove in horse-driven chariots on those roads, apart from the dignitaries, the warriors on horses and the elites?' Banto thought. 'Could Princess Yashodhara be going for a drive with her royal husband!'

Suddenly he blurted out aloud.

"Why did such a perfect queen marry an austere person like Siddhartha?" "Because he wasn't austere since birth. He was quite lively like other children and lusty when young."

Banto looked around and saw his mentor smiling, he got up and questioned, "Really?"

"Yes. Whenever he was disturbed, he would run to his pleasure house and spend time with the dancing girls. He was very fond of them, as if they were his family. Do not keep thinking Monkey, start writing about Siddhartha's beloved." He advised.

"Sure, Master, I'll start tomorrow."

Both the Chinese scholars walked back towards the main building as temperature dropped and pleasant breeze brought to them the fragrance of Juhi.[1] They both took a deep breath. Hieun Tsiang spoke softly, "Nalanda has azure pool winds around the monasteries, adorned with the full-blown

1. Jasmine.

cups of the blue lotus; and the dazzling red flowers of the lovely kanaka hang here and there…"

Banto felt his heart melting in the poetic ambience. He did not want to throw a pebble, of even a word to disrupt the liquid silence of the moment.

Next morning after breakfast, instead of going to the library Banto again came downstairs and sat in front of Buddha's statue with his writing paraphernalia. He imagined Queen Yashodhara's stunningly beautiful face, her compassionate dazzling smile while Tathagat looked on with half-closed eyes. He started drawing her life in words. When the sunlight dimmed and jumped to the top of the walls, he gathered his writing material and left the shadowed ground.

*****

---

* Monkey King is a mythical figure. Some scholars believe the character originated from the first disciple of Hiuen Tsiang, Shi Banto. He was considered very powerful and could carry heavy mountainous stones on his shoulders. His inspiration comes from an amalgamation of Indian and Chinese culture possibly influenced by Hindu deity Hanuman.

* Hiuen Tsiang's travelogue was translated, by Renegrosset.

Chapter - 2

The Koliya Princess

A QUEEN WAS BORN WITH BONY LIMBS,
SILKEN HAIR YET HEART SO BOLD.
HER FATHER'S PRIDE, HER MOTHER'S CHARM,
SHE WALKED THE PATH WITH FIRM RESOLVE.

The small town of Devdah was situated at the foothills of Shivalik range of the Himalayas, sitting in the lap of beautiful natural surroundings. It was seventh century BC. River Bhagirathi snaked down the mountains, southwards and gave out a tributary, Rohini which dissected the land between Koliya and Shakya Kingdoms; east and west. Carrying with it the rich minerals and silt to make the regions fertile and prosperous. Even in comparison to the great kingdoms of Kaushal and Magadh. Where Kings Mahakaushal and Bimbisar ruled respectively. The two rivers continuing southwards, joined the Hiranyavati river, and then surrendered themselves into the loving arms of the holy Ganga.

Amongst the firs, pines, hemlocks and colourful rhododendrons of the forests, roamed beautifully striped Bengal tigers, wild elephants, wild water buffaloes and red pandas. White rumpled-vultures circled above in skies looking for dead meat with their sharp vision.*

It was the month of Vaisakh. The Lumbini garden between the two cities of Kaplivastu and Devdaha[1] was bustling with activities. The place

1. Lumbini was collectively maintained by the youths of the two republics. Mayadevi's father Anjana was the King of Devdah. His wife was Rummindei or Canchan, meaning beautiful woman. A rich householder had built a pleasure grove for recreation near Devdah, the capital city of Koliyas. The Queen was so fascinated by the garden that she asked her husband, "Please buy this for me." King Anjana replied, "I can't do that but I promise to get one made for you, even better than this." Thus, a different garden was created in a nearby spot,

was being swept clean and sprinkled with water. Arrangements were being made because Queen Mahamaya of Kaplivastu was visiting the park reserved only for women. There, on the trunk of a tree was carved a statue of Ma Bhawani, the Goddess of fertility.

A water reservoir with purple and pink lotuses always extended its helping hand to women in need of a dip. Melodious sounds of chirping birds were pleasing at dawn.

The queen was coming here to pray before going to Devdah for her first delivery. Her mother from Devdah was coming with a surgeon, a midwife and her women companions. So that she could escort her daughter back home. The child was overdue. Hence she was anxious about her. The only male in the gathering of women was the Ayurvedic surgeon sitting aloof with his surgical equipment in case he needed to provide his services, en route.

A tent was already erected for Queen Mahamaya to rest, along with her mother, sister and attendants. The doctor had seen her and told them, "The Honourable Queen has waited too long to go to Queen mother's palace. Let's see what Bhawani has in store for us."

As soon as Queen Maya lay in her temporary bed she dozed off with fatigue, while her mother, Rumindei, covered her with a sheet. An attendant squatted down in front of her watching the patient. The elderly one came outside and sat on the stone bench next to Prajapati, her younger daughter. The weather was warm but comfortable under the shady tree. They both sat together and heard the late afternoon stillness, to subdue the restlessness within. Unpredictably a wolf howled long and loud tearing the still air. Rumindei shivered and spoke, "Bad omen Praja."

"Ma, please think positive."

They heard Maya moan. Prajapati went inside, to find her sister still sleeping. Her full belly was going up and down with each breath under her red blanket. The sound of her breathing was music to her sister's ears, however laboured it may have been!

The faded evening broke from behind the trees as a dust storm hung in the air.

Maya woke up and after giving her some water Praja helped her freshen up. "Sister, I desire to walk a little."

---

with abundance of water resources and varieties of trees. Lotus flowers grew on land and in marshes with green meadows around it. The garden was named Rumindei and later it was distorted to Lummindei and much later Lumbini. Queen Rummindei's daughter Mayadevi was most probably, born there. * Some of these animals are extinct now.(geography net).

“Sure,” and she held her hand carefully.

“The bag has burst sis.” Maya whispered tragically.

Panic spread like wild fire. Outside the tent, the gynecologist came running. The female attendants surrounded her with an enclosure of sheets, while her sister supported her on her shoulder. Maya held the branch of a Sal tree with one hand and her swollen belly with the other.* A maid was sent to calm her mother down.

“Don’t worry Mother Queen, your daughter is very keen to have this baby. Ma Bhawani will help her.”

“So be it,”she uttered absentmindedly.

Maya screamed as she tried to push the baby out. Rumindei held the maid’s wrist. Tight.

The child who had been ten months in the womb was probably too big for the birth-canal. Sweat was streaming down queen’s pale face. The summer breeze was slowly wiping it away. Everyone waited full of anxiety as Maya’s mother dawdled hither and thither, with a worried expression.

The mid-wife lent the surgeon a helping hand with the sterilised instruments. One sheet was held between Maya’s face and the Vaidya’s. He asked the women to encourage Maya to try hard and push the baby out. He was extremely worried because Maya’s pulse was slowing down. He signaled to Prajapati and whispered, “The situation is grim, and the child’s neck is tangled up in the cord. It could be lacking fresh air; I have to cut open the Queen to bring the baby out and then stitch her back.”

“Won’t that be dangerous for her life?”

“Caesarean operations have been successful before when the woman is strong. Take a quick decision or we lose them both.”

Praja urgently talked to her mother and soon, Maya, under mild sedation, was washed, cleaned and an incision was made on the left side of her abdominal wall. A stream of red blood sprouted out. Once the enlarged, pink uterus was visible, its wall too was cut opened and stretched to save the new life.

The mid-wife cleaned the boy while the women banged a big brass round tray with a heavy ladle to produce a din to make the child strong against loud sounds of the wars, in future. The crying baby was wrapped-up in soft muslin and laid next to his unconscious mother who was being stitched by the vaidya. When she gradually came to, she looked dazed. Her searing pain somewhat subsided after looking at the wriggling, pink bundle of flesh and bones, next to her.

---

* In those days women delivered a child while standing.

At a distance a temple's gong was clanging on and on and the bellowing of conches was heard as the evening 'arati,' and prayers were in progress.

Queen Maya was made more comfortable against a tree with the help of pillows while she held her prince in her weak arms. The cavalry that had followed the chariots of Maya and her lady companions was told to inform King Shuddhodan about the good news. Two horse-riders shot towards Kapilavastu while the rest of the entourage got busy to arrange food for everyone.

The good news spread like a jungle fire. The city of Kapilvastu was drowned in an uproar of rejoicings. Drummers beat up, people deaf. The euphoria made them forget the caste taboos and everybody sang and danced together. Most were drunk by midnight. Next day,General amnesty was proclaimed by the court to let the convicts free from the jails.

More tents were put up since it was clear now that the royal family would spend some days at the Lumbini Forest. Too much of blood loss had made Maya anemic and feeble. The surgeon was on twenty-four hours duty, administering natural medicines, painkillers and antibiotics. Vegetarian healthy diet was provided. All were jubilant. And waited for the king to come and rejoice to see his heir kicking his feet.

The village-women had started coming with gifts for the prince, and sang songs of congratulations and blessings.

King Shuddhodan had reached from Kapilvastu Palace on a galloping steed, after hearing the long awaited news.

The breathless king sat next to his beloved wife, holding her limp hand before even looking at his precious crown prince. His jubilation at holding his future heir in his arms did not last long when he realised that the love of his life might be slipping away from his grasp forever. Clinging to a tiny straw of hope he handed over the child to Prajapati and took the nutritious cup of black gram and vegetable soup from her hands and held it at his wife's unwilling lips and smiled.

"You want to get up and go home soon, don't you? Drink this or I'll ask them to prepare chicken soup for you."

"No!" Her ailing voice faintly protested. "You know I am a staunch vegetarian." "I know sweetheart! So, drink this."

Each passing day faded his hopes of her recovery. A maid was whispering to another, "It is as if a flower in full bloom is wilting and withering away to waste."

The king talked to the Raj-Vaidya[1] in privacy, who explained to him, "Our Queen has just gone through a very complicated[2] childbirth. I tried my best but now all depends on God."

The surgeon bowed his head regrettably. If it would have been a harsh monarch he might have ordered him to be beheaded. Since tribal-chief Shuddhodan was a true republican who played by the rules, he did no such thing. He asked his treasurer that the doctor be paid for his labours. He thought, 'This is what Maya would like.'

The king was seen smiling when he faced his wife again yet was crying from within. Queen Maya couldn't hold on to the flimsy thread of her young life after seventh day.

The life at the beautiful garden suddenly screeched to a halt. And she passed away quietly while her husband was holding her frail hand, delicately. That day was silent as death. The fowl lost their voices as the women wailed; the breeze became suffocating and the flowers forgot to give out fragrance and drooped. The dark clouds of grief, burst and came pouring out of everyone's eyes.

Prajapati the king's junior wife had taken charge of the prince while preparations were going on for the funeral of the most kind and pure soul, Queen Mahamaya.

The bier, a bamboo ladder was cushioned with Kusha grass and covered with a cloth on which lay the much loved fragile queen; after being given her last bath by Rummindei along with Prajapati and covered with a red shroud, denoting that she died a 'suhagan,' leaving from the care of her loving husband. When, after being dressed up in a red brocaded sari, her hair-parting was filled by Shuddhodan with bright vermillion just as she use to perform the daily ritual after her bath, with loving pride. The women cried louder and flopped down on the ground beating their chest.

The funeral procession was led by Queen Mahamaya in her eternal sleep, never to wake up again, to look at her precious son. The bier was carried on four shoulders turn by turn by the closely related men. But morose Shuddhodan never left his post. King Anjana, Maya's elderly father straggled behind the bier with dried-up tears. Siddhartha's mother was cremated at the bank of Rohini river, under sandalwood logs, with

---

1. The Royal physician *doctors who had studied Embryology and Gynecology took care of pregnant women.
2. Abhinishkramana Sutra According to ancient text Maya's son was born from the left side of the abdomen. He couldn't come out through the vagina. Surgery was done during old days. According to Wendy Garling (Stars at Dawn p.60) and other earlier scholars Buddha was most likely a Caesarean section.

great sorrow, surrounded by Suprabuddha, her brother and other close relatives. The women had stayed behind.

'Was the infant prince imbibing everyone's pain of loss, as well as his own? Did he sense something was terribly amiss?' no one knew.

In the two cities straddling the Rohini River celebrations abruptly came to a halt. Devdah's King Suprabuddha, Maya's brother and queen Amita had also been blessed with a girl child, the same day the Prince was born. Yet the rejoicings stopped. However, though Maya's demise broke her husband's heart, yet he did not neglect his new-born. The little one was the only connection, he had left with his beloved Maya. Prajapati and Shuddhodan came back to Kapilvastu, in a royal chariot while his junior queen held the baby in her arms.* There was no procession following them. No bards were heard, all the way to the palace. Only sad clatter of the chariot wheels shattering the road while the hot wind blew dust in their faces.

Although Maya's sister had an infant son of her own named Nand, she handed him over to a wet nurse and took care of her sister's newborn.

Afterwards it had been decided by the nobles at the 'Sansthagrih' assembly that Prajapati was most suitable woman to bring up the crown prince.

*****

Inside the palace of Devdah, Chief Suprabuddha was bent over his infant daughter whispering in her ear her name, Bhadrakanchan. The name was calculated by the priest according to the position of the stars at the time of her birth. It meant the one who has complexion like gold. The queen and the maids watched with interest. One young girl was holding a bowl of a mixture of 'ghee', honey and curds prepared beforehand. Her father fed the baby, her first meal with a gold spoon, saying tender words, "I wish you grow up healthy, strong and gain knowledge of the Vedas, long life, prosperity and the protection of the goddess."

The baby gurgled and cooed, expressing her delight. He knew now his little girl would never forget his voice.

Anita gave him a languid smile and whispered, "Aren't we treating her just like a son?"

"She is more precious to me than a son, my first-born. Look at her lotus eyes and how she looks at me!"

---

* Bas relief.

Amita did not have the heart to tell him that newly borns could barely see, although they could hear. After the mother and child took their bath, the umbilical cord was buried in the garden. Ten days were supposed to be observed for purification of the parents. But after seven days the sad news of his sister Maya's demise had reached Chief Suprabuddha. Heart-broken he went to attend her cremation. And stayed there for thirteen days of mourning.

After forty five days Amita along with her husband and Bhadrakanchan left for Kapilvastu. They stayed with the bereaved family of her brother, Chief Shuddhodan till the Brahaman-Bhoj feast.

*****

After they returned to Devdah an auspicious day was fixed by the priest for horoscope of the princess to be read. The astrologer in presence of her relatives predicted, "Our princess would be intelligent, brave and proficient in many arts including dexterity in Martial Arts. She would be strong willed and marry a king."

To which Suprabuddha replied, "She is already a queen. My girl shall have all the luck in the world."

The astrologer was silent, as if a snake had just sniffed him. He did not want to spoil the king's exuberance by telling him anything further.

When the princess was four months old she was taken to the temple of Kuladevi.[1] Her head was placed towards the Goddess for her blessings.

The same day Prince Siddhartha was going through the same ritual, at Kapilvastu. But with a difference. Whenever his head was turned towards the idol he would cry and squirm till his kicking feet were towards the goddess. When his resistant howling grew louder, King Shuddhodan gave up because he couldn't stand his crying. Queen Mahaprajapati was glad too because she wanted to bring him up according to his instincts.

A maid whispered to another, "He doesn't want to bow his head to the goddess."

After visiting the Goddess, the heir of the throne was presented in the court for the benefit of all members of the assembly at the time of his naming ceremony.

---

1. 'Ancient India' by Jeannene Auboyer, p. 164.
   Tutelary Goddess. Belief in mother goddess was present in pre-Aryan cultures before a pantheon of Hindu Gods was created to represent the various aspects of the natural phenomena. This also proved the tribal nature of the republic. *Steven Collin's trans.-Aggnna Sutta: believed to have words spoken by Buddha.

The court priest studied the child, covered only in a silken sheet. His feet, as well his fingertips and the whorls on them were observed carefully. Asita Kaladevala then turned towards Shuddhodan's anxious face and announced in a joyful loud voice.

"This child has thirty two auspicious signs on his body. He will either rule over the people of a kingdom or, on the hearts of the whole world." A few astrologers were studying his horoscope, as the baby was busy sucking his big toe. Quite unaware of the rejoicings around him.

When the Royal Chaplain saw the fallen face of the King he added, "For those who rely on clan, the Kshatriya is the best in the world; (but) the person endowed with wisdom and (good) conduct is the best in the whole universe."*

*****

At Devdah when Princess Bhadrakanchan was six months old, the ceremony of 'Annaprsanna' was performed.

Chief Suprabuddha was sitting on a davenport next to his wife, who held the tiny Princess in her lap. Malti, her nurse-maid was holding a silver bowl with a mixture made up of rice, ghee, and honey. Her father fed his daughter joyfully, her first bite of solid food with his fingers. The pink tongue licked and slurped while a priest kept chanting Sanskrit shlokas.

Soon Bhadrakanchan was toddling around the seraglio courtyard pulling wheeled toys made up of burnt clay, wood, or ivory. Chariots, monkey, dolls and an elephant. Some times she would joyfully shake her silver rattler and feel proud of her musical creation.

Before the children were old enough to play outside in the garden, they stayed indoors and played in the courtyard and enjoyed hide and seek in the dark corners of the secret chambers of basement. Those were constructed for hiding the children and ladies in case of an enemy attack. There were also tunnels to be used as escape routes.

Malti, her wet nurse took care of Kanchan since she was a baby. She moved around her like a shadow and even slept in her room at night. She attended to the upkeep of her night-lamp, 'Ratnadweepa', a jeweled lamp that burned all night and protected the princess from demons and ogres.

The princess had sat in her lap screaming when during the ceremony of 'Karnchedan' her ear-lobes were pierced to save her from various diseases. At the age of three her education began.

Koliyas were an offshoot of the Shakya clan who usually called the chief of their tribe 'Maharaj' and the members of their oligarchic republic as 'Rajan.' Who were either governors of the smaller republics or, their adult family members. The seat of power lay at Kapilavastu, ruled by chief Shuddhodan. All the judicial and administrative matters were discussed at the 'Sansthagriha' or the Town Hall, in presence of their royal ladies. This moot[1] hall was situated in the centre of the city within Shuddhodan's fort.

Shakyas belonged to an indigenous non-Brahmanical society[2] and they considered Kshatriyas the warrior-class superior to the Brahmans or the scholars. Because they performed the most important task of protecting their people. Yet had to keep a priest in their court for presiding over various rituals, specially animal sacrifices to please their class and the superstitious public. This knowledge was beyond them.

The two cities of Devdah and Kapilvastu were fed by the constant stream of Rohini River which nurtured their farms but as the population grew, scarcity of water often led to dissensions between the farmers of the two cities. A dam was built to sort out the issue.

At some point of history, Shakyas and Koliyas had become vassals of the Kaushals. However, they were still the proud descendants of Ikshvaku[3] Dynasty with many great names to mention. Raja Harishchander of Kashi, Raja Ramchander of Ayodhya and twenty two out of twenty four Jain Tirthankaras also belonged to this lineage. The clan followed the solar calander, thus called Suryavanshi. Some priests also pointed the 'Chandra' (the moon) at the end of their names. Hence their faith in the Lunar calander as well.

Suprabuddha, and King Shuddhodan were relatives linked by inter- marriages. Queen Amita was the sister of Shuddhodan. Whereas Suprabuddha's two sisters were married to him and his third sister Mangala to Dhrotodan, King's older brother. The fourth one Vibhawari became the wife of Shuddhodan's younger brother, Amritodan. And the Fifth one got married to the youngest brother Ghanitodan.

There were four gates in the four cardinal directions of the palace. The main gate use to be decided upon, according to the horoscope of the owner of the house. Armed guards protected the four entrances, wearing their brown tunics, crimson sashes at the waist and matching turbans on a white uniform. Armed with lances and swords.

*****

Princess Bhadrakanchan was playing with her friends in the front

1. Shakyans also had a moot hall at Chatuma. Mallas of Khushinagar and Licchavis of Vaishali had their own Sansthagriha, or the moot halls.
2. After the Buddha period north-west was experiencing mixing of the emerging Brahmanical and ancient tribal cultures. Wendy Garling. pp. 19-20 – stars of Dawn.
3. Ikshvaku – Iksh means sugarcane.

palace garden. Whereas the boys were playing in the backyard practicing archery and wrestling. The girls were squealing with delight as they ran after one another.

At a distance the glaciers had started melting, warmed up by kisses of the sun beams. Summer was planning to move over. Green and brown patches of undergrowth became visible on the snowy mountain slopes. Yet, there was a lingering nip in the air.

The princess was groping around, blindfolded. With outstretched hands. She was running in circles barefoot on the grass to touch her friends guided by their sounds.

"Kanchan"! One of them would whisper in her ear and dart off as soon as she turned around. Her best friend Renu, poked her with a finger in her back and ran away yelling, "Kanchan I am next to the Ashoka trees, come and get me."

Upset princess tucked her long skirt a little higher and ran following the fragrance of the orange and red Ashoka blossoms and the sound of her tittering. As she neared the lotus pond the wet grass warned her to go slow but she was too fast to come to a halt and skidded right into it. She splashed with a gasp and removed her red blindfold as her dark tresses dripped streaks of water.

The lotuses shuddered and the swans flapped their wings. The game was over. Everyone was concerned. The two maids attending the children came running and one of them, covered her wet shoulders with a towel while helping her out. Two girls were snickering behind there cupped hands. Shivering child with muddy feet couldn't care less while Renu asked with concern, "Are you alright my friend?" Kanchan shook her head with tearful eyes.

An eunuch came down the steps of seraglio to call the children for lunch in her masculine voice. She wore a printed sari and her long hair were oiled and coiled in a bun at the nape of her neck. The princess was led inside to bathe and change, before going to the dining courtyard.

The men of the household had been served earlier, after the king. The courtyard was cleaned and prepared for the ladies and children. There were attendants flitting about the dining area getting ready for serving the delicacies. Everyone sat on individual cushions on the floor, facing their own small little tables with short legs. A bronze platter like thali[1] was placed in front of each one with silver bowls and no spoons. They ate with their fingers. Saffron rice, puries[2], vegetables, chutneys and pickles

1. Round Tray of metal.
2. Deep fried flat bread.

along with, yoghurt, bean curry or dal[1]. In the background Veena[2] and other instruments were being played softly. Some girls were handling palm-leaf fly whisks.

As soon as Queen Amita entered she asked a girl as usual, " Has the King been served?"

"Yes my lady, today he ate in his own chamber." "Thanks."

The ladies were all vegetarian. Only men ate non-vegetarian, the warrior's diet.

After the sumptuous meal some maids helped everyone to wash their hands with warm water in basins of bronze on wooden stands. They wiped their hands with towels held by women and turned towards the tray laid with quids of paan,[3] diced betel nuts and small cardamoms; to freshen up their breaths.

"Mother, may I also have a paan?" Cajoled the little princess.

"No darling it is too harsh for your sensitive palate."

"Then why do you take it?"she harped.

"Grown-ups can tolerate it. Besides it has many health benefits. To begin with, green betel leaf acts as a good source of roughage. You ask too many questions. So let's start walking towards our rooms while we talk."

Amita continued while walking, wrapped within her pink silk sari with graceful steps.

"The stuffing in the paan is splattered with slaked lime which is calcium for bones. The betel-nut too has the same property. The cardamom in it is a blood thinner and prevents formation of clots. Edible camphor freshens up the mouth and gulkand, a sugary rose preserve gives out a sweet flavour but can be replaced by a spice or tobacco, which could become addictive." She said it all in one breath so that the inquisitive girl is satisfied once for all.

"Wow Ma, you know it all."

"Everyone does, about paan at-least. Sorry!" Spoke the mother. "I forgot kattha, an extract from the bark of catchu tree. It is pungent but helps to diminish mucus."

"Well mother all I like about paan is that it colours your lips and makes you look pretty."

"Then why were you asking so many question, you naughty girl?"

---

1. Lentil soup.
2. Bow Harp.
3. Folded betel leaves with stuffing.

Bored Kanchan was bouncing along the colonnaded corridor where inverted-funnel-shaped, round-bottomed, tall pots were decorated at intervals.

"Why are they all black polished with floral and geometrical designs all over?" Asked the inquisitive child once again.

"These are the symbols of our modern period. Before us, grey pottery was made at Kuru and Panchal Kingdoms." Answered the patient mother.

"Aren't Panchals the overlords of Kaushal Kingdom?"

"They were, long time back. Under some treaty in the past now Kaushals are free but might be paying some tribute to them. Who told you about it?"

"My geography Acharya. Aren't these Panchals the same we are told about in the Epic War of Mahabharat fought 2500 years back? The clan to which Draupadi or Panchali, Arjuna's wife belonged.

"Yes honey, but put the rest of the questions in front of your Acharya."

"Just one more."

"Go ahead."

"Ma, are you an encyclopedia?"

"Hush. Now go back to your room for your afternoon nap."

*****

The stony wall of the pointed Himalayas, shone with white snow all year round. It also helped the monsoon winds to hit and pour down rain thus watering the seasonal crops and filling the lakes and wells.

The Fir and Sal trees dotted the outline of the nearby hills and the receding sun was peeping from behind, in orangish hue. Bhadrakanchan's pets, a deer, a baby elephant and the goose now romped about the garden freely as the children had left ending their last game. Champa and Chameli flowers still spread their scent around while the Nagishari passion flowers played hide and seek through their dark foliage and heard Mittra trumpeting.

By evening, queen Amita and her daughter were sitting on the staircase, coming down the seraglio. The patrolling guard on the ground moved further to give them privacy. At a distance small chubby clouds were nestling in the arms of nearby mountains. The heavier dark ones seem to be rolling down the slopes running after each other. The lapping waves of Rohini River were sighing in anticipation of the rain. Far away a peacock screamed, calling its mate.

The curvy path to the river where they often strolled, was tinted with an evening glow. Amita started humming under her breath. She covered her shoulders and head with the loose end of her red sari. The magic of the instance was touching her soul. And she sang, with Kanchan's head lying blissfully in the crook of her arm. The melody was in 'raag' Malhar[1] from Sama Veda[2].

"O dusky clouds do not scare, with your sonorous rumbling sounds.

Which pierce my heart with lonesome arrow, as my beloved is not around. Go kiss the swans on their lofty flights, hug the mountains and leave.

I'll pine for him, if you melt your drops, procrastinate! The wait is long."

The melody hung in the air as they lingered on, spellbound, till the evening shadows lengthened. A servant girl came to light the lamps in the mouths of the two sitting marble lions at the end of the staircase. As they were coming up Bhadrakanchan whispered, "Mother!"

"Yes darling?"

"From where did you learn this haunting composition?"

"All our classical music comes from Sama Veda."

"I too have written a poem."

The queen looked down at her nine year old. "That's amazing my child show it to me tomorrow since it is dinner time now!"

They came up, as king Suprabuddha too left the conference room where he had been discussing with his ministers about the forthcoming event of the boating competition in Devdah. Where his superiors Shuddhodan and king Mahakaushal from Saraswati were to be invited along with the chiefs of minor republics.

After having his dinner, in the room of his choice, he walked towards Amita's bedroom for her relaxing company and wise counseling.

*****

Next day Amita was reading her daughter's poem in the garden. While the jasmine flowers rolled their fragrance, touching everything around and the peacock in the garden danced with vibrant wings.

"I use to spend the nights thinking, who the heck am I !

Now I spend the nights dreaming for a better life.

1. Tune
2. Raaga Malhar a classical melody sung in rainy season at night. It's composition is described in Sama Veda. The veda about Indian classical Music.

Is it too good to be true?

I turn on the light and look inside the mirror, and see a face with shining eyes.

And better still, with a broad smile.

The dark dull me was nowhere in sight

It's past not the present. Oh, I am set free! Set free! Set free!

And I love the new incredible me."*

The mother was astounded at the talent in such a young girl. She wiped her swampy eyes and got up to keep the important 'document' safe in her chamber.

She asked her next, "May I make some corrections in your fabulous poetry?"

"No way mother, no way!" And Bhadrakanchan hopped, skipped and jumped all the way to the library, in her crimson long skirt raised a bit.

---

* Poem by Jiya Kapoor. (Ten year old-1923- student of class 5th Melbourne)

Chapter - 3

The Boating Competition

THE BREEZE WAS BLOWING YET WATERS CALM,
CROWDS WERE GATHERING IN SUNS'S WARMTH.
THE FLASHING BOATS DID STREAK THE RIVER,
AS THE TREES AND PAVILIONS SHIVERED.

That morning Bhadrakanchan woke up to the gentle alaap[1] of Raaga[2] Bhairavi as usual. Malti left a tumbler full of water with lemon and honey stirred in, by her bed-side for her to drink.

Near the bath area surrounded by curtains a woman was grazing a piece of sandalwood to prepare a paste used as a bath salve. The princess got up yawning and stretching. When the time came for a bath, she could hear the melodies of the lute, fife and cymbals. A female attendant helped her rub her teeth with a neem twig; and then with salt and mustard oil. Her gums were massaged with honey while she sat on a low marble seat inside a tank. Two girls poured perfumed water on her salved body and washed it away rubbing gently with a loofah. She was dried and helped into a long blue skirt along with a white blouse with silver trimmings. Her ears were adorned with small pearl studs.

Her Dhayamma, Malti led her to sit on a cushioned stool with ivory legs ending into tiger paws. Bhadrakanchan's pet goose was circling around her and she picked it up and petted her, saying sweet nothings. It pecked at her tresses, while Malti brought her hair dressing kit with ivory combs and lifted the goose up kindly from her lap to place it on the floor. She oiled Kanchan's hair and carefully removed the frizzy tangles between her 'ows and eeks.'

1. Alaap = long chant in varying notes.
2. Bhairavi Raaga = an organised dassical mode of different groups of notes, sung in the morning.

"Amma please go slow. If you pull my hair like this I'll grow bald soon and Siddhartha would refuse to marry me."

"Really? I didn't know that you have made up your mind."

As she got busy braiding her hair with expensive pearls and clips. Wearing iridescent shoes in myriad hues, the Princess was ready for breakfast of milk, honey, nuts and fruits.

In front of the palace, preparations were going on for the departure of the royal entourage to the west bank of River Rohini. A boating festival was to be held along with some other competitions like wrestling and chariot racing. Amita the Maharani and other ladies of the seraglio came down dressed up in fineries and laden with heavy glittering ornaments. There were pearl and ruby strings woven into their lustrous black hair. Most of them were chewing paan or scented betel- nuts or simply cardamoms. Some young ladies were vying for Suprabuddha's attention. But he preferred the hand of his chief queen. The rejected ones grimaced behind her back and giggled deliberately over the loud sound of singing bards.

One after the other the array of chariots was driven near the palace steps. First, the chief boarded and occupied the front seat under a white parasol held by a well-dressed young boy. He was flanked by the royal chaplain and prime minister. The army commander was standing next to his stallion ready to mount. The back seat of the king's chariot was engaged by the dignified Queen, her little princess and carer Malti. Thus, all the carriages were filled up and the procession started, with high-ranking officials and soldiers in the lead and at the end.

The caravan moved through the main thoroughfare and the king waved to cheering crowd. The colourful stoles of the chatting courtesans flared with the breeze oozing out perfumes. The girls seldom left the upper palace so were delighted to get this chance for an outing. Ladies and children from their balconies were throwing flower petals from above. Men were lining the sides of the narrow road and shouting, 'Hail chief Suprabuddha.'

The gentry soon reached the soggy, sandy beach of the river, where a crowd had already gathered. They hailed the king till he alighted and proceeded to the royal pavilion. On top of which three flags were waving. The river bank had turned into a huge camping ground with individual tents in bright colours.

Soon the sounds of drumbeats, gongs and cymbals announced the approach of guests from Kapilvastu. Once they settled down, another cacophony arose. This time, even louder. The Kaushalan overlord of the Shakyas and Koliyas, King Mahakaushal with his small son Prasenjit, was advancing with a bard in front, singing the praises of his ancestors; followed by his battalion of army which had been placed in Shakyan and Koliyan areas for observation. People didn't like them because they were enemy soldiers to keep a check on them and needed to be fed at their expense.

King Mahakaushal looked at the top of the royal pavilion with approval where his flag was fluttering higher than the other two. As he alighted his thoroughbred he again looked around to survey, whether the arrangements were worthy of his presence. Once satisfied he paid attention to the welcoming committee. Shuddhodan and Suprabuddha came forward and garlanded him and the little prince, while their higher officials saluted him. He was led to his throne where he was introduced to the family of the two chiefs. Amita welcomed him by waving the holy lamp in front of his face and marking his forehead with auspicious saffron and rice. He was offered the sweetmeats. Amita asked smiling, "Maharaj I don't see Maharani Mallika."

"She had a headache so I let her rest." She then turned to children and introduced them to Prasenjit. To Devdatta's chagrin, the King was charmed by Siddhartha and Bhadrakanchan, the small chicks. Siddhartha was the same age as Prasenjit.

After King Mahakaushal was seated in the central high ivory chair, Shuddhodan and Suprabuddha sat on his two sides followed by their brothers. Then two rows of the priests and high ranks and eventually the ladies, in priority to their status. Amita became happily engrossed in chatting with Prajapati while Devdatta's mother Mangala felt ignored and tried a conversation with Amritodan's wife Vibhawari, whose husband was a governor outside Kapilvastu.

Bhadrakanchan, Prasenjit and Siddhartha were perched aloof on top of a sand-dune with Prince Prasenjit in the center. Since all was set, court priest Sage Asita blew the conch with full lungs. The sonorous loud sound reverberated through the wind. The first sports event started unfolding. Children's attendants sat at a little distance, enjoying the show as well as keeping an eye on their aristocratic wards. The dignitaries at the royal pavilion were drinking fragrant 'sherbets', drinks of juices and nibbling at delicious snacks while watching the proceedings at the waterfront.

About thirty boats were lined up on the western bank of Rohini River,* flowing between east and west. They were to take a rights turn and then proceed towards the mountains in the waters of River Bhagirathi till they come to a colourful, fluttering barricade, and take a U-turn before heading back. All the boats except for the two most ordinary ones, belonged to the princes of smaller Shakyan states, or to sons of rich merchants. There were personal little flags waving at the front tips of boats. The two simple yet clean boats belonged to the sons of the chiefs of their guilds. The names of the participants were announced as Pothapada and Bhima. Pothapada was younger and did not keep a mustache or a beard whereas Bhima was proud of his thick upturned whiskers. Both were expert in their individual arts, of Iron and wood. Bhadrakanchan yelled for Malti and when she came, "Please Amma I want to talk to the two artisans, after the race."

"Why not! I will bring them to you." She assured her, "I'll take care of that."

Bhadrakanchan diverted her attention to the sport. Announcements declared, "The owner of each boat would also be its coxswain. He would have to have a plan of action where he does not exhaust his 'manjhis,' the rowing crew, too soon. Or he would need to take them over one after the other. The safety of the boat and the crew is his responsibility."

Shuddhodan got up from his chair and bowed slightly in front of King Mahakaushal saying, "Sorry to leave Your Majesty, I too am participating in the race. My boat is number seven."

"You too Rajan?" He said with a glint in his eyes. "That's the spirit. May I ride with you as a passenger? I want to forget for a while that I am a powerful monarch."

"It'll be an honour Maharaj! And you sure are powerful. In no way less than Panchals, Licchavis or Magadhans!" They both walked towards the boats with measured steps.

"That's my father!"announced proud Siddhartha and Kanchan responded, "Oh yes! My mamaji uncle is climbing into boat number seven. Even Prasenjit was thrilled to see his father, leading him.

"I wonder to which cities these other participants belong to! Their bows[1] are decorated with their tribal flags,"chirped the little princess.

Malti who was not only Bhadrakanchan's carer but also her teacher answered from behind. "Princess, the participants are from nearby states. Maybe from Cátuma, Khomadussa, Sámágram, Shilavati, Nagaraka, Medatlump, Shakkra and Ulumpa." While she was reciting the names of nearby Shakyan territories, Kanchan was counting them on her fingers.

"That makes it eight, Amma, two fingers are left," Malti smiled, "Sorry darling I can't recall the rest."

Soon, the three children saw the elderly sage Asita, the royal chaplain of Kapilvastu wave the green flag. Kanchan announced excitedly, "Here comes the auspicious moment!" Prasenjit, focused on the waterfront and

1. Forward end of the boat; the curved front.

shaded his eyes with his plump hand to avoid the glare, while with the other hand he was still eating some sweet. Soon his attendant rushed forward to shade him with a royal umbrella and offered him a handkerchief to wipe his pouting lips. Siddhartha kept sitting on the sand dune, morose.

Before the green flag was waved, Koliyan and Shakyan guards on horses, had started pacing the two flanks of Rohini River. Ever watchful! Many life-guards too, dotted the banks, ready to plunge. The boats were searing the waters. Boat number seven, with the state insignia of Shakyans, a white elephant, also had a Kaushalan flag fluttering on the beautifully carved ivory bow. Bhadrakanchan and Prasenjit climbed down the dune, sand filling their shoes. The two hopped up and down clapping. Kanchan looked at Siddhartha realising that he is not sharing the excitement.

"What's wrong?" The child prince opened his palm and the princess sat by him to look closely. A baby snail was wriggling inside its tiny shell yet peeping out. "Yak! Aren't you scared of the slimy creature?" Kanchan made a face.

"No, he is the one who is afraid to be crushed under our feet," replied her perceptive friend.

Egoistical Prasenjit who was listening to their babble irritably picked the snail from his hand and throwing it on the sand, crushed it under his boot.

"Do you mean like people in a war?" "Exactly."

"My dear friend your tenderness touches my heart. We cannot rule, without resorting to war."

"I know. But force necessary to control one's kingdom is one thing but going to the extreme of tyranny is another."

"My dear little wise fool. shouldn't we be watching the astonishing race, with our fathers participating in it. Instead of being so serious about an insignificant creature?"

"Nothing is trivial in this world," responded Siddhartha yet got up and tried to join them, in their exuberance.

"Look, look! My father seems to be giving instructions to the man holding the white parasol above King Mahakaushal. The attendant now has tilted it so that the north westerly wind becomes an asset rather than an hinderance to speed of the boat."

Due to the windy conditions, narrow boats were becoming hard to handle. Shuddhodan had kept a bowl full of pebbles in the centre of one of the boards. As soon as the boat tilted to one side and the bowl skidded, the king would instruct the paddlers and managed the rudder at the helm with the steering handle. He advised the rowers, "Keep the boat in the middle of the river. The waters are deep and less choppy."

He then sat down at the end of the boat in front of the drummer, facing its bow and gave instructions to the rowers who had their backs towards the front. It became easier now, to manage the rudder as well.

"Boom-boom-bang! Boom-boom-bang!" The drummers pounded to encourage and synchronize the rowing crew. The crowd shouted and cheered as the concerto built up.

All of a sudden a boat zoomed past them, recklessly. The Shakya chief steered away. In the process the boat tilted dangerously and they all screamed and huddled together on the opposite side to save the kings from splashing indignantly in the icy water.

"That hot headed Tapodan!" Shouted Shuddhodan.

*****

At the Maharaja pavilion, conspiracies were being hatched between Dhrotodan, the elder brother of Shuddhodan and Suprabuddha against the chief of Kapilvastu.

Shuddhodan's father Sihahanu had five sons. Dhrotodan being the oldest. But his gambling, drinking and other vices made him unfit to become a King, although he was the rightful heir to the throne. Besides the members of the 'Sanstha' confederation, too did not approve of him. Second son Shuddhodan was expert in warfare and swordsmanship. He was ambitious yet caring towards his people. So he was chosen the chief of Shakyan council. The third and the fourth princes were given governorship of other cities while the youngest Amritodan stayed at Kapilvastu palace with his family and assisted the King along with Dhrotodan. Whose problem was that he wanted his son Devdatta to become the Chief after Shuddhodan as he was elder to Prince Siddhartha. King Shuddhodan was still deeply in love with his deceased wife Maya. So he was determined to make Siddhartha occupy the throne after him. Although his first born from Prajapati, Nand too was older than Siddhartha. Dhrotodan and wife Mangala were always conniving and plotting and pressurizing their son to do something to regain his father's lost seat of power.

Soon Amritodan joined the two conspirators and placing his hands on the backs of their chairs exclaimed innocently, "Look at that fool Bhima! He is making the U-turn at full speed. His boat might overturn." And it did. Tapodan's tailgating boat right behind, banged into it and stalled. Shaken, the arrogant chief of Pathoragarh wiped the splashed water from the scowl on his thick-browed face. He gave the wheel to his second in command. A disappointed chorus rose from the public, as the multi colourful triangular flags on the demarcation hemp cable were dancing with the wind. Bhima and his crew clung to the upturned boat, shivering. The watchful guards dived in the cold waters to save the crew. But Bhima had lost his face as his proud whiskers were dripping water from the two ends downwards. Seeing that Tapodan twisted the ends of his own mustache upwards and ordered, "Move! Move!".

Bhadrakanchan opined to Siddhartha, "Bhima became arrogant about his strength. His overconfidence clouded his thinking."

"You are right Kanchan, arrogance forebodes destruction."

A cracked voice came from behind.

"How come our little cousin becomes wiser when my brother is around! By the way I do not agree with both of you. A little arrogance is good for a man who strives to be on the top."

Kanchan made a face and retorted "You are not a man yet Dev even though a few years older, so save your arrogance for the future."

Prasenjit, who was listening to their squabble butted in, "I agree with Devdatta."

"See!" Spoke Dev, proud to get his support. "And you little girl should come and play with me instead of hanging around with this shrimp, cousin of yours. I am very strong too, I can even carry you on my shoulder."

Siddhartha retorted sarcastically.

"You mean the way wicked Ravan stole Sita on his shoulders from Panchvati and flew her in his flying vehicle to Lanka?"

"I am not worried," snapped the little girl proudly, looking at Siddhartha. My Rama will save me."

"Won't you Siddh?"

Prasenjit intervened, "Please stop your 'Ramayana Gatha'[1], the race is so engrossing."

Devdatta stomped away yelling, "Little brother you better be careful. I still have to take revenge from you for the 'Shot-Swan

---

1. Story of the Hindu Epic Ramayan. *River Rohini flows southwards and separates Devdah and Kapilvastu. Devdah being on the east. —'Let the Sakyans and the Koliyans see you, facing the west crossing the Rohini River'. (Theragatha verses;527-33.)

episode'[1], when I was humiliated in front of everyone at the Rajyasabha court. Just because you were lucky enough to be the ruling king's son!"...And his voice trailed off as the crowd screamed. Two boats running too close to each other had collided but not upturned. The hue and cry went on as the accident victims continued unabashed.

An interesting spectacle was underway. Charged by the moment, Shuddhodan and Mahakaushal had replaced the rowers and sat side by side to row their boat dexterously and safely. They were not swinging their oars frantically like the others but were steady yet forceful. They successfully maneuvered the U-turn at the end and swung back expertly, slightly titling the boat to one side and the bowl full of pebbles skidded too fast and hit the bottom of the boat. No one cared. The crew was focused on giving them instructions. The horde of people clapped and whistled while jumping and thumping each other. The excitement was searing up as the royal boat, number seven zipped pass the other boats, and headed backwards. Everyone watched with bated breath as the rowers approached the finish line. Suprabuddha and Drotodan had a frown upon their brows. Amritodan clapped with vigour.

At the bend a few accidents had happened. So the kings took a wide arch away from every boater and reached the final win. As they got off panting, they hugged each other and grinned like little boys, instead of monarchs.

That was the day when their political relationship turned to friendship. So Shuddodhan invited Mahakaushal to Kapilavastu, who agreed to visit for a few days before returning to Sarasvati, his Capital. He thought, 'This way I could even inspect my territories and troops stationed at various posts.'

Prasenjit had wandered off to find the older prince Devdatta.

Bhadrakanchan saw Malti coming followed by Bhima with dried up and slightly upturned mustaches, and Pothapada. They both wished to the royal children and Bhadrakanchan spoke to them respectfully. "Thanks for coming gentlemen. I had a few requests to make." Impressed by her polite demeanor they responded together.

"Anything for you young lady, just let us know what you need!"

"Please Bhima make some exclusive wooden toys for me."

"Sure princess! Would you like a chariot for your dolls?"

---

1. Swan episode : Devdatt had shot a swan in flight with his arrow. When Siddharth found the wounded bird and nursed it back to health along with his play mate Kanchan. A conflict arose between him and his cousin. The court's verdict was that the savior is greater than the killer.

"No, thank you. I would like to have a dollhouse looking like a palace and a few small animals. An elephant, a deer and a goose! And above all a prince like Siddhartha and a princess like me living in it?" While she looked at Siddhartha with adoring eyes who was still looking at the crowd of colourful people who had started moving towards the wrestling arena.

Bhima replied, "Although I haven't made any animals before, but I'll do my best!"

"And what choice can you offer me Pothapada?"

"Princess, I am only an expert in making the best tips of arrows which never miss their mark. I'll ask Bhima to make your size bow and I'll provide you with a quiver and arrows."

"Wonderful Potha I would love that." Satisfied Bhadrakanchan looked at Malti.

"Amma, please give them some gold coins."

"Oh no! No need for that," interrupted Bhima. "I make chariots for the king for free. How can we take money from you, Princess who is the sun-shine of our town? It'll be a pleasure to serve you." Potha shook his head in affirmation. Then they turned towards Siddhartha.

"And what is your desire dear prince?"

Siddhartha smiled sweetly and replied, "Nothing for me please you are already building a palace where I can live with the princess." He was craving for some solitude.

*****

Chapter - 4

Ancient Legends

THE GLORIOUS PAST OF SINDHU CIVILIZATION,
CAME ROLLING BACK AS, TIDES IN THE OCEAN.

Princess Bhadrakanchan loved to know about the early Vedic period and her ancestors. Before bedtime she would curl up in her bed and pester Malti for stories connected to Vedas. Being an educational topic, she was always obliged. One night while pressing her feet, Malti started a story from one of the Upanishads, treatises on the Vedas. She informed her, "My grandfather was highly qualified. When I was a little girl, he would narrate many stories to me he knew through the oral tradition."

"Narrate them! Narrate them!"chirped the green talking parrot in his cage and started nibbling at the green chili Malti had fed it.

The lights were dim in the bedroom and all was quiet. There was a fire burning in the stone fireplace at one end to keep the princess warm. Malti had made sure that no firewood was used, as it made the chamber too hot. Sandalwood was fragrant but too smoky. So, she only used cotton or silk cloth to burn at night. That made the room just comfortable enough. She was sitting in a vicar-chair, wrapped in her multi-coloured shawl, while her beaded bronze necklace glinted in the light of torches hung at certain spots. She spoke at length while Kanchan and Mitthu the parrot, were all ears.

"Her name was Ghosha. Her grandfather was a renowned scholar. Who's name was Dharmatama. He along with his son Kakshivate, wrote hymns in praise of the heavenly Ashvanis and sang them. The Ashvanis were twins with heads of the horses, and were wonderful physicians.

Ghosha developed a skin disease which left random white patches on her body. Due to which no one was ready to marry her. She was advised by her father to pray to the Ashvani Kumars for cure.

Malti cleared her throat gently and continued. “Ghosha beseeched the demigods to give her the boon of good health and a clear skin so she could enjoy the fruits of a happy marriage. She composed two hymns of the tenth book of Rig Veda. Each containing forty verses.”

“Really! She must have been intelligent, if the Ashvanis gave her the desired boon.”

“She sure was, like you. If you want you too can be wise like her and write poetry.”

“Go ahead with the story Ma.”

“Well the Ashvanis were great surgeons too. They had the ability to perform organ transplanting surgery.”

“Were they the ones who fixed baby elephant’s head on Ganesha[1], the God of Wisdom.”

“No one knows but there has to be some plastic surgery going on in the ancient past. However, the moral of Ganesha story is that if one listens more and speaks less he’ll become wise. Anyway coming back to the main theme, the Ashvanis performed a bloodless surgery on Ghosha by special techniques and she was healed. Her skin glowed and she prayed to the two Gods every day to express her gratitude.”

---

1. According to a Hindu myth, once Hindu God Shiva went away for twelve years to meditate, leaving his wife Goddess Parvati. One day before taking her bath she was cleaning her body with a paste of turmeric, wheat flour, cashew nuts and mustard oil along with some other ingredients.
   When the dirty paste came off leaving her body glowing, she made the figure of a small boy with it and made it come alive with her divine powers. She told him, “Son Ganesh, guard the entrance of my bath chamber.”
   Shiva returned from his trip without her knowledge and came to meet his wife. Ganesha stopped him and said, “You cannot go in Sage, because my mother is having a bath in privacy.” “And who are you?” Shiva questioned authoritatively.
   An argument followed and irate Shiva wanted to teach the obstinate child a lesson. He chopped off his head and flung it far-far away, never to be found.
   Parvati hearing the commotion came out quickly and seeing her son’s headless body started crying. Shiva, on hearing her story tried to console her and sent his minions to find the head of any child who was sleeping with his head towards north. They found a baby elephant’s head for Parvati’s son. Parvati cried even louder. However the head was transplanted on the child successfully and Ganesha woke up. “Now he won’t argue rudely with his elders and would listen more with his big ears,” said Shiva but his wife was still unhappy. So Shiva told her further. “He’ll become so wise by hearing more and talking less that the world would pray to him before any other God. That to some extent satisfied his mother.
   Our bodies are magnets so is earth. If we sleep with our feet towards south our vitality suffers.

"Did she get married then?" Kanchan's eyes rounded up with curiosity. "Oh yes! I attended the marriage myself."

"You fibber!" and the princess threw a small pillow at her, in jest. Both of them laughed wholeheartedly.

After a few days it was time again for a bed-time story. Princess quickly finished her saffron-laced warm milk and settled against the soft silk bolsters on her canopied bed. She faced Malti who was busy settling her ample body in a comfortable chair.

"So ma'am, who is going to be my next model of inspiration?"

Malti shuffled, as soft strains of music played with the dim lights and shadows in the room.

"Her name was Gargi Vachaknavi. A famed philosopher and learned scholar of Veda. She had thorough knowledge of Brahm Vidya."

"What is that?"

"Knowledge about the Brahm, the creator of the cosmos."

"I wish I had met her!"

"No chance dear! She belonged to the period of King Ramchander of Kaushal or Saket. Her father was Vachaknu. His name is mentioned in the 'Griha Sutra' of Ashvalayan scripture. But so far it only exists in the oral tradition…or may be its been written down, but it is too lengthy for a little girl to read."

"Okay."

"It was known that Gargi could awaken her kundalini powers." "And what is that darling Amma?"

"It is one of the highest stages of Yogic practice where the dominant energy at the base of our spine is awakened with the help of Mantra, Tantra, Yantra, yoga or meditation."

"Oh my God that sounds complex."

"Yes! And dangerous too, if not done under a proper guidance. So don't even think of it."

"Okay! Okay!" And the princess raised her palms as a truce.

"Returning to the story," Malti continued. King Janak of Mithila organised a debate on Brahm Gyan known as Rajasuya Yajna in his Capital, Janakpurdham. Many famous sages of the times, participated, namely, Bhujya, Ushasta, Ashvala, Artabhaga and many more who competed with the most renowned and powerful scholar Yajnavalakya and lost. The only contestant left was Gargi. After asking preliminary questions she specifically asked about 'existing environment' in the world and 'theory of origin', of all things existing and their interconnectedness in this universe. Finally, she asked, "that O Yajnavalakya, which is above the sky, and which is beneath the earth, that which is between these two, sky and earth. Across what is woven warp and woof?"

When Yajnavalakya answered 'space', she asked, "Across what is space woven, warp[1] and woof ..."

Finally, "What is Brahm?" She knew that 'It is the world of the imperishable or the ultimate reality' yet she wanted to hear his opinion.

The proud scholar was getting a feeling that Gargi knew more than the rest of the participants. He, afraid of losing from a woman put an end to the debate by snubbing Gargi. "Dear lady do not go any further or you might go crazy."

Gargi did not want to bow him down so she gracefully withdrew.

Before the function was over however Gargi was given the title of Brahmvadini[2] to the chagrin of Yajnavalakya. When everyone left after refreshments, only Yajnavalakya and Gargi stayed along with the King Seeradhwaja[3] Janak. The scholar who had defeated everyone in the contest asked the king: "O King, why did you give her an epithet of 'Brahm-vadini? Wasn't I the top-man in the 'Rajsuyayajna'?"

"Yajnavalakya, I have no doubt of your superiority but you did not let her finish. She would have in the end, discussed the theory of 'time-warp'. A hypothetical eccentricity in the progress of 'time' that would allow movement back and forth between eras or that would permit the passage of time to be suspended."

"Oh that! I do not have much faith in hypothetical scientific ideas." And he looked at Gargi with disapproval and left the moot hall after thanking the king and collecting his award in gold."

The princess who was sleepy by now, came out of her bubble of imagination and looked at Malti "O Amma, this time-theory is too heavy for me to retain. I am more of a fun girl. So please relate the next story in a lighter strain. But I do like the courage and self-confidence of Gargi who was not intimidated even by an established philosopher of her times. Like her I too do not like being dictated to!"

1. Warp means the basic foundation or material of a structure or entity. 'Woof' = the weave of fabric. (The set of yarns placed lengthwise in the loom, crossed by and interlaced with the weft and forming length-wise threads in a woven fabric). Brahmvadini, means Professor with knowledge of the cosmos.
2. Full name of Sita's father and King Ramchander's father-in-law.
3. In modern times, first recorded in 1950-1955.

"Good! But some times humility adds grace to one's demeanor."

Malti got up and covered the princess properly. Who said, "Good-night Amma, and thanks for the story. I hope your treasure-chest of ancient tales is always full, for me to peek into."

"God bless you princess, I'll make sure of that. Sweet dreams."

The Family History

Princess Bhadrakanchan was getting thirstier and thirstier for more knowledge. So, she often visited the palace library. She would go through the palmyra palm-leaf texts written in Sanskrit, about the past. Although more information was floating around in oral traditions or in the songs of the bards. She often bombarded her Acharya with questions, who taught her history, politics, astronomy, Sanskrit, grammar and other subjects. Her teacher was Malti's brother.

One day, she found a copy of the family history. Which had been written and rewritten for survival. Her curiosity knew no bounds. She thought, "It'll be interesting to go back to my roots. But if Ma sees me with the book she'll say, "Kanchan, put it back right away. The palm-leaf 'parna,' I mean page is fragile… study your school books!" Bhadrakanchan who was generally an obedient daughter, this one time, hid the book in her stole and hopped away to her room.

She read late into the night despite Malti's admonishing. She even told the veena- girl to stop playing. The story started with Lord Ram of Ayodhya, which was the capital of Kaushal kingdom, about three hundred years ago. Ram had created an ideal monarchy. He was devoted to his people and presented himself as a perfect example to follow, in values. His people adored him and later generations worshipped him. After Rama, Treta Yuga[1] ended and morals of people started deteriorating.

After Treta Period the new millennium of Dwapar, was fraught with tensions. Brothers fought with each other for property. About 1000 B.C. the great battle of Mahabharat was written down though it was fought, about 3000 BC where brothers, Kauravas and Pandavas fought with one another.

When King Krishna, who was also Arjun's cousin and his political advisor in the war passed away, the Kali Yuga or the dark age commenced. The kings became indisciplined and lost strength of character. Apart from their queens they started keeping concubines, to entertain themselves. The

1. Hindu philosophy divides the life span of earth into four epochs. First, Satayuga, (when people have highest sense of ethics and morality); Second, Treta Yoga when bad people like Ravana are around. Third period is Dwapar (when Krishna lived) and last is the Kali Yuga or the Dark age.

weaker people were bought and sold at auctions as slaves. The priests became counselors to the kings and encouraged animal sacrifices to ward-off the results of their sins, for a fat 'dakshina' or fee. And went laughing all the way home. The rigid rituals started becoming unaffordable to the poor. Brahmans did not always follow the high code of conduct prescribed for them by religious norms. Those who were pious and straight, stayed poor.

Princess Bhadrakanchan was feeling sad and right away spoke aloud, "The naughty Brahmans!" She laid the book aside for next day's read.

Her disturbed mind even next day kept on haunting her about the plight of the poor masses. She was riding her mare with her instructor but the images of sick and helpless people in her own town kept on flashing in her thoughts. She had drawn her father's attention to it. But a small republic's chief had his own limitations. On major issues a discussion always took place in the assembly at Kapilvastu. More priority was given to spending money on strengthening the army rather than trying to ease the life of the poor.

By evening princess sat down cozily in her bed against the pillows to continue reading the text regarding her family history. She carefully untied the red string holding the bundle of sheafs together, written in Sanskrit.

About in Ninth. B.C.E. the Kaushala King Okkaka exiled his four sons along with his five daughters of the chief queen Sujata who had passed away. His low-caste, jealous junior queen made him promise to enthrone her son Jamtukumar after him and send the nine children to the forest. She was a former maid-servant, named Disha.[1]

All the royal children of Okkaka of Iksh'vaku dynasty left Saket and started walking towards north. They reached the valley on the southern foothills of Himalayas. The land there was lush green and marshy with a promise of being fertile. The girls were fascinated by a pond of blooming lotus flowers. They walked a little further and found a lake of crystal-clear water and a rishi's hermitage. Deers with shiny, spotted skin darted about: rabbits hopped and amphibians came in and out of water. Ducks swam and geese squawked, wondering about the identity of those new people on the scene. The widespread vista was full of trees. The boys put down their bows and quivers against a huge boulder, under a Sal tree and stretched alongside it on the cool grass while the girls got busy picking up fruits from under the heavily laden boughs. They ate, drank and fell asleep.

On waking up they saw at a distance a Yogi figure sitting still under the sacred Pipal Tree, deep in meditation. Undisturbed by the evening chirping of the mountain pheasants.

1. According to Dathvansa – Buddhist source.

The royal children took a dip in the lake and lit a fire to dry themselves up. The oldest princesses left a pile of washed up fruits in front of the Muni and waited for him to come out of his 'Samadhi', which he soon did. A pink hue spreading across the horizon, was falling on his salt and pepper hair. He opened his eyes and looked at the dying fire at some distance and the young strangers around it. Then he looked at the fruits in front of him. By this time they all presented themselves. The boys prostrated, and the girls touched his feet for his blessings. He raised his right palm, in response. Observing their demeanours, he spoke gently,

"Royal protégés, what purpose all of you have in this 'aranya'[1]? Were you too banished like Ramchander due to a jealous step-mother, Kakei?"

"Unfortunately, that is exactly the story of our present situation. We, like king Rama are from Kaushal kingdom", answered the oldest prince, Ulkamukh. For a moment the learned one thought and introduced himself.

"My name is Kapil! You can see my hermitage. It'll be nice to have some Kshatriya warriors around me. I'll feel safe while meditating and performing religious rituals without interruptions."

"It'll be an honour Sir!"

"My suggestion is, if you decide to make your home here, it is a good spot. A tributary of Ganga River flows by. The forest is abundant in trees. You could think of clearing a patch of land by burning their woody trunks which of course is quite a cumbersome work. Then start by building bamboo huts with thatched roofs. You should plant some more trees at the boundary of your new village, and have a fence erected, for safety. The soil here is marshy, so hard to till, but very fertile for arable farming. Rice, sugarcane and vegetables grow well here. There is plenty of game available for meat eaters like your clan. Start a new life and propagate." The friendly sage was helpful in guiding them.

"Thank you, Sir, for all the well-wished advice but where would we find proper matches for ourselves?"

"We shall see that later."

Kapil decided on a piece of land for the exiled royalty and marked it with the golden sand mixed in water.

The nine aristocrats worked day and night to build their small hamlet, and named it Kapilvastu.[2] The land was so luxuriant that apart from giving

1. The description of the forest is based on an ancient story from Mahavastu – translated in English by Jones
2. Vastu = science of architecture

good crop, 'the burnt tree-stumps sprouted again'. They all were noticing and learning new clues about their environment.

One day, the youngest thirteen year old princess came running home, from fruit gathering. Her eyes were wide open with fear while she pointed her finger towards some bushes at a distance. Her older brother couldn't gather anything from her stammering. So, he went to look for himself. As soon as he neared the bushes, he saw two blood-shot eyes prying from behind a thorny shrub. He went closer and the leaves rustled. The creature disappeared leaving the echo of his feet behind. When Kapil muni was free, the curious prince described the incident to him. To which he answered.

"There are many primitive tribes in this forest. They have dark faces which they like to paint with natural dyes. They think that the Brahamans and Kshatriyas of lighter colour belong to some foreign tribes and have no right on their forests. They should stay in their cities. When faced with the intruders, as they visualise them, they try to kill. If it is a trader, just crossing the jungle, they shoot an arrow just for the loot. Once in a while some caravans of traders pass through the northern route.[1] But they do not dare to attack a large gathering! These thieves and murderers are called 'Dasyus'. Their almost naked nymphs are expert archers. Beware of their tribes. They are head-hunters.[2]

"In contrast to them are some other tribes generally more pliant but not docile at all! One group wears cobra hood on their heads and live in the caves called the Nagas. Whereas a declining group wears Garuda[3] hood, with vicious looking beak of a bird of prey. These two tribes are enemy to one another. No one should ever get caught in their cross-fire. Anyway, the Nagas, are slowly moving towards eastern hills of the country. Those who are left, they worship snakes and collect their venom for various purposes. They are industrious and keep to themselves."

Soon the small village of Kapilvastu prospered. The oldest princess was given the position of the mother and the rest married among themselves since there were no decent folks around, far and wide. Thus, Ulkamukh, Karakandu, Hasteenika and Sinipura got married to Supriya, Ananda, Vijita and Vijitasena.

The Royal Mother developed leprosy. She was taken to an isolated part of the sal forest to live in a lone hut. The king of Varanasi named

1. Uttarpath
2. The one who collects maximum number of heads would become chief of the group.
3. Garuda in Hindu mythology is an enemy of snakes. His eaglike beak, wings and talons look like that of a vulture.

Rama had also developed the same infectious disease and he too was passing his time in the same grove after giving his kingdom to his sons.

One day the princess was attacked by a lion and the king saved her. They became friends and cured themselves with a herb called, 'Kol' and by sleeping under the sal trees. Her skin became shiny and she looked beautiful. They both got married.

Help came from Varanasi. The kol trees were chopped off and a settlement established. The hamlet was called Ram-gram, village of Rama and also as Kolnagar, town of the Kol Trees. Their main road was named Vyagrapath, the 'Path of Tiger.' The two major cities of the Kol Janpad, (district) were Ramgram and Devdah. And the tribals were called Koliyas. Their kingdom was situated on the opposite bank of Rohini River to Kapilvastu.

*****

However, King Okkaka who was worried for his children sent a secret messenger to find out about their well-being. The king was shocked to hear about their unethical liaison but exclaimed.

"Shakya vata bho kumara parama-sátyáváta bho rájkumára!"

(Capable indeed are the noble princes; it could be considered appropriate for them-brothers and sisters-to become husband and wives at the extremely difficult situation.)

Hence the name, 'Shakya' for their clan; meaning, powerful and talented. As the city became populous and prosperous, it's name spread far and wide.

The wild tribes started moving away from urbanisation. Many fairs and festivals were organised to encourage economy. Merchants came and it became a busy trade centre.

It was late when princess Bhadrakanchan finished reading the historical manuscript. Malti was already fast asleep. Princess knew now why all the Shakyas, including the Koliyas were so proud of the purity of their race. They would only have marriage alliances amongst their own clan. Two hundred years have passed since, yet the Shakya tribe continues the same practice. She thought that it wasn't prudence. It was arrogance and some day the clan might end up paying a heavy price for it.

'In any case, I wouldn't have a problem marrying Siddhartha,' she thought.

*****

Next day when the princess Bhadrakanchan visited the palace library to return the book about her family tree she found another interesting text. It was translated from Myanma or the language of Mranma Pran (Burma), a history of the ancient royal dynasty of the country. Soon after lunch, she started reading again, missing her afternoon siesta.

'A few centuries earlier, the Koliyan and Shakyan were still insignificant in comparison to the western, powerful kingdoms of Kaushal[1] and Panchal. At one point in history the King of Panchal was victorious over Kaushalas. And wanted to further enhance his status by getting the pure blood of Ikshvaku dynasty and have high born descendants like Shakyas. He asked for a Shakyan maiden's hand. But caste proud tribe refused. Humiliated Panchal king attacked the two republics and destroyed them. Most people were killed, some saved themselves by hiding and others escaped under the leadership of Abhiraja, towards Kamarupa (Assam) in the east. With great difficulties they crossed the mountains bordering Mranna Pran (Mayanmar or Burma) and reached the land between Chidwin and Ayeyarwady rivers.

The open-minded and hospitable people of the land noticed their expertise in governance, they welcomed the refined refugees and accepted Abhiraja as their ruler.[2]

Panchal, after defeating the Shakya, made Kaushal kingdom independent again, under certain conditions of a treaty and allowed it to rule over the small republics since it was nearer to Sarasvati, the capital of Kaushal.

The days were flying by. Bhadrakanchan was twelve. Her jealous father never let his family visit Kapilvastu. Amita missed her brother and her daughter missed Siddhartha. Small shreds of news would reach Kanchan's ears. She had come to know that the crown prince wasn't allowed yet, to go out in public places, on his own. What she didn't know was that recently, sometimes he would sneak out of the palace with Channa, his charioteer to look at some girls. Most of his time however was spent in schooling and training as a potential warrior. With his sharp intellect, he quickly memorised the Vedas, a part of the syllabus.

The Shakyan family at Kapilvastu conducted a school of archery called Vedhanna, where students from neighbourhood came to learn. Devdatta too was one of the students along with Siddhartha. Princess Kanchan too had had enough practice of archery at home. First with her little bow and

1. Capital of Kaushal had shifted from Ayodhya to Sarsvati.
2. King Abhiraj founded the kingdom of Ta Gaung – seventy miles from the present city of Shwebo. Evidence of the old city are still present.

arrow and then by a full size one. Her main passion however was a ride on her young pet elephant, Kunj, whom she lovingly called Mittra or friend.

One night, she was asked by Malti while combing her hair before bedtime, “Why such a long face today, Princess?”

She burst out, “Amma, I saw some poor children in the street, from the terrace. They were in dirty rags with disheveled long hair and legs like stilts. Why do the destitute suffer so much?”

“Darling it is the result of their accumulated past life ‘Karmas’, I mean actions. They alone can atone them in their present lifetime and collect good karmas for their future.”

Her hair was done so the inquisitive girl climbed in her bed saying, “Sometimes I feel Amma that the ‘Karma’ theory is a little too far-fetched. It is just a pseudo-balm on the wounds of people, unjustly treated.”

“Throw the disturbing thoughts out of your window, before sleeping. I’ll tell you a story about another outstanding personality, tomorrow.”

“What was her name?”

“Lopamudra!”

“Someday I’ll relate, how electricity was generated with an experiment by our ancients.”

“You mean, like the lightening in the sky?”

“You got it.”

“Why don’t you tell me a story now?”

“You are tired, my child.”

“Oh no, I am not!” And she sat erect.

“If you insist, I have no problem.”

“Thanks Amma,” and the princess settled her delicate body against the royal-blue bolsters with a shimmery white piping. Her dark tresses framed her ivory complexion, and her bright eyes became wide-open in anticipation; as Malti was busy settling herself in a wicker chair. Her greying hair at the temples were glistening in the flickering light of a tall lamp. Her plump jowls moved as she tried to finish her paan rapidly. After chewing up the last nutty bits, she got up to drink some water, to clear her throat.

Her voice boomed in the dimly-lit room.

“There was a king who ruled the kingdom of Vidarbha. There was also a sage who was always busy in his spiritual and scientific pursuits.

The sage wrote about his scientific experiments in a book named 'Agastya Samhita' in which was given the method to prepare a dry cell, to produce a direct current of electricity."

"You mean the energy which is found in the lightening of the clouds which acts as a torch to the lost travellers?"

"I guess so! My son who read the methodology tried the experiment at home and it worked. He is such a curious lad! Anyway, he took an earthen pitcher and placed Zink filings, mercury, wet sawdust and two copper plates in it."[1]

"Was copper discovered then?"

"Yes, copper and bronze were the commonly used metals. Iron was discovered later. Anyway, he filled up the pot with some compound of copper and a current was produced."

"Amazing!"

"However, the real story is that in our most important Rig Veda there are dialogues given between Lopamudra and the sage. She was very intelligent, pious and loyal to her husband, as well as refined and cultured, since she was brought up at the palace of the King Vidarbha. Who had given her to sage Agastya because he had asked for her hand in marriage. She had looked after her husband well but was fed up with the austere life because the sage had vowed for a life of celibacy and poverty. She wrote a hymn of two stanzas in such moving terms about her loneliness that her husband broke his vow of celibacy and started giving her loving attention. Soon they were blessed with a son named Drisdhasyu."

"What happened to him?"

"Nothing he became a renowned poet."

"And what is celibacy Amma?"

"You'll understand when you grow up. Now go to sleep my child." And Malti extinguished, all the lamps except Ratnadwipa which was suppose to ward off evil.

*****

1. 14 Feb 7673 B.C. Research by Dr. Mandyam Kumar. Ancient India – Jeannine Auboyer.

Chapter - 5

The Excursion

TINKLE TINKLE RANG THE BELLS,
THE ELEPHANT WALKED WITH GRACEFUL STEPS.
THE HONEST LAUGHTER OF INNOCENT GIRLS
THE CHILDHOOD CRADLE SWINGS WITH JEST.

One morning when Chief Suprabuddha was busy with his courtiers, Bhadrakanchan entered his chamber. The Rajan was delighted to see her. He told his ministerial staff to wait.

"Excuse me gentlemen! I'll be a minute."

"Sure Sir!" they gladly obliged and looked at the rosy cheeked princess who was wholesome like a breath of fresh air.

"Father I want to go for a ride on Kunj through the city. You know he is my friend."

"Sure honey I hope, the eleph…oh, sorry darling I mean your friend is grown enough to go through a crowded bazaar."

"He sure is! He can flap his ears and move his trunk all over and listens to his carer Sadhuji. He is a big boy now." She said raising her hands above her head.

A smile spread on everybody's face and the chief answered,

"Okay, if Sadhuji is taking you, it is fine."

"Thanks, I like his sagacious company, anyway. I also appreciate your not calling my 'friend' an elephant."

"I dare not!" and the King raised his eyes upwards, and everybody laughed while the princess narrowed her eyes reproachfully and pouted her lips, before leaving.

Queen Amita was standing at her balcony, looking at her daughter with her friends as they were leaving through the palace gate on the swaying elephant. She believed that a little exposure is always good for children. Her thoughts turned to her parental home. 'I wish my brother at Kapilvastu, would also let Siddharth go out of the palace and see for himself, the kind of kingdom he would rule in future. Otherwise when he grows up he may not have the strength to face the realities of life which may be too ugly especially for a prince.'

Musing thus, queen Amita walked towards the kitchen to check on the menu, for the day. The kitchen was muggy and hot due to the steam oozing out from various vessels and the fires burning. So, she quickly gave her instructions and called her maid, "Ganga, please come to my room and press my feet before lining them with 'alta.'"

The chief cook had been sitting cross legged on the floor since morning. As soon as the queen left, he got up to stretch in relief. His round belly was peeping from under his sweaty vest and wobbling a bit at his every movement. He rubbed his eyes, burning with smoke and looked around if all was in order. He noticed his errand boy shunning his duty, so he shouted.

"Hey, you donkey, what are you staring at out of the window?"

"Nothing Sir, I was shooing the dogs away who were trying to climb up the window."

Satisfied, he said, "Alright! See to it that no crows also come inside to steal away the kitchen food. I can hear their cawing. The food inspectors is about to come to taste everything. Stay at guard!" He ordered in a hoarse voice.

Two women in a corner of the huge, partially open kitchen, were constantly rubbing pots and pans with the clean and cooled ashes from the hearths where wood was burnt from early morning to late evening. Whereas two stout men were non-stop replenishing the huge pitchers of water. The head cook got busy again stirring his curries with long ladles and at the same time blasting off instructions to the errand girls. Since it was almost time for the King's lunch, he laid two round trays with food. One for the sovereign and the other for himself, as was the custom. The chef would taste every item before the king, from the tray of his master's choosing. So that there was no chance of him poisoning the chief-in-power.

*****

The princess of Devdah and her friends were going for a pleasure trip to the city park. The thrilled girls were giggling and chatting all the way.

After leaving the palace gates their pet elephant reached the main road which went through the central market, where every vehicle and pedestrian walked through the crowd jostling with one another. The 'torandwar' or the main gate was decorated with yellow marigolds and the auspicious mango leaves. As soon as they passed it a flower dropped in Bhadrakanchan's lap and she squealed with delight. The elephant's bells tied at the knees and ankles were warning the pedestrians of its approach. The girls were experiencing different sounds and smells and for a change were quiet. They noticed how four palanquin bearers were dexterously weaving through the crowd sweating profusely. While a four-wheeled buggy crossed them painfully and some rich young men seated in it laughed and joked playfully. The buggy stopped for a moment and two fellows got off as the vehicle moved on. The two young men headed for the tavern door, up four steps on a veranda. The well-dressed one, waited outside while his servant went inside the tavern to get a jar of perfumed wine for his masters to enjoy at the park they were heading to.

Through the myriad smells and sounds of bazaar a whiff of 'ghee' aroused the apetite of girls. Princess raised her voice above the bedlam and shouted, "Sadhuji, please stop at the 'Halwai' milkman. we want to have sweet 'Jalebies.'

"Not here my child, let's cross the market and park our Kunj somewhere safe. I'll send someone to get the sweetmeats you desire."

"All right!" she resigned with disappointment and their ride advanced out of the cramped lane.

Once the crowd thinned, they came to a clearing where some snake-charmers and monkey trainers were gathering circles of crowd around them. Sadhuji sent two servants to go and fetch jalebies in a basket. While rest of the battalion on horses stayed with the princess and her friends. They watched the going ons around them. A man came, up on a bullock cart while a cow was following it, tied to the tail board. The cart was loaded with two sacks of wheat from his farm. After haggling with the plump shopkeeper he exchanged the wheat for five jars of oil and bartered the cow for ten bales of cloth which he would sell in his village. Satisfied he left with his sari-clad wife who was still squatting in the cart watching the princess with interest while, the transactions were going on.

The boys reached the sweetmeat shop and climbed the steps up to the veranda, avoiding the street dogs waiting for the crumbs. There were a few people before them, waiting for their turn. So, the younger boy looked towards the road[1] for some diversion.

1. Hieun Tsang in the seventh century described a network of winding, narrow lanes

A peddler was moving tall in the crowd holding a bamboo pole with horizontal reeds on which dangled cheap trinkets on hooks for young girls. Glittery strings, clips, ribbons …; a woman walked with a child straddled on her one hip. Gongs sounded from the nearby Shiva temple situated in a narrow lane. Two women squabbled over the cost of flowers with the florist next door. Some children played in the narrow balconies of the residential quarters above their father's shops, which were windowless small cubicles, on both sides of the road.

Suddenly trumpeting, of an angry elephant sent a warning signal to the crowd. It had already pulled down the bamboo structure at the entrance. Panic stricken 'mahaut' was desperately trying to control the irate mammoth with his hooked goad. Mayhem that ensued, was making people scuttle out of its way, elbowing each other. The peddler who found himself facing the beast, hit its trunk forcefully with his mobile shop, and then slinked away before the elephant could even think of trampling him. His treasure of glittery knick-knacks flew in all directions. A red beaded string landed on a Pandit priest's 'shikha', or the top knot, and hung there. Right then he had lost all faith in God as he crouched under a vacant cart. From his hideout, the Pandit's beady eyes could see a straw hat flying and then landing on the head of a donkey, carrying two bags of sand. Blinded by it he went, helter-skelter, hee-hawing and hit a fat lady in a yellow sari, who plopped into a fruit seller's basket, placed on the footpath. His crushed watermelon, splattered the pink juices all over his face and shaggy graying beard, dripping. The innocent lady held on to his vest trying to retrieve her balance, while her curvaceous behind felt all wet and juicy. The dirty, sticky vest of the vendor, couldn't bear the muscular pull and tore all the way down. Luckily, her son was following the woman and helped her get up to run and climb the veranda. The fruit-seller threw away his torn vest and fled to safety.

The crazy elephant after turning the carts upside down, snatched a toddler by its trunk and threw it upwards like a toy. Its mother screamed and fainted. But the young alert peddler, jumped up in the air and clinched the shocked child in his secure grasp. Shouts of 'aha's and 'bravo' were heard all over, as the baby clung to him screaming his head off.

Just then people noticed that the travesty tantrums of the uncontrollable animal were tapering off. They looked up at the terrace of an arms shop where stood, a dark strong man with bow and arrows. He had shot the elephant at a tender spot, behind one of its ears and was shouting to the mahout, "Please do not worry about your ward. I have given him a mild

going towards the interior of the city of Kapilvastu. *Red-lac dye for decorating the feet.

tranquilizer. When he slows down, remove the arrow gently and the wound would heal with a paste of turmeric and mustard oil. Take him away before he gets too drowsy."

The mahout pressed his big toes in his neck behind the elephant's ears but the prick of the arrow tip and its pulling-out, had put the animal in a last burst of rage. He pulled his skinny master down and threw him at random, on the heads of the people. Some people ducked while the poor guy came flying and landed on the stout shoulders of a young labourer. The startled man tried to shake him off. The victim jumped off his perch and profusely thanked the hefty man for unknowingly saving his life before running towards his charge. To everyone's relief, the pesky beast was slowing down and led away from the street.

The business resumed as the tamasha-fun was over. Panditji came out of his hideout and adjusted his 'dhoti'[1] and 'Janeu'[2] before walking towards the narrow street of Shiva's temple, chanting "Shiva, shiva, shiva, fervently." A sadhu[3] dressed in ashes and a langoti[4] however walked away nonchalantly. The cuisinier came back to his seat and sat cross-legged on his dirty cushion, near the burnt up jalebies in a 'kadai.'[5] He removed them from the oil and reduced the heat in his wood stove before piping out new ones from a bundled up cloth with a hole. When they were golden yellow, he removed, strained and dipped those in sugar syrup. Once drenched the circular jalebies in irregular shapes were offered to the customers in 'dona' bowls made of dried leaves. The item was weighed on a tula[6] with a graduated arm and a suspended pan. He was paid in punch-marked coins.[7] The latest trend for cash, gradually replacing the barter-system.

As the two boys reached the spot where they had left the princess and her entourage, no-one was there except an eunuch from the palace. She informed them, "The princess was restless and headed for the park nearby. Where were both of you?" The 'Trans' demanded angrily. "Sorry, we couldn't help it. The market was more crowded than usual due to 'Navratras' and the approaching festival of Dassera[8]. Besides a mad elephant created havoc."

1. Dhoti – tangle of a light cloth around the waist and groins.
2. Sacred thread. +Tamasha=fun and games.
3. Sadhu – a sannyashi or renunciate.
4. Jockstrap type thong
5. Kadai – a wok with two opposite rings to hold.
6. Weighing balance.
7. The punch marked coins were minted by the 16 – Janapadas (clans) in copper, silver and gold from 1000-600 B.C.
8. Dassera festival is celebrated to commemorate the victory of Rama over Ravana of Lanka.

"Okay! Okay! The delay is already enough. Hand me over the basket of sweets."

She held it with one hand and the reigns of her horse with the other and galloped away kicking dust.

At the park Bhadrakanchan was running after a butterfly when the long awaited goodies reached her. She did not complain about the delay and thanked the eunuch profusely. After wiping the 'Ashoka donas'[1] clean, the young girls roamed around the garden observing various trees. Some Sal trees were full of pale blue junthi flowers. The tamarind trees were laden with green, juicy and sour tamarinds, a temptation for young girls. Some girls were already picking up the dropped ones. The palace eunuch following them, bought some from a vendor with a basket on his head and a twisted wicker stand stuck under his arm. He placed the basket on the now erect stand and handed the mouthwatering treat to the princess, whose attendant paid in cauris, the shell money.

There were many teenager girls and boys promenading around, giving each other sly glances. The slightly older young ladies were scattering lightening glances to bolt young handsome men, right where they stood. Some couples were whispering in the bowers with fragrant flowers hanging down. Birds were chirping and hopping. A peacock screamed at a distance. The charged ambience was full of life.

A group of boys passed by ogling at the palace chics, but the eunuch accompanying them fixed the Romeos with her hard glare. Soon these girls, laughing and gossiping reached the other end of the park where some local boys and girls were practicing a play. One little fellow was holding a bow made from a twig and a crooked arrow. Another was hopping around with a limp tail made from a strip of cloth tied to his waist. The girls were amused and since it appeared that they were enacting king Rama's life[2], they requested to join the group. A tall girl came forward and eyeing their expensive clothes asked authoritatively, "Where are you from?"

"From the palace", Renu answered. And they were invited to participate. The princess acted so well that she was allowed to bag the coveted role of Sita, Rama's wife. By this time the eunuch was settled comfortably on a nearby bench, chewing a quid of tobacco. She ignored the loud bickering of children. No one wanted the role of Shabari[3], a low

1. Bowls made of dried Ashoka leaves.
2. Ramayana in Sanskrit was originally written by Valmiki who was descendent of Sage Bhrigu. It was called – Ram Charit Manas.
3. Shabari was living at the ashram of Martand Rishi when she met Ram who was going to Chitrakoot hills during his fourteen year exile. Shabari was not her name but was the name of the tribe she belonged to. Her real name was Sramana.

caste tribal woman who adored Rama from the core of her heart. At that point Bhadrakanchan introduced herself, “I am the princess and live at the palace with the King and the Queen, my parents. I have someone in mind who would like to do this role.”

“Who?” There was a questioning chorus.

“My sweeper’s daughter! I’ve only seen her once but she’ll do.”

“We can’t do that,” the director came forward, indignantly.

“And why not?”

“Because it is a religious show. No low-castes, above all sweepers please!”

“God Ramchander, the great king ate the berries offered from her hands which had been tasted by the low-caste Sramana beforehand. Are we even superior to him? Tell me!”

“Shabari Sramana belonged to a jungle nomadic tribe. She did not collect night soil and clean up the ceramic pots containing the foul smelling excrement, even though it may be from the royal chambers,” contradicted the tall macho girl.

Confused director, a chubby boy tried to mellow things down, “Please Shikha, don’t be that fastidious. I am sure the girl herself doesn’t do that.”

“But she lives with her mother. Doesn’t she? Outside the boundary of our city. Even their shadow can pollute a brahman so they constantly strike a pair of clappers together when they need to move outside their village to warn people of their approach. And low-castes are not allowed in the temples or study the Vedas,” insisted the persistent brahman teenager.

“They would be allowed in my temple!” And the princess moved forward and placed her arm lovingly on the tall Shikha’s shoulder and took her aside.

“Listen friend I don’t mean to antagonise you but out of compassion give her a chance to come near the superior beings like us. It’ll be revolutionary. She would be given a purifying bath in a secluded corner of my personal garden with raw milk. Besides we won’t tell anyone who she is! There would be expensive gifts showered by my father on the actors…you don’t want to miss out on that. Do you? And remember that there won’t be any performance at the chief’s palace, if she is absent from the drama. You can perform wherever! At the same time, for your information, grownups recruit actors from the lowest classes.”* The princess then smiled with a smirk, while the eunuch stood behind her like a shield.

* Jeannine Auboyer: Ancient India.

In spite of any indications or expectations to the contrary, the play of Ramlila was enacted after the 'chaumasa,' of monsoon rains. In the private garden of Princess Bhadrakanchan at the palace; near a white marble statue of a 'yogi' sage, on a tall pedestal. There was water flowing out of his cupped hands, toward east.

Somehow, the statue reminded the princess of Siddhartha. Because she had heard that when King Shuddhodan once took him to a ploughing ceremony at the fields, eight year old couldn't stand to see hard work done by farmers and pain that the bulls endured. Disturbed, he had gone and was found sitting under a rose apple tree, in meditation, like a Yogi.

*****

After much practice in Kanchan's garden along with lavish foods and drinks, the day of the long awaited event arrived. Sramana, however was made to practice in a remote corner of the garden. The princess requested Malti and Renu, "Please check that everything is in order."

"We will, but what to do about Sramana Shabri, she is still not able to get her accent right. Her tongue, despite her efforts, smacks of her village dialect."

"Don't worry, that'll only make her role more realistic! I'll instruct her myself, she needs to be given more encouragement to boost her confidence."

"What if your mother comes to know about her?"

"She is not as narrow minded as my father or others. I'll talk to her and she'll manage them if they come to know. She would be let in our little secret just like Malti Amma. Okay!"

Malti was grinning to hear her little ward's high sounding suggestions. Though she knew 'if the king does come to know, she would run the risk of getting whipped or rot in jail for ever.'

The stage was a simple raised platform and the audience had wicker chairs to sit on. Of course the royalty had the privilege of soft cushions under their soft behinds. The serving staff squatted on the ground in front, on a cotton carpet. Some guards stood at the back in their uniforms. The background sheets of the stage were in different colours, according to the mood of the scene. Two women held them on either side. Yellow for heroic action; dull looking for a sad scene; multi-coloured for a farce; black for gruesome and red for violent scenes. The front curtain was only white, held by two chubby boys standing proudly on stools for the important assignment. Drums and instrumental music was prepared for creating the right milieu. Soon after breakfast, the show began which was squeezed into one day instead of ten.

As soon as the curtain went up or rather dropped down a 'Sutradhar,' compere came on the stage and invited the bard to sing in praise of the ancestors of the Shakyas and Koliyas. And the show rolled on. Small, little interludes took place. If a child forgot his dialogues, someone from the background took over while the actor only moved his lips and a squeaky childish voice would get transformed into a mature woman's. Once as Ravan was carrying Sita forcibly on his shoulders and she was throwing away her jewels, one landed in chief Suprabuddha's lap. He smiled at his daughter's enthusiasm, while she dressed as Sita exclaimed, "I am sorry, I missed."

When Ram came collecting the ornaments, he jumped down the stage and rolled to one side. Audiences grinned in an unobtrusive manner. Embarrassed, he got up and fixed his bow in place, and saved his dignity before collecting the last piece of jewellery. While trying to climb back he dangled precariously at the edge of the stage in a yellow 'dhoti', panting before heaving himself up, struggling with his bow and a childish paunch.

Anyway, the function was a great success. The dance performances were cute but the final chorus, children sang together with discordant voices, turned the finale of the concert into a comedy. The audience couldn't help grinning behind their hankies.

After the play there was prize distribution. The instrumentalist, drummer, the make-up and the costume-man, all were awarded. The artist with arched eyebrows and a hooked nose had painted Sramana's face so well that her fresh taut skin looked full of wrinkles and she bent double at the waist holding a shaft like a very old woman. She wore a necklace of fine grained and well polished sandstone beads and two iron bangles. Since low castes were not allowed to wear any other metal. She was awarded a third prize. She thanked in a shaky, feeble voice. Her dialogues had a natural touch of a low caste's tongue, whose part she was enacting. That was the most glorious day of her otherwise painful life. After the secret was found out by the brahamans, her father was beaten black and blue by thugs sent by brahmans. To teach them a lesson in propriety.

And then the name of the second prize-winner was announced. "The second prize goes to, Raghav who enacted the role of an angry young man, Laxman, prince Ram's younger brother." Finally, the queen announced, "The receiver of the first prize is,—" everyone caught their breath. "Devdatta!" Cheering and clapping went on for a long time. Nobody knew that he was in Devdah on a visit. He was given the role of Ravan at the spur of the moment. He performed a powerful act. Consolation prizes were given to Shikha and Mahendra, the directors and Bhadrakanchan.

The sun was throwing its last rays filtering through the trees from behind the hill-tops. Outside children had left with their parents except for Sramana who trudged the long way home alone, through the nearly empty streets. Except for a few drunkards who might have tried to molest the young girl had the princess not ordered a guard to follow her home.

Kanchan and her friends walked towards the 'ranivas'. Just then a scream was heard and Gopu, dressed as Ram, fell as a yellow scorpion crawled away with its stinger tail held high proudly. Renu ran inside to get some home remedy. The princess was rubbing Gopu's sting with an iron key, to neutralise the venom.

"Thank God it wasn't a snake I am so scared of the creepy creatures." As the boy was sweating and twitching his foot, an eunuch came and picked him in her strong arms and took him to his chamber. A sugar and water paste was applied to the red spot as he drank hot turmeric milk. Just then queen Amita entered with a concerned expression but was relieved to see the child's pain subsiding.

---

* According to nineteenth century archeologists.

Low castes were only allowed metal jewellery in cheap iron. 'Ancient India': p. 30 Auboyer.

Chapter - 6

Kapilvastu

A SMALL REPUBLIC WITH PRIDE AND VALOUR
IN THE SCENIC BEAUTY OF LOFTY PEAKS.
WAS CULTIVATING RICE
IN THE FERTILE PLANES OF BHAGIRATHI.

The fort of ancient Kapilvastu was the stronghold of the republic. An area was used for permanently stationed officers, 'mahamatras' who were in charge of the army and their equipments; troops ready for action whenever the need be. 'Chalak's or billeting officers took command over the 'Pindadayika' or soldiers of the supply corps, storm troopers (pakkhandino) and 'Cammayodhimo' or warriors in leather cuirasses.[1]

The armoury contained the armours to protect different parts of the body— 'shrastrana'(head covering), 'kanthatrana' (for neck), 'kurpasha,' (torso), 'kanchuka' (knee-length coat), 'varavana' (full-length coat), 'patta' (an armless coat) and 'nagodarika (gloves). Some armours were made-up of hides, hoofs, and horns of selected animals; tortoise, rhinoceros, bison, cow and elephant.

The fort was within high boundary walls made of layers of bricks about fifteen hands[2] wide, thus was huge in length and width.[3] The walls[4] were not straight due to Rohini River flowing on the side, which was somewhat curved giving the pentagonal shape to the land covered inside. The tall boundary wall all around was surrounded by a deep and wide moat full of

1. The list is from the Buddhist Pali Sources; cuirass was a defensive armour for the torso made up of leather, with a front and a back plate. (Second source—Dr. Awantika Lal)
2. Approximately 10-12 feet wide.
3. 1600 feet from north to south and 1000 feet from east to west.
4. Description of the wall is based on Buddhist scriptures and excavations Lalithavistara.

hungry 'ghariyal' species of crocodiles. The fort had four gates in the four main directions. Inside the village-like palace ground were many smaller palaces, ponds and temples. The whole complex was situated in the center of the capital city of Kapilvastu.

Outside the castle were some important factories.[1] Smiths of the metal workshop made utensils like huge water jugs, copper pots and frying pans; the agriculture equipments like spades, chisels, hoes and axes were made from the newly discovered iron along with various weapons. Metals were smelted in the furnace. There was also a mint where copper coins were casted.

The king and his ministers were busy in the conference room discussing the economic conditions of their kingdom and various business projects, before the meeting of the Sansthagriha assembly. A few important merchants were also asked to join. The minister of treasury named Pradyuman was a middle-aged man with greying hair at the temples. He sat next to the minister of justice who supervised the state revenues. King Shuddhodan asked,

"Pradyuman, please tell everyone about our financial status."

"Sure your majesty. Actually, we are generally financially sound, except during the wars. However, I would read out the details as well."

After listening to the details the King advised a few changes for the upcoming budget and stamped it with a seal. On which was written in Sanskrit, 'Saknasya Nigama.'

The ivory merchant a young handsome man with dark mustaches requested, "Ivory being a lucrative item to sell, specially at Sarasvati, I need some support from the administration. After paying our taxes to Kapilvastu and Sarasvati, our profits become small so further investments dwindle."

The king thought for a moment and asked the revenue officer, "What should we do Shantanu?" Who answered, "Your Majesty many poor people are also not able to pay their taxes. Confiscating their household items does not do us much good. It's only the welloffs who sustain us through their taxes and voluntary donations."

"Okay Laxman, I'll look into it and see what I can do about the ivory. I am going on a business trip to Sarasvati and would be meeting King Mahakaushal and talk to him about your problem."

Next, an older man in a pleated 'Paridhan,' with grey hair and upturned whiskers spoke about his issues. "O, Maharaj! This year the sugarcane harvest was not good due to shortage of water in the Rohini so please

1. T. N. Mishra Bidari.

allow me to increase the prices of those wines which are distilled from sugarcane."

The king addresses the treasurer, "What do you say Pradyuman?"

"Fine Maharaj, if the prices of the other wines and meads made from palm, coconut and honey are stable it is alright."

The King asked again.

"And what is the situation of imported wine?"

"Highly taxable as usual!"

King Shuddhodan smiles, "To appease the Bahaman intelligentsia, I have banned alcohol drinking but who stops?"

The meeting went on like this till the evening bells were chiming in temples. Just then a guard entered and told the prime minister Mahanaam softly, "Pandit Ambattha had been waiting outside for hours for the meeting to end. He wants to talk to the king." The minister looked at the king who shook his head in affirmation.

When Ambattha entered, no one paid any attention to him. The Brahaman felt humiliated. He like others of his class believed that the non-Brahamans were suppose to respect and serve them, since they were sacrosanct and were exempted from any kind of criticism or severe punishment. The most harsh punishment they could be meted out with, was the removal of their topknot which meant excommunication from the Brahmans society.

The annoyed Ambattha, was struggling with his thoughts. 'The members old and young, are seated in the hall on grand seats, making merry and joking together, nudging one another with their finger; and not one of them even offered me a seat. These Shakyas, menial as they are, mere menials, should neither venerate, not value, nor esteem nor give gifts to, nor pay honour to Brahmans.'[1]

Embittered Ambattha forgot that the 'Shakyas were of hardy' independent spirit and rejected the social pretensions of brahman superiority.[2]

Ambattha who had come to the King expecting gifts and donations, left full of resentment for him, without clearly telling him his purpose for coming. When he was gone the king felt bad for him but could not make anything out of his non-communicative visit. He shrugged his shoulders and called out the attendants for a round of drinks.

1. Ambattha Sutra – Trans. By Trevor Ling. The words were spoken by him to Buddha much later.
2. Trevor Ling – "The Buddha", p. 110.

The climax of the meeting was celebrated with rich snacks and intoxicating brews. Young girls in flowing garments came to serve them after drawing the curtains and lighting the fragrant lamps.

*****

After dinner King Shuddhodan went to his chief queen Mahaprajapati's room and while changing, told her, "Tomorrow is the spring[1] ploughing festival, which I need to attend with you and inaugurate. Please prepare Siddhartha too, to come with us. I want him to get a feel of what all he might be doing once he grows up and is the crowned prince."

"Sure Arya[2], I'll see to it that he is ready in time."

The light from the lamps was throwing an iridescent glow on the jewels of his queen Praja. The king looked at her pretty face lovingly and added, "Also remind me that I need to go to Sarasvati on a business trip, two days after that!" "Sure Rajan."

When the couple settled in bed, the king fondly started taking off her jewels one by one. And then started removing the hair pins stuck in her lustrous black hair. He always enjoyed the ritual.

*****

The ploughing festival of spring was about to commence at a government farm near the North-Road, main highway passing through the city of Kapilvastu. 'It was one of the main staging posts, the major commercial and cultural artery of the day.'

It linked Kapilvastu with Magadh kingdom in south and Kaushal kingdom in the north. The highway continued a further long distance towards west to Takshakshila the capital of Gandhara.[3] Wealthy merchants moved their goods and religious pilgrims, their ideas on this route till the vast Persian lands of west. One could reach Vrijji and Anga Janpads towards the east.

The humming of the traffic had started becoming audible early in the morning as the farm folks were awaiting king Shuddhodan's arrival. The Shakyans were farmers who cultivated rice, millet, mustard seed, lentils and sugarcane. They also raised cattle, sheep and goats for meat and milk.[4]

1. New year coincides with spring equinox. Jeannie Auboyer: 'Ancient India.'
2. The Superior one.
3. Confessions of a Buddhist Atheist – Stephen Bachelor. — unworthy of his throne: Mahasupina Jataka—
4. Confessions of a Buddhist Atheist – Stephen Bachelor. — no. 77, I, p. 190. (Trans. Auboyer.)

Siddhartha was eight years old when his father King Shuddhodan was taking him and some of his friends to witness the ritual of ploughing of fields. His mother queen Prajapati Gautami dressed him up with great care according to what the occasion demanded, and he was excited to go with his father for this formal function. Devdatta, Bhadiya, Mahanaam, Kimbila and Kaludai who went with him were also his schoolmates.

On reaching the farmland they got off their chariots amidst cheering crowd. There were colourful small, triangular flags and banners at the entrance gate of road leading to the farm. The track had been sprinkled with water to settle the dust and lined with white lime-powder used in whitewashing the buildings to ward off insects. The king and royal children walked majestically, smiling in response to the people around. People on two sides of the cordoned road were waving and yelling, "Maharaj ki Jai"; Hail the King!

The procession reached the farm, where high ranking officers, Brahmans and royal guests were moving around in bright knee-length long cotton coats over twisted silk Dhotis, covering both the legs and turbans. On one side a long table was laid with cooling drinks and tasty snacks. Some girls were attending to the table. Minstrels and musicians were playing their music among people. The boys served themselves and sat on a grassy patch enjoying their refreshments.

As the ceremony commenced, the priests started chanting 'shlokas' in Sanskrit. It went on and on for such a long time that the boys, finishing their picnic ran away where dancing and music was entertaining the public. The hot sun was making the dancers sweat and their fancy dresses were getting soaked.

After chasing each other for some time the boys got hot and tired. Siddharth left his companions to look for some shade. He came to a rose-apple tree and sat under its cool relief. His eyes were still itching due to the glaring sun. So, he closed them and rested, oblivious of what was happening around him. He might have dozed off while sitting against the tree trunk.

By the time the ceremony was over, everybody started looking for the Prince. His mother found him sitting under the tree in yogi-posture with closed eyes. She thought he might be meditating so she asked the ordinary children playing nearby not to make too much noise. They slunk away to play elsewhere. When it became too quiet Siddharth opened his eyes and asked his mother, "Is it over?" Prajapati answered, "Yes son, let's go. Your father is waiting for us."

"Okay mother but I feel, reciting the scriptures does not make the corns grow bigger and better. It is neck breaking labour that does it. Didn't you see how hard the poor oxen were working to pull the heavy plough and the skinny farmer's back was burnt due to sun and streaming with sweat. The holy men reciting the 'mantras' and the dignitaries, were under huge umbrellas. While the hired farmer was busy whipping the poor animal to urge."

However, when Gautami told the king that she found him meditating under the rose-apple tree. He got worried. Sage Asita's warning, was constantly hanging over their heads like a sword. He knew that he would only die in peace if someone as capable as Siddhartha would take charge of the kingdom after him, otherwise all could be lost.

*****

Siddhartha was turning more and more good looking every day. He was studying and practicing marshal arts with his cousins and friends. He was way above everyone and that irked his cousin Devdatta the most, who was always competing with him and yet loosing. Siddhartha never considered himself superior due to his accomplishments. But Devdatta's childhood complexes never let him rise above his petty jealousies.

By the time Siddhartha was twelve his father took him around on business trips to Sarasvati so that he could get a glimpse of the administrative aspect of running a domain. On such occasions he would meet the Kaushal Prince Prasenjit and they had become friends.

The royal carriage, followed by some soldiers had reached Sarasvati by dusk. It was the new capital of Kaushal Kingdom after Ayodhya. Siddhartha's young eyes were eyeing the magnificent buildings with awe. The city was pulsating with vigour and energy. Yet the hum of the crowds was refined. Sophisticated young well-dressed socialites were going in carriages or sauntering about in the parks. The prince clutched on his father's arm fascinated as the palace of King Mahakaushal became visible. They were stopped at the gate for identifications and the vehicle moved on to the drive crunching the red grit. They got off near the steps and were welcomed by the Chief Minister.

King Shuddhodan and his ward were then led to the side veranda where king was having a drink in privacy along with his queen Mallika. On seeing them he welcomed the Chief of Kapilvastu and looked at Siddhartha who bent and touched his feet.

"So this is the heir of your kingdom! Welcome my son, you have grown as tall as Prasenjit. Now have a soft drink or water before you meet Prasenjit with his friend Bandhul at the end of the lawn practicing archery."

Siddhartha looked at the two figures almost his age at a distance on the green grass and moved towards them. The minister introduced him to Prince Prasenjit and Bandhul, son of the governor of province of Malla.

"So here comes our little wise fool!" Exclaimed the arrogant prince lightheartedly. "Are you still harping about non-violence or are you trying to become a great warrior?"

"Both." He smiled while Bandhula looked at him with curiosity. "I practice the marshal arts diligently but I still believe in the concept of non-violence."

"Forget your emotional tug-of-war, shoot the target with my bow."

"Bull's eye," screamed the boys. Impressed by his expertise they soon became close friends.

*****

When Siddhartha was fourteen he became more interested in religious scriptures, Rig Veda and Atharva Veda. He realised the importance of the 'mantra' chanting. The words and sounds seem to hold great power which could influence the human mind and body and its natural surroundings. He also studied the 'Brahamans' and 'Upanishads', the latest scriptures. But when he tested them against the realities of life, he always found something amiss. Poor people stayed poor, however religious they were.

Siddhartha also studied under the guidance of his Acharya, the Manu Samhita which was originally called the Dharma Shastra or the Book of Ancient Law. Manu, in remote past had divided the society into four groups according to the aptitudes of different people. Those who were good in studies were made the Brahmans. They became more educated than most people and came to understand the mysteries of the cosmos. The warring tribes, the Kshatriyas were essential for their protection while they studied, so they were considered second in the social hierarchy. Since Brahamans did not have time to make money for their own sustenance they needed the generosity of the moneyed landlords and the traders who had an insight into money-making business, and were known as the Vaishyas. The dull ones could clean up the mess of everyone else. As the time passed the different classes became rigid and turned into castes. Which eventually became the shackles of Hindu society.

However, during the ancient period, anyone could change his caste, if one was better suited for some other profession despite what his father professed. The class division was for convenience and was flexible. With the passage of time when guilds came into the picture, it became narrow minded and stiff. Brahmans became arrogant and money-minded. Their greed was slowly becoming their downfall.

Siddhartha was determined that when he becomes the king he would try and dissolve the rigid boundaries existing between the four castes into the ocean of oblivion. His reverie, however was soon interrupted by his mother's melodious voice.

"Siddhartha come soon, we need to go for the evening Samai Ma's temple and light the lamp for the Goddess," called his mother, the queen.

Siddhartha came and asked, "You mean to say that the all powerful 'cosmic power' cannot see in the dark?"

"Come on son, logic and faith do not go together."

To please his mother, he followed her to the temple of the family deity, mother goddess. He looked at her benign face and many bejewelled arms holding her weapons and blessing her devotees one palm raised towards them.

*****

Chapter - 7

Ashoka Dona Festival (Youth Festival)

YASHODHARA THE DAUGHTER OF THE GREAT MINISTER
WHOSE FAME WAS KNOWN IN EVERY LAND
SELECTING A FORTUNATE DAY FOR HER MARRIAGE
APPROACHED AND ENTERED WITHIN THE ROYAL PRECINCT.*

When Bhadrakanchan was about to be sixteen, Suprabuddha and Amita often discussed marriage prospects for their daughter. Not knowing that she has already chosen her match. She had told her mother one day, "Ma I shall either be Siddhartha's wife or no one's!"

"Your father would never agree my dear!" "Why?"

"For two reasons! One, that after marriage, he would go to Takshakshila leaving his wife with her parents. When he gets back after two years only then the ceremony of 'Gauna'[1] would take place and marriage be consummated."

"Then why marry him at all?"

"His father insists. Probably to bind him to the palace of Kapilvastu. And the second reason is as everyone knows Sage Asita's prophecy."

"I am sorry Mom, I can't do what father wants. I had been his wife in every life-time. I cannot quit now. This is our seventh and the last life together."

"How do you know that?"

"Sage Dipanker prophesied to me in my dreams a few times."

"Isn't it childish to pursue a possibly painful life based on a dream?"

---

1. 'Gawna' – in the villages of northern territory of India the tradition was and still is to marry children young. Even at age of ten or twelve. Once they come of age, the girl is brought with fan-fare to the boy's house, for good. Nepal was Indian territory before the British rule. *Romantic Legends, 92 : Beal.

"No mother I know it is true! Uncle Shuddhodan is organising 'Ashoka Dona'[1] festival to give gifts to young girls. And Siddhartha would choose one to be his wife. Please ask father to make arrangements for me and my friends along with Malti Amma to attend the function."

"Leave Malti aside, she is not too well. I'll do the rest!"

*****

The aristocratic chariot was speeding on the road between Devdah and Kapilvastu. Six soldiers were escorting the princess and her friends to youth festival. An eunuch followed them as a special guard. They called her 'Amma' yellow curtains on the windows of the vehicle were fluttering in the breeze, coinciding with Bhadrakanchan's heart. There was a distance of two yojana[2] still left, so the princess tried to relax in her seat. She rested her head on a beige coloured silken pillow and closed her eyes.

She saw herself in front of a shrine, in the city of Paduma where Saint Dipankar held his residence at that time. Her name was Sumidha and she was selling flowers outside, when a young monk came to pay his homage to the saint. He wanted to take some flowers for him, but he had no money and the florists were all sold out. He requested the flower-girl, "Give me one blossom young lady to offer to the saint." The girl who was smitten by his good looks, charm and saintly demeanor put forward a condition.

"I'll gladly give you five flowers out of my seven for free if you marry me."

The monk looked at the beautiful young girl and answered – "I am sorry, I am under an oath of celibacy, I cannot marry anyone in this lifetime, but I promise to marry you in the next."

"I'll wait!" And she handed him the entire bunch of lotuses,[3] before getting the sage's blessing.

Just then a slight bump in the road woke the princess up, from her trance. The image dissolved yet had appeared so real! Their chariot had come to a screeching halt. She poked her nose out of the window to inquire from the coachman, "What is wrong sir?"

Before he could answer Eunuch Amma came forward and answered, "one of the wheels has gotten loose due to the long and rough road."

"What do we do now?" the princess asked with a frown.

---

1. Ashoka Dona – a bowl made from dried Ashoka tree leaves. *Beal – Romantic Legends.
2. 15 km.
3. This is a story from Jataka Tales, where stories based on previous lives of Buddha and Yashodhara (Bhadrakanchan) are described.

"Nothing. You girls get down and enjoy the scenery while we fix it. I too would get a chance to stretch my tired old legs." And she dismounted her horse with a groan. One of the girls giggled, 'Amma is always grumbling about her advanced age. Once I saw her head covering removed and her bald head shone like a boiled, peeled potato."

As Bhadrakanchan and her companions alighted, the girls were still laughing away. Princess scolded them, "Please girls we need not make fun of the elderly." And she moved a little further away from them.

Once alone, she took out the flyer from under her stole and started reading the requirements prince Siddhartha wanted in his would-be bride. It was sent to the parents of all the girls who were invited to attend the 'dona' festival by King Suddhodan at Kapilvastu.

"She should dress modestly.

She should lovingly obey.

She should be adept as a courtesan in knowing the arts of love….

However, caste or status of family is not important."

As the princess was engrossed in reading, her friends admired the surrounding mountain tops where the glaciers were beginning to thaw and the patchy slopes were sprouting grass.

"Come Princess, the wooden wheel is fixed."

Eagerly she boarded the carriage followed by other young maidens. Her sallow complexioned, loving friend Renu, sitting next to her asked, "Why such a worried look on your face?"

"I am afraid of getting late for the evening proceedings lest the prince chooses some other girl to be his future queen."

Renu teased her, "So what! You can easily find better suiters than him. You haven't even seen him in last ten years. What if he has turned ugly like a toad?"

Kanchan slapped her lightly on the shoulder, "As long as he is wise and compassionate as before I want him, ugly or handsome!"

The horses were galloping hard as the sun was sinking behind the mountains. So was Kanchan's heart, she closed her eyes to shut the anxiety out but it persisted.

The magnificent palace of Kapilvastu had its south entrance adorned with garlands and beads. Burning torches were lit in the mouths of the two white elephants with trunks raised in a salute at the top of the gate-pillars. The intelligent and responsible 'dwarika' officers checked the credentials of the coachman and recognising the flag of Devdah let them rattle in till the steps of the palace entrance.

Devdatta, in all his finery was standing with his friends to welcome the guests. The princess got down gracefully, with her fair feet adorned by anklets and 'alta'. After seeing Devdatta she quickly veiled her face with her shimmering white stole. Before he could make his welcoming speech Amma quickly led the girls inside. He stood there agape with arms half stretched, questioningly. Nand patted his back and enjoyed a chuckle at his expense . "We are done here cousin, lets go inside."

The Kanchukin or the guardian had been recruited from among the eunuchs; cane in hand, clad in a white tunic over her sari, she protectedly followed the maidens.

The main hall was well-lit and filled with fragrant excitement. Delicate murmurs were floating among the best dressed gentry. The last recipient was receiving the most expensive jewel of the evening. Shuddhodan had told his son, "This is for the girl you like most." Since he did not like anyone in particular, he gave the necklace to the beautiful girl called Mrigi Gautami, the doe-eyed maiden who had fallen for Siddhartha at the very first sight. She eyed the gorgeous necklace with approval and fluttered her eyelashes, darkened with anjana kohl, at stunningly handsome prince of her dreams. Who was tall, fair with dark curly hair and eyes. She spoke coyly, her voice dipped in honey, "O generous prince should I assume that I am the chosen one for you?"

"Your beauty is dazzling no doubt young lady but you received this jewel simply because you were the last participant and that was all, left with me to give."

Their attention was drawn towards the entrance as a swan-white glittering figure glided towards the prince, veiled. By the time the young Koliyan girls reached the prince, Mrigi stomped away, feeling rejected. She sat on a vacant chair, looking at her diamond necklace with three emeralds set in gold at the center wondering, 'Who is she now? The beautiful and expensive piece is not worth missing out on Siddhartha.'

Princess's attendants gracefully left her as she reached Siddhartha. They watched them from a distance. Ganga spoke mischievously eyeing the dashing crown prince, "She will knock him out. After all the beauty treatments she has gone through; ointments, perfumes and what not! Us, fumigating her clothing for so long over the fragrant smoke!"*

Mrigi looked for her friends but they were busy admiring young handsome men covered in jewels, flowers and perfumes. Devdatta had left his group of friends and was amusing himself with pretty faces around, holding his cup of imported wine in one hand and combing his dark wavy tresses with the other. He noticed pretty Mrigi moist eyed sitting aloof and came to her with a gallant demeanor. He asked charmingly, "Without a companion pretty lady?"

Mrigi looked up at his tall figure and handsome face, yet averted her gaze as she glimpsed a savage look in his eyes. She was in love with Siddhartha's loving and compassionate personality.

Devdatta sat next to her without being invited and switched on his best manners.

"Your name has to be Mirgi[1]."

"Why do you say that?" Mrigi was curious.

"Because your eyes are as pretty as a doe's."

"You really think so! Siddhartha doesn't."

"Don't mind my brother he is a fool. You are a beauty to behold."

"Then why is he giving away his own emerald necklace and the signet ring to another girl when the ceremony is already over?"

"Oh, he gave away those things to her because he has known her since childhood."

"Do you think he'll choose her as his bride?"

"I hope not! Would you care for a drink?" he asked getting up.

"No thank you, my mother doesn't approve."

He got his hint and moved away to look for greener pastures.

Mrigi knew that like other kings or princes Siddhartha too could have multiple wives. She still has a chance of becoming, 'at least his junior queen'. She was lost in thoughts and didn't even notice that prince Nand, Prajapati's son was also interested in her and was nearing. Mrigi couldn't stand it anymore. She smiled at Nand briefly and treaded towards her father Dandpani. He was a rich, respectable man who owned a staff of solid gold. His family's reputation was good and his mansion, no less than a king's palace.

"Father, I want to go home."

"Why child? Dinner is being served, we'll have it and leave. We would be coming tomorrow again to witness the tournament where all the young princes gathered here would get a chance to prove their expertise in marshal arts."

"Okay father!" She answered dejected. She wasn't use to hearing a 'no' but somehow wanted to find out more about the new arrival.

---

1. Mrigi means deer. *Mahabharata IV.

In the meantime, when the king and the queen saw Siddhartha with Bhadrakanchan engaged in a conversation they couldn't resist their curiosity. The prince was saying, "May I know your name lady and your introduction. You see, the actual ceremony is over but since you have come for me, I feel honoured and obliged to give you some precious gift. But I have nothing left. The princess visibly flared up. "Why didn't you save one for me?"

"I didn't know who else was coming! Specially someone with a veiled face." The prince was enjoying her tantrums. "It seems you are not good looking that is why are hiding behind your teasingly beautiful stole."

"Oh really? We shall see that later. I shall only show you my face if you can guess my identity."

King Shuddhodan and Queen Prajapati moved closer to the couple unobtrusively to eavesdrop, on their son's reaction to the mystery girl who was saying, "I shall show you my face only if you can guess who I am!"

"Hmm, any clue?"

"You have met me before."

Siddhartha's mind zoomed in on a little chubby girl by his side when he was nursing the wounded swan hit by his cousin Devdatta's arrow, as a child...; or watching the boat race. Also once as a teen, while returning from Bhagirathi with Channa during autumn, they had stopped near some rice fields where he had seen a girl's back and side profile, in a simple sari. Nursing the sick children and washing their soiled clothes, at a poor hut. She appeared like a goddess with a healing touch as she cleaned their infected eyes and applied ointment as well as gave medicines to those suffering from fever. She had been bandaging the wounds due to infected boils or otherwise.[1] While their mothers were busy working at the farms, doubled up in the watery rice fields, singing melancholic songs, nearby.

He heard Bhadrakanchan saying, "You are routed, O Prince."

With a sudden rush of realisation, he spilled the beans.

"You are Bhadrakanchan," he said wagging his finger at her. "My paternal or should I say maternal aunt't daughter." With a flash the princess flipped her veil grinning broadly.

Sixteen year old Siddharth was hit by Kama's[2] double-strength arrows. He gently took her silken hand and led her to his parents who were right behind.

1. The stars at dawn.
2. Kama = Cupid.

"You have turned out to be so beautiful my child", Prajapati admired her with a hug and told Siddhartha to give her the gift. He answered, "Mother there is nothing left."

When his mother hinted with her eyes, he took off his precious emerald necklace and adorned her neck with its beauty. Yet she frowned. So, he gave his signet ring too.

When the princess touched King Suddhodan's feet, he blessed her and asked, "Haven't your parents come dear?"

"My father was not in favour of this match if it might take place."

"Is it due to sage Asita Kaladevala's prophecy that Siddhartha might become an ascetic one day?"

"Yes Sir! But I was adamant and convinced him that I'll take care of the situation if and when it does arise."

"I admire your confidence my child. Keep it up!"

"But they would be here tomorrow for the three-day long military training competitions."

Her aunt Praja looked at Bhadra dotingly, while Mangala passing by, made a face at them. Devdatta was cursing Siddhartha, standing at a distance. He had always had his eyes on Yashodhara, since childhood and now she was slipping out of his hands just like the crown.

He had been remorseful of the fact that though his father and then he himself were the rightful heir to the throne yet his grandfather had preferred his second son Shuddhodan to be the ruler. Mangala too had her grievances. Being the oldest daughter of king Anjana of Devdah, she should have been given a chance of marrying Shuddhodan the king, yet she ended up with his good-for-nothing older brother. Her husband Dhrotodan was busy socialising and conniving so Mangala gloomily sat next to Mrigi, knitting her eyebrows.

Bhadrakanchan and Prajapati were exchanging news while the king listened.

The king advised his wife, "Please make the best arrangements for them." "Sure Rajan!"

*****

During the sports event, each evening ended up in festivities and merry making. Sumptuous food and drinks were served while dancers and musicians entertained the guests who were mingling with one another for the possibility of any future alliance – political or matrimonial. After all the prince would choose only one bride to be his chief queen. The rest of the girls had a choice of joining Siddhartha's seraglio as his courtesans, which wasn't such a hot idea after all.

While the young girls and boys were busy flirting, Dhrotodan and Suprabuddha conspired in hushed tones. The Koliya was saying, "How do you stand the domineering attitude of Shuddhodan?"

"Do I have a choice? I am the eldest of my five brothers yet my father rejected me for the post of the chief. My younger brother is the king and I need to maintain decorum for mine and my family's interests."

"When Siddhartha would ascend the throne you would have to bow your head to him too."

"Unfortunately that seems to be my destiny." He spoke bitterly.

"Change it! Change your destiny. We are not a monarchy like the kings in the planes. We are republics where the Chief is voted by our Kshatriya members."

"That is only in theory. In reality the tradition is that the oldest prince of the Chief has the first right if he is worthy. Actually Shuddhodan is a very disciplined king who is popular amongst his subjects. And Siddhartha is capable too. The Chief never gave anyone reason to complain till he created a township outside Kapilvastu, where all the sick and the elderly were shifted so that his son could be kept away from any grief. Yet he provided them with dispensaries and other amenities. But those people missed their relatives and friends."

There was sweat on Dhrotodan's agitated brow.

"Let's move away from under this chandelier. It is too hot. My throat is parched. I'll get us drinks. Which wine do you prefer, Greek or Persian?"

"I'll go for Persian."

He clapped his hands at a passing serving-girl dressed in Greek tradition and picked a gilded goblet of wine from the silver salver, for himself. Next he waved to a girl dressed in Persian attire and wine from that country appeared.

Suprabuddha took a few sips from his cup before resuming their conversation. Before he could open his mouth Dhrotodan commented, admiring the Greek serving slave girls.

"These 'Yavani'* dames are so graceful and sexy!"

"You mean just like their wine? But I prefer to look at the luscious lips of those Parsi girls through their translucent niqabs."

"Do you really? I thought you were not the kind!"

"No I am not! I didn't want to appear rude by not participating in your enthusiasm. Anyway never mind them for now. I was putting forward a political strategy. King Mahakaushal and his son are quiet friendly with me. But I don't want to put down Shuddhodan with their help."

"Why?"

"For two reasons. One, although Mahakasushal's daughter is married to Bimbisar, King of Magadh he likes Suddhodana and his family. He is bound to pressure the Kaushal king not to go for war. Secondly, if he destroys Shakyas, he would definitely come after Koliyas as well. Our republics are no match for the powerful kingdoms of Kaushal, Magadh or Kashi and others. Our lands are hard to till but fertile enough to become greed of our dominant neighbours."

"You mean there is nothing anyone can do to shake off the chief from his throne generation after generation."

"Actually, there is something we can do! He said with a twisted smile. Start up a secret campaign against chief Shuddhodan by seducing the members of the federation in our favour."

Dhrotodan became thoughtful. They both looked at some distance and saw Maha Prajapati approaching them. Dhrotodan slipped away tactfully so that she could talk to her brother in privacy.

The crescendo in the hall was ascending by the passing moments. People were eagerly awaiting the final outcome of the evening.

Though Siddhartha did not much care for the marshal arts, but to save his teacher Acharya Kondiya's honour, he had excelled in all the competitions due to his excellent focus and concentration. The participants were supposed to prove their expertise in archery, sword fight, pole fight, wrestling, hand to hand combat, spear, lasso, iron dart, club, battle axe, thrown iron discus, and trident. At the same time excel in swimming, horsemanship and ability to aim from a moving chariot. Even mathematics was considered important for a warrior. There was an exciting race too of the two wheel war chariots led by one horse, in the arena. Prince Siddhartha was announced man of the day. Princess Yashodhara's heart was bouncing in her chest. She clung to her mother in excitement.

The most jealous person due to his success was Devdatta, his cousin. He had tried every trick in his arsenal to beat his sworn-enemy but to no avail. He was busy thinking, 'In every way I am better than Siddhartha but he gets away with success because he is the king's son. I hope Sage Asita's prophecy does come true and my cousin becomes an ascetic. Then I shall get the throne as well as Yashodhara'. While he was lambasting himself his stream of thoughts was interrupted by his three friends, who came to check on him.

At night, after an extravagant feast the polite conversations reduced their tempo. The gentry tried to focus on the dancers. While the politicians played their piddling games. Their acrimonious onslaughts on the oppositions were spoken softly to their comrades.

Some dignitaries had started stepping on to the stage. Commencing with the king and his brothers. There was a scattered stir amongst the audience. Some feminine hearts fluttered; others pretended to stay calm. A small number however had someone else in mind so they preferred to be rejected. Realising the significance of the situation the dancers gracefully withdrew. Suddenly the dying noise turned to stillness and quiet. Slicing the calm, king Shuddhodan announced in his deep and eloquent voice.

"Dear honourable guests I deeply appreciate your kindness for joining the happy occasion of this youth festival, where the prince would choose his bride after proving to the girl and her parents that he is a worthy match. Today only the wedding ceremony would take place. After which the chosen princess would go back to her parents' house and 'gauna'[1] would be celebrated after two years, when the Prince returns from Takshakshila University after finishing his higher studies."

There were loud whisperings among the gathering.

Suprabuddha and his queen Amita looked at each other. Amita warned Bhadrakanchan, "Look daughter, this is your chance to withdraw. You are sixteen, if you do not want to wait there are many fantastic options for you right now!"

"Father, since I was a little girl I wanted to marry Siddhartha. Please mother, I don't want any craping about it now. Even I can, study some more, while I am waiting for my would-be husband to come back."

"Your plucky attitude would drown you one day in sorrow," warned the concerned father. The princess just bowed her head, in resignation.

Her parents looked at the stage, absentmindedly where the king was inviting his older brother's wife Mangala to come and make the important announcement of the evening. He also requested Suprabuddha to come and grace the stage with his benign presence. Giving a remorseful look to his loving daughter, he left. When Mangala appeared, Shuddhodan helped her climb the steps. She was smiling from ear to ear as she stood between Shuddhodan and Suprabuddha, feeling important; under festoons and bright chandeliers.

---

1. The act of consummating; completion of marriage. *Yavani: Greek.

The kings were wearing knee length long coats with brocaded, vertical central panels, and gold embroidery at the hem and the edges of the armholes. The 'Paridhan' tapered towards the hem giving it a flair. There was a sash in the middle. Their necks were adorned with all kind of precious studded necklaces and pearls and on the pierced earlobes, dangled solid gold balls on small chains. The tips of the plumes on the crown of Shuddhodan had glittering droplets of gems. He had a handsome mustache, the tips of which were twisted upwards and a trimmed beard along with dark wavy shoulder length hair. To top it all he wore a fabulous long- sleeved 'Angarkha' in turquoise. Suprabuddha had thrown a crimson silk 'Uttariya' over his left shoulder. His crown was, however no match to Shuddhodan's.

The backdrop of the stage was of purple velvet curtains with golden trimmings. Tall Mangala was clad in a precious sari, woven with silk and gold threads. She cut a pretty picture till she opened her mouth to speak. She took enough time to let her presence be felt. Then adjusting her red brocade stole and turning her face towards Prajapati, her voice exploded in the hall.

"Congratulations, sister-in-law, your precious daughter-in-law would be"... and she paused, slow-rolling the announcement. All eyes went to her. Shuddhodan had a frown.

"She is Yashodhara", she still kept everyone in the limbo. The king was uneasy at her audaciousness. The boom came again. "Yashodhara is the new name for our well-known Bhadrakanchan, our King's niece!"

The hall resounded with thunderous clapping, willing or unwilling.

Before Prince Siddhartha and Princess Yashodhara were brought to the stage, another announcement was made by Chief Shuddhodan.

"One thing more, illustrious gentlemen and charming ladies, to-morrow we shall have a royal procession to commemorate the auspicious marriage of our crown prince and his beautiful bride. Your graceful presence would increase our joy manifold. We'll be happy to make arrangements for those who intend to stay, at the palace!"

The dancers reappeared and danced with a gentle slow rhythm. While the priest looked with concern at the wedding pavilion, nearby. There were cut banana trees fixed in the four corners around the big, square vessel ready for the ritual of sacrificial fire.

After making the couple exchange garlands on the stage in front of everyone, sacred fire was lit with the help of camphor chunks, in the huge copper vessel. Prince and princess had been led to the pavilion by priests to perform the main ceremony. Close relatives followed them and took their seats on cushions. Chiefs Shuddhodan and Suprabuddha sat along their queens, opposite to one another while their two priests were facing the betrothed couple. Fragrant herbs, ghee sandalwood powder and rice were sacrificed on the ignited logs of mango trees, to the devas. The couple went circumambulating around the holy fire seven times and pronounced their pledges to one another. They took blessings of the priest and the family elders by touching their feet. Yashodhara did not veil her face as per the custom. Siddhartha took off his turban as he was sweating. His gold like complexion shone further.

Many a maidens sighed regretfully, and one even dropped her gift, which she was holding, absentmindedly.

The parents and relatives gave expensive gifts to the newly married royal couple. Yashodhara had received a pink Kashi-silk saree interwoven with real gold thread from Prajapati. The gold ornaments were intricately carved out of almost pure gold and encrusted with rare gems. Ladies of the family were looking at the trousseau and evaluating it. The prince received from his wife's parents a thick, gold wrist band, a heavy gold-chain and silver and gold, bars and coins along with silk garments. While the women were busy ogling the trousseau and the dowry under Mangala's supervision and running commentary, the priest was still chanting the wedding mantras in his nasal tone as the couple was made to act like puppets on his instructions. The pundit in the end blessed them, "May you both have a joyful future and healthy progeny."

The ambience was full of excitement and happy vibes. Bells chimed, to ward off evil, incense burned and so did many hearts. Devdatta and Mrigi had their spots knocked out. Their dreams shattered, they both stood exchanging verbal onslaughts at the expense of Siddhartha and Yashodhara, with bitterness. They went till the gate together busy in vindictive and vicious talks. Most of the crowd seem to have left happy.

Next day, soon after morning chores and light breakfast the regal procession of the married couple started from well decorated palace gates. There were marigold garlands, strings of semiprecious stones and banners which hung all over the city. From balconies, terraces; over temples and trees. The Shakya flags were erected at the fort and other public buildings. Lengths of silk and linen were hung in scallops in front of palaces and houses. Sweepers had cleaned and sprinkled water with goat-skin bags on the royal road. 'Heaps of sandalwood and aloes were positioned at intervals along the route, to be ignited when the moment came so that their aromatic smoldering should perfume the air.' Torches were placed on each side of the main boulevards.*

A young healthy mahout was ready with a fig wood throne fitted on the back of the royal elephant over velvety, gold trimmed sheet hanging on its two sides. It was painted in crucial spots with natural vegetable dyes. A parasol with a gilded staff was stuck high at the back of the howdah. Musicians, dancers, priests and officials were assembled at the eastern gate of the fort to follow the King's magnificently embellished chariot.

As soon as the married couple came surrounded by their entourage and a ladder was placed for them to climb up, the orchestra started bellowing conches and beating gongs, cymbals and drums to the utmost. The effect was nerve wrecking rather than melodious to the Young bride. She held prince's hand nervously under the privacy of her gossamer silken shawl. He reassured her by pressing her hand gently while looking straight ahead.

Ladies followed the dancers in the procession; then the elites flanked by guards in their dazzling, sharp uniforms. A group of nobles on the horseback was followed by a throng of people on foot, completing the column. Colourful streamers were waving above their heads, brightening the streets.

Ladies and children were squeezed in their balconies, bending double to look at the newly wedded royalty. Men were lining the muddy roads. Mrigi, at her home was painfully aware of the happenings along the thoroughfare and had told her maids, "Do not bother me. I have a headache and I am going to sleep it off." She blocked her ears with silk cushions till the sound faded and sulked and wept to her heart's content.

The procession was proceeding on the wide ring road circling the capital. At last they reentered the fort with palaces within, to poor Yashodhara's relief.

After a late lunch the virgin bride left Kapilvastu with her parents and some troops, for Devdah.

*****

---

* Yavanzi: 'The slave girls in the seraglio were either 'born in the house' who were practically members of the family. Or had been bought for a nominal price; or received as a gift. These young women were often brought from Greece by merchants in their trading vessels and were sold for their expertise in singing and dancing along with the claims that they were from noble families.' Greeks were called Yavanas in India and their girls, Yavanis.
Note:

* The description of the procession is partly based on J. Auboyer's 'Ancient India,' p. 280.

Chapter - 8

Takshakshila

FAR AWAY IN THE DISTANT LANDS
AT CROSSROADS OF CULTURES DISTINCT;
HE SALLIED FORTH TO QUENCH HIS THIRST
FOR INSIGHT, WISDOM AND LEARNING.

Soon after her marriage to Siddhartha, Yashodhara went to her parents at Devdah and resumed her further education. In her free time, she would teach some poor children or take care of their medical needs. She craved for Siddhartha's company but she knew she has to be patient. No one forced her into the situation. It was her own choice. Whenever she was overwhelmed with emotion, she would write poetry. Her favourite companions Renu and Rohini never left her side.

Yet, when he was sent for further studies to Takshakshila he was glad to leave the monotony of a small backward city. Fear still lurked at the back of his mind about the unfamiliar surroundings. He had made his father king Shuddhodan promise that Channa would stay with him and also study at the same university as a poor student. Poor and bright students were allowed to study for free, due to the donations proffered by the rich and generous.

Queen Prajapati had tried to dissuade her husband from sending him so far. "There Are good colleges in Sarasvati too," but the king was firm. "Praja if Mahakaushal's son can study there, why not mine. He'll learn worldly wisdom apart from making good contacts. I am grooming him to be the best king ever. Right now, he does not know, how to deal with the conniving world. He is too honest and straight."

Without further arguments Queen Gautami quietly started packing his ornamental metal trunk, with tearful eyes. 'All new clothes but less fancy so that it doesn't look like he is flaunting his princely attire around,' she thought.

However, he wore his diadem on his father's insistence, a few rings, his wedding chain and gold bracelet along with his signet ring. His father said, "You need the exposure son. Takshakshila though established by Kaushal king Ramchander's brother is at present under the rule of Persian Achaemenid Empire[1]. It is a magnificent growing city famed for its wealth[2] and rock architecture. Takshak was the name of Prince Bharat's son and 'shila' means rock."

"It's good to know its history father. I also know the city existed parallel to the most ancient Sindhu civilisation of the Hindus. I am willing to go and meet all kind of people from different countries."

The palace was very quiet the day Siddhartha was to leave. No singing or dancing was heard in the ladies' quarters. It was as if someone was taking away the soul of the palace. Shuddhodan, his uncles and aunts came till the main steps to bid him farewell. The ladies from the upper floor of the palaces were struggling to get a last glimpse of their prince. Queen Prajapati Gautami came out with a silver plate and waved a lighted lamp in front of his face. She marked his forehead with saffron and sprinkled some rice on him. Some sweet meats sweatened his tongue. Her eyes were brimming with tears and heart, with blessings. However, Devdatta could barely conceal his smile. With Siddhartha gone he'll try to make some place in the king's lonely heart, for himself.

Siddhartha left early in the morning, with Channa on a four-horse chariot, escorted by six soldiers, lest dacoits, ferocious animals or head hunting wild tribals intercept them en-route. People had gathered outside the palace gate to look at his handsome, kind face which won't be seen for next few years. A bard praised and blessed him. While the people threw flower petals on him. When he passed the street where Mrigi lived. He heard her voice, "I'll wait for you, my Prince." Embarrassed prince did not look up at her balcony.

Their next stop was Sarasvati, where they stayed the night in an inn. His cavalry- men found their own lodgings, while Channa attended to the horses, specially Kanthak. Siddhartha was already missing home and his women so couldn't sleep well that night.

Their journey was long. The wheels of the coach were making gritty sound on the road. The clip-clop of the horses was creating a rhythm. There were meadows and green farms on the two sides of the trade route. The

1. Ramayana.
2. Ramayana.

Shakyan flag, between the two front stallions was waving in the pleasant breeze. Overwhelmed with joy Channa started singing and Siddhartha played the flute as an accompaniment, enjoying the ride. There was all kind of traffic on the road. Wagons and bullock-carts carrying villagers or goods covered with water-resistant hemp sheets.

Their melodious fusion lingered in the breeze for magical moments and then was taken over by occasional traffic's cluttering. Then the Prince spoke softly. "You sing beautifully Channa."

"I must have got it from my great grandfather. In his times professional bards were still the royal coachmen who would entertain their masters while driving."

Stopping now and then at villages to replenish their stocks of food and change their horses. They moved on for a period of one month to cover three hundred 'kose.'

At last, after passing rivers and mountains; the dreary, rocky landscape, dotted with animal carcasses or human bones they neared the city.

Dusty and exhausted, they could see at a distance the huge central dome and the spires of the university. As the horses sensed that their destination was near they galloped and leapt.

The group took their lodgings in a public house for that night. Next morning, Siddhartha wrote a letter with a quill dipped in ink on a palm-leaf sheet.

"Dear Father and Ma

I have reached here safely and would go to the 'Mahavihara', tomorrow with Channa for our admission.[1]

With Regards.

Your son Siddhartha.

The short note was sent though one of the homing pigions they had carried with them in a wooden cage. His escorts reached back home after another month. Leaving the prince's chariot behind which got a parking spot next to the high boundary wall of the institute, made up of blocks of stones. Many stables for the horses were also available. Kanthaka stayed there, in the familiar smells of other horses. Channa after giving a test in music, started his free education. His basic schooling, in the past had been due to prince's generosity.

There were students from many countries, apart from all parts of India. The foreign students were mostly from Greece, Bablonisa, Arabia and

1. Siddharth's visit to Taxila is not mentioned in any texts but might have existed in oral tradition, as some scholars believe.

China. Rishabha, the first of Jain Thirthankars had visited Takshakshila. His colossal feet were carved in the foyer. The list of the subjects taught was long.

Siddhartha's main Acharya who taught him philosophy was a Jain. He also trained him in meditations by which the state of consciousness achieved a higher plane of a formless realm. 'A sphere of nothingness'. He also revealed to him the theories of social science and politics. For the practical aspect of warfare prince was under another teacher.

Siddhartha liked the cosmopolitan culture of the institute. Being a prince of a small republic was no big deal there. He was treated only as a student like others.

He was beginning to find his own individuality, in this context. For once he wasn't thinking of his dancing girls. But he kept in touch with his queen via the 'air-mail' service. His bright intellect quickly let him absorb his courses and opened up his mind. His favourite subject was philosophy. Sitting in the huge library he poured over the six 'darshanas' or philosophies of the Vedic religion along with Greek, Chinese or Zoroastrian. He was even taught Arthashastra which only existed in the oral tradition.

He exchanged his philosophical ideas with his classmates from other countries. His Acharya told him, "Siddhartha you are lucky to belong to an era which may be called the 'pivotal-age'* as far as religion and philosophy are concerned. A moral revolution is underway. Since last hundred years, as I have heard from people of other countries directly or indirectly, 'the spiritual foundations of humanity are (being) laid simultaneously and independently in China, Hind, Persia, Judea and Greece.' China's Materialism, Skepticisms and Nihilism; Persia's Zarathustra, as a struggle between good and evil and Elijah's monotheistic belief, that God is present in the quiet voice of inner conviction. If we believe that the only God is Yahweh then so it is!

Siddhartha was impressed by the idea of a deity[1] of 'wisdom' in Zoroastrianism of the Persians ; the 'middle path' of Greek philosopher Aristotle and the atheism of the Sankhya yoga, propounded by Ashtavakra which believed in deep reflection and independent experience. Even independent of the Vedas. He stopped believing in the superiority of the Brahman hereditary status or that the Vedanta was the best Hindu philosophy among the six 'darshanas.' He preferred Sankhya Yoga. Which did not believe in God.

---

1. Deity of wisdom – Ahura Mazda. Islamic Arabia's indigenous polytheistic beliefs were practiced side by side with various forms of Christianity, Judaism and Zoroastrianism *Pivotal Age=Axial Age, word coined by German philosopher Karl Jasper.

He realised that the law-giver Manu, who divided the Indian society into four sections or guilds was forming his divisions dependent on the kind of work people preferred to perform rather than by birth. Suddenly a window opened in his mind and he could see clearly and logically that the people followed traditions blindly without questioning what is right or wrong. They felt that they would be insulting their ancestors if they did not believe in doing, what was told to them. Follow the leader was not Bodhisattva's[1] game. It was as if he was getting glimpses of the ultimate reality but not the whole picture. He wanted to go to a secluded place, without any swords hanging over his head, and sort things out on his own; calm his turmoiled mind. He did not believe in Taoism founded by Lao Tze of China, who taught that a spiritual force underlies the universe and is found in all things. Even though it is a part of all things, it is greater than all things. It is the ultimate reality." But Siddhartha did not believe in going with the flow as was suggested by the renowned philosopher. He felt, that a man's destiny is in his own hands. Our free-will should decide what kind of future we want and go for it. However, he liked the point that 'a Taoist should be selfless and without ego and thus free of anger.'[2] Mahavira's Jainism on the other hand believed, that man is given only limited free will depending upon his past life karmas. Thus, his complete destiny can't be entirely under his own control.

*****

Those were the most formative years of Siddhartha's youth. He was establishing his own principles and was gaining confidence to believe in them.

Despite the fact that they may not conform to the existing values of the society, or to be precise, he thought, 'to the members of the council at Kapilvastu.'

He was in his mid final year when he started becoming restless. He felt, 'the courses I am studying are not providing anything new to me now. I know the gist of them all. Why should I continue here?' He had started missing home and wanted to quit. He talked to his Acharya and asked for his opinion. Who replied, "You have a keen mind, Siddhartha, I am proud of you. I know that you can learn more about the practical aspect of warfare here but in other subjects, there is nothing more to learn for you. But if you quit in the middle of the session, you won't get any credits or your

1. Bodhisattave – one who is striving to be a Buddha. -+- German philosopher Karl Jasper.
2. Taoism was a recently developed philosophy at that time, of China by Lao Tze. *Pigeon mail

'Sanatak' undergraduate degree. Your father would be disappointed in you. He might even feel humiliated."

"Acharya, I have listened to him and the other elders of my family all my life. Isn't it time, to listen to my own voice which I am tired of suppressing."

"Suit yourself! You are an adult and above eighteen. Be your own master. I wish you good luck son. Remember your fee would not be reimbursed! Yet give it a second thought."

"Okay sir, how about if I leave four months before the due time. Would I get my 'degree.'

"Sometimes this kind of privilege is given to great donors."

"I'll organise that quickly." He sold his diamond studded diadem to give an early exam, along with Channa; four months ahead of time.

As a 'Guru Dakshina' fee to his class-teacher, the prince was planning to give his Acharya an expensive umbrella along with a simple one; two pairs of wooden sandals and a few turbans. To his other teachers, he would gift an umbrella, a pair of wooden sandals and a turban each.

Chandak had nothing much, to offer as his only possessions were a bronze ring and a necklace of ivory beads which had been gifted to him by Siddhartha. Since there were still four more month to go, he stopped thinking about it.

*****

While Siddhartha was busy imbibing the best education available in those times. Yashodhara was pining for him. The young princess, passed each season writing verses for his beloved. During spring the entire nature, takes on a golden hew; flowers suddenly bloom; butterflies flit on them, frolicking about in the fragrant garden, sucking the nectar. The pleasant breeze plays with Yasho's silken locks. There is no one to caress them back in place.

"Takshakshila lies far beyond the moon[1]
A whirlpool of grief, churns deep beneath my mind,
Bees come for honey when it's flowering time
Why is it sleep comes not to me tonight?"

To which Siddharth would reply,
"Do not get drowned my dear, in the pool of stress,

1. 'Six Seasons without you' from a Srilankan poem by an unknown author (from Palm Leaf manuscripts) translated by Ranjini Obeyesekre in 'Yashodhara'.

You are mine strength, be Yashodhara's too.
The moon, reminds me of your fair countenance,
dark clouds of your lustrous, ebony hair.
Your lips, as red as Karkandhu fruit,
Your eyes as blue as the deepest of lakes.
Be calm as a mountain in billowy tempests."

Winters were the worst season for the lovelorn Princess. When the heavy rains approached at nightfall, she craved the warmth of Siddhartha's arms around her curvaceous body. In the mornings she would watch, from her balcony, the rollicking mists meandering through valleys and pathways. Till the sun shone, shyly through.

*****

Sometimes, when free, the two young students of the university would go for a ride on their horses towards the trade routes. One, called the 'Royal Highway' by Megasthenes, was coming from eastern India; the second from western Asia and third from Kashmir and the central Asia.

"Takshakshila was also called the city of cut-stones", Siddhartha had told Chandak, during one of their jaunts.

"Quite an appropriate name", Channa had replied.

The prince also explained the 'snake-sacrifice' to him. "Arjun's grandson and Abhimanyu's son, Parikshit succeeded his grand uncle Yudhishter to the throne of Hastinapur. The Kuru king was a successful ruler till he had to perform here, the snake-sacrifice."*

"Really? That means this city might have been founded at-least five hundred years ago. Wasn't it?"

"Yes." Raja Parikshit and his son ruled between 1200–900 B.C.

Surprised Channa was still digesting the information when Siddhartha suddenly pulled the reins of Kanthaka and dismounted his horse to pick a broken bit, which looked like a piece of some woven basket. "What is it?"

"I am not too sure. It appears to be ancient. A slurry coated woven basket used in the manufacturing of items made by casting. I'll have to show it to Guru Ji. King Parikshit belonged to the Iron Age. I wonder… anyway let's go back! I remember I need to collect firewood for his wife."

"Oh yes even I need to go and fill water for my teacher's wife and join her in singing the evening aarti prayer. She likes my voice. I need to feed my pigeons as well."

Before mounting Kanthak, once again, Siddhartha patted him and whispered in his ear,

'You're the bravest steed that ever I back'd;

mark how ye crossed yon cataract?

From hoof to hoof I should like to measure the space ye clear'd.'*

*****

At Takshakshila the preceptor housed his own pupils who paid for their board and lodgings in cash or in the form of services to the teacher and his family.[1] Siddhartha paid in cash yet helped Guruji's wife. Her name was Savitri Devi. She became very fond of the prince for his refined demeanour and conversations full of wisdom. He called her 'Ma.' He found shades of affection in her voice like that of his mother's.

Brahmanical influence in Takshakshila was not as rigid as in the backwaters of Kapilvastu. Hence Channa too did not feel segregated due to his low caste. He was practicing his lessons well.

Siddhartha was tossing in the five streams of thoughts of his times. The ancient Greek philosophy for the first time, without denying Greek Gods, diverted towards the study of phenomena. Water was considered the first cause of life. He was stuck with this idea, that the natural elements not god created us.[2]

Siddhartha's felt a reflection of Plato and Aristotle. Plato advised the individual's moral and ethical obligation to self-improvement for its own sake and the good of the greater community.

Siddhartha thought, 'If the modern Greek philosophers can deny Gods, going against the ancient Greeks, and say, our phenomena has created our

1. Brittanica.com.
2. * Hindu philosophy – 5 elements cause life – air, water, fire, earth and 'ether' (sky).

* Adam Lindsay Gordon; 'The Roll of the Kettle drum.' A.H. Massina & Co. - Printers & publishers *Howey Street. - Melbourne.*

** Snake sacrifice: One day while going hunting in the forest, King Parikshit got tired and thirsty. He entered the hut of sage Samika, who was in deep meditation and did not respond to his salutations. Angry, he picked up a dead snake from outside and coiled it around his neck. Later when his son Sringin heard about the incident, he cursed the king that he would be bitten by Takshak snake and die on the seventh day. So Parikshit enthroned his son Janamejaya and spent the last seven days of his life listening to the discourses by Sage Sukadev, son of Rishi Vayasa. The discourses were compiled in a book, Bhagvata Purana. With its knowledge, his fear of death was absolved.

bodies and an individual's thoughts can create his destiny that means the environment and the individuals or societies are the truth about the ultimate reality not the various gods which have grown out of need in different imaginations of different cultures of the world.'

Gautama felt that his century might be an age where ancient beliefs in gods would slowly and gradually fade, and new more revolutionary ideas emerge. In Japan, old Shinto religion of various gods and deities was slipping in the background when Confucianism and Taoism were becoming the modern religions. China in ancient times believed like Hindus, "The gods, spirits and ancestors could affect crops, the weather, childbirth, the king's health, warfare and so on. It was therefore, important to make sacrifices to appease them." Yangshuo culture of the Yellow River Valley prospered between 5000-3000 B.C. in China. They, likewise believed in life after death so would leave daily items in the graves and tombs. Same had been the case with Egypt.

Whenever Siddhartha's thoughts ran in that direction, he would have a discussion with his Guruji, who could give him only limited satisfaction. Then he would sit quietly and meditate under a tree. All his women were forgotten at these interludes. That is when he felt comfortable in his own skin and at ease in his own space.

He would often mix with other students when the university had its annual gathering. His five best friends were Prasenjit, Bandhula; who's pet name was Handsome, Ahinsak, Mahali; a Licchavi nobleman from Vaishali and Jeevak, Amrapali's son studying medicine. Other outstanding one's were, Panini who later wrote 'Shabda-Vidya-Shastra' on Sanskrit Grammer; Chanakya who wrote his 'Chanakya-Niti' on political science; Vishnu Sharma became famous for writing 'Panchtantra' while Charak wrote his 'Charak Samhita' on ancient medical science, Ayurveda. Ahinsak was studying Tantra-Vidya magic. He was son of the royal chaplain at the court of Sarasvati, named Savatthi Brahaman. Ahinsak was charismatic and appealing to women. Besides he was strong, powerful and a bright student. He was the pet of his Acharya as well as his wife. No one disliked him except his fellow students.

All the teachers resided in loosely connected buildings where they taught. Rulers use to make donations. There were sixty-four subjects offered including the art of finding treasures, decrypting encrypting messages. Entrance exam use to be very difficult and only 3 out of 10 students passed the admission test.[1] Channa was only admitted due to his expertise in singing.

1. Scholar Harold M. Tanner.

Ahinsak's classmates became jealous of him and one day when he was away on some household errand other students told the Guru a cooked up story that he had an affair with his wife. When the unaware boy came back, he was disheveled and his clothes were torn. He gave vegetables and flour to the lady, who laughed aloud.

"What happened to you handsome?"

"I was chased by a street dog at the market."

"Go take a bath and change before dinner." She ordered affectionately. She liked him because he did more work for her than any other student. His Guru became suspicious due to her joyful, tinkling laughter in Ahinsak's presence.

Eventually the time came to depart the university. The education being almost complete everyone was looking forward to going home. Students were planning to buy gifts for their teachers and were asking them as to what they would like to have as 'Guru Dakshina'.[1]

After finishing his exams, Ahinsak politely asked his teacher, "Guruji, what 'dakshina' may I offer in your honour?"

"Forget it, you can't give me what I want."

"No Guruji, I am sure I can do something for you."

"If you are so sure then get for me one hundred chopped little fingers of men." The Guru thought, 'this way he soon would be caught by the police.'

One of the rogue students quipped, "Why not hundred and one Guruji?"

"Stay out of it and get lost."

Ahinsak was shocked. He asked the teacher "You don't want to turn me into a murderer Guruji?"

"Yes, I do. Either do it or forget it."

"No Guruji I have to fulfill my promise."

He left with frustration and tears in his eyes, after touching the feet of the lady of the house who had fed him. She became so emotional that she hugged and blessed him in front of her husband and kissed him on his forehead.

Coming back to his village Ahinsak had only one aim in life, how to collect those little fingers. At first, he requested people politely so that he could pay his debt of gratitude to his teacher. But no one agreed to part with their fingers. So, he waylaid people passing through the Jalini forest in the Kaushal Kingdom where he had shifted, leaving his home. When people

1. Gift to teacher.

struggled, he tried to control them forcefully and then cut their fingers with a sharp blade of a weapon. If they became too much troublesome, he would kill them.

Slowly and gradually he became numb towards his sins and turned into a serial killer. People never passed through the Jalini forest alone or without a weapon. As he collected the fingers, he would string them together to form a necklace and hang it on a tree near his home, a cave on top of a mountain. His grown hair, whiskers and beard made him look even more savage and formidable. His eyes were always red-shot due to consumption of some intoxicant leaves. Whenever he would see travellers passing by the hill he would come running down with a sword or a scythe and kill them even when they stopped struggling. The police from Sarasvati was always on the lookout for him but they couldn't catch him partly due to their own fear.

The necklace of fingers hanging on a tree was often attacked by carnivorous birds. So the murderer wore them on his neck. He got the name of "Angulimal' or the one who wears a necklace of chopped fingers.

*****

After giving all the gifts to his teachers and shawls to their wives, Prince Siddhartha and his coachman had started for home, four months ahead of the due date of their departure. Their chariot had a roof to save them from the sun, rain or the cold. However, the rainy season of the four months was over. The long road, they knew would last forever. This time, the protection of soldiers was not there, because he wanted to surprise his mother. So, the two of them would have a stopover as soon as the sun got ready to go down. Usually, they would follow a caravan of ten to fifteen horse-carts laden with goods. The traders travelled even during night as the dacoits were afraid of their numbers. One man would lay in one of the empty carts, looking at the stars to guide so that the caravan should not lose its way in the dark. Once in a while they would see human skeletons strewn in the jungles, attacked by some raiders or animals.

Approaching Sarasvati, after an exhausting journey, Siddhartha felt that they were almost home. Yet there were few hours left to reach there. Channa wore a long-sleeved jacket, tailored to fit. It had a high collar open at the neck, decorated with braid, plus breeches and leather sandals. The prince was bare-chested and devoid of his diadem. Siddhartha told him, "You look dashing in your new clothes just like worn by the foreign grooms, who come to sell the horses from across River Kizilirmak in upper Asia."

"That's a strange name!"

"It is also called the Red River."

"Thanks prince but I was more comfortable in my usual attire. Yet, since it was your gift …"

"Oh come on, I just gave you this to make you look stylish."

Suddenly both the young men stopped talking as they heard faint sound "Clippety-clop! Clippety-clop," from behind.

They heard the nearing staccato of the hooves. Siddhartha craned his neck through the window to see backwards. Amidst the clouds of dust he saw the silhouette of a bandit. The prince shouted to Channa, "There is no point in galloping faster, just stop!" Channa slowly brought the chariot to a halt while his master grabbed his bow and sword. Channa hopped down with a lance, followed by Siddhartha. They both faced the masked men with dirty clothes and dirtier looks. A struggle was expected but the prince instead addressed the leader with a grey beard politely, "Friends, let's not spill blood unnecessarily, What do you want?"

The elderly thief grunted aggressively as his companions surrounded the duo."Anything of value and your horses." Siddhartha took off the gold bracelet he was wearing, his chain and the rings except the royal signet. "These are all yours enjoy them without guilt." He said with kindness. "But my horses, I would not give up without a fight."

The chief bandit gawked with mouth agape at the precious gem-studded jewels and spoke, "Due to your invaluable gifts and your courage, I shall forget the horses. You are a brave man. Sarasvati city is just a few hours away. We too are going that way, we'll follow you till the town so that you don't get nabbed again."

"So be it!" The prince then offered the bandit chief to sit with him for a chat not minding his smelly presence. Now they started moving as a group. Siddhartha was talking to the thief. "I know that the reason for increase in crime is due to the great divide between rich and the poor. The administration should reduce this gulf between the two extremes. Once the bellies of the poor are full they may not easily resort to crimes.

"Well said, O' Prince!" I am impressed by your genuine concern. I wish when you wear the crown we could join your army. My men are good fighters. They only need some disciplinarian training." The prince laughed. "Are you really serious my friend? Because if you are, I'll seriously give it a thought."

"Prince I am touched by your noble thoughts. I used to think that kings are only after the blood of criminals."

"I believe every man has some good left in him. Given a chance it could come to the surface and change his life altogether. If your intentions are pure, you don't have to wait for my coronation. You come with me right now and I'll recommend you to my father. I won't let your past ruin your future. Unless you are planning to break into my palace for loot."

"No way! Not anymore. I respect you. Please consider me your fan. I can prove to be a very good spy. I know the underworld people well. I could be an asset to your republic!"

"You sure have transformed during the ride my friend. I can hardly believe that I am having this conversation with a seasoned robber, turned into law abiding citizen! But I am happy for you. You can come to me whenever you need assistance."

Siddhartha then casually told his companion that the two items he was given were his wedding gifts. The Head of the thieves became thoughtful. The Prince meanwhile emptied his pockets and brought out gold and silver coins. If you care, I shall give you all this cash for returning my gifts from my new bride. If you come to Kapilvastu and meet me you'll get even more of it.

By this time, they could see the distant twinkling lights of the city as the dusk was dissolving into the arms of night. Looking far away into dwindling light of the dipping sun behind snowy peaks the robber announced.

"In the city we'll go to a tavern for drinking, eating and lodging with our friends."

"All highway-men and thieves, I guess?" the prince remarked in jest.

"Who else would befriend our ignoble company."

"You know what, Channa and myself can also dress as thieves and learn what goes on in these taverns and then maybe I'll give you the job of a spy."

"I don't mind if your high status does not get offended!"

"You know you sound like an educated person What's your name?" "My name is Astic I was once well educated, but when robbers came to our village, killed my parents and burned our house, I forgot all my education and belief in God.

"I am sorry to hear that."

While getting off at the tavern, Astic told the prince, who was looking like a very handsome thief indeed, in borrowed dirty clothes. "Better be prepared for the crude and dirty language of the low class society which frequents this place. Loud arguments and brawls are a common factor. The prince answered, "If we are uncomfortable, we can always walk away."

Channa was apprehensive and yet he kept quiet and followed the master quietly keeping his dagger hidden in his clothes for his ward's protection.

The hustle and bustle of the cosmopolitan trade center was enjoying its night life activities. At some places they could hear instrumental music and tinkling of anklets. Young couples were laughing and loitering in the parks. Beggars were begging for alms near the temples from where the peels of the temple bells were filling the vibrant milieu. The milkman and the flower sellers were doing brisk business. Vendors and hawkers were yelling their throats dry. Roads were well built, broad and lighted.

At some distance, there was a roundabout with a fountain in the center. Around it were a few taverns with 'mashal' torches burning at the entrances to light the pathways. The six men entered one of the inns. All eyes went up in their direction. Some filthy looking men waved at the newcomers and they joined a large group of merry makers. There was 'churat' (cigarette) smoke drifting in layers, in the dimly lit hall. Siddhartha was embarrassed deep within because many inquisitive stares darted towards his face. Yet he kept a stoic expression. Pretty soon he got a hang of the loose language that was flowing along with the fumes of local 'toddy.' Channa whispered in his ear, "You are a good actor."

Two suspicious looking characters in nondescript dark garments sat in a corner table. Their faces were partially covered with the tails of their black turbans. Their heads were bent low as they whispered in undertones.

Channa looked at his master meaningfully who winked back. Channa took off his iron bangle and let it roll towards them. Before they could realise he bent low on the ground to retrieve his item and heard, "…governor of the province would be sent to war shortly as soon as his valiant son returns from Takshakshila. It would be the right time to infiltrate his mansion and kidnap his wife. King Prasenjit is infatuated by her."

Suddenly the speaker bit his tongue as Channa turned back towards his own table picking his bangle up. Siddhartha hinted him to be quiet for the moment.

One 'tipsy tongue,' at their table also lowered his voice and head and reported the latest rumour, after gaining everyone's attention. "Our king Prasenjit is looking for a new queen from some high caste clan."

Another woozy villain promptly replied, "He should marry my daughter I am from the highest family of bunglers. That is why my thefts often go wrong and I end up in the jail."

"Good idea, we'll talk to the king tomorrow." The young lad with shaggy hair answered with pretended seriousness.

A third one spoke, “Blokes he wants to marry a Shakyani girl”.

“What?” Everyone squawked, Siddhartha being the loudest.

“To my knowledge they never marry outside their clan”, he informed.

“So what? They cannot refuse their sovereign. Soon an envoy would be sent to Kapilvastu with the proposal.”

Astic clarified, “This man our colleague operates in and around Kapilvastu, so he knows.”

“Yes” Siddhartha and Channa answered together.

“But why haven’t we seen you before? I hope you are not the Chief’s spy?”

“Shut up!” Elderly Astic shouted. “No one who comes with me can be a spy. Would I put my friends in a risky situation!”

The bubble of tensions building up burst and normalcy returned to their group. The gossips went on and the jars of local wine were being guzzled down the thirsty throats along with oily snacks. Siddhartha’s gullet was on fire due to the crude intoxicant so he was hardly sipping. When no one was looking he quietly let the liquor flow out to the dirty floor and tried not to let even a shadow of discomfort cross his countenance. The bald thief with grey beard, across him bawled. “Some bloody scoundrel pissed under my feet.” He shuffled his chair and got up to holler. “Clean up the mess boy!”

At dinner time the prince could barely swallow the rice and lentils. The starving men however were gulping down the food avidly, which was too greasy, salty and sprinkled with chilies. Busy, licking their dirty fingers they had no time to notice the runny noses and watery eyes of the outsiders. After the loud sounds of guttural belching ended, Channa paid for all of them, to their rejoicing. One guy who’d stood up and was wiping his fingers with his already soiled white turban, snatched a bottle of Toddy from the counter and drunkenly spoke, “Pour your generosity on this one too my friend.” Channa obliged.

By the time they left, barely anyone could remember his own name. Astik, bade farewell to his new friends and stayed the night at the tavern, while two of his roly- poly ones, were literally rolling on the floor. The tavern keeper asked his boys, “Shift the full ‘barrels’ to their room.” One boy came close between the two on the floor and shouted, “police!”

The snoring pair shot up alarmed and ran helter skelter upstairs.

Siddhartha and Channa came out and broke into an uncontrollable guffaw. Prince mentioned, “At least now we know from where to get secret information.”

They were outside in the cool breeze planning, 'where to go next,' when the secretive black turbans walked out and went in opposite directions. Channa asked, "Should I follow one of them?"

"No need, I know who they are talking about! We don't meddle into our short tempered sovereign's affairs."

Their next concern was to locate a decent and clean inn to spend the night.

"It's a good thing Channa, we did not keep all our eggs in the same basket or we would've been pauper by now."

"You are so right Master." He returned the leftover gold coins to his prince.

*****

Siddhartha next morning decided to spend the day at the modern city of Sarasvati before starting for home. The capital had everything to offer except good sanitation. After breakfast at the inn the prince along with Channa toured the city. Which was situated at the junction of heavily travelled trade routes, on which rich merchants with fancy attire stopped to take a break, before moving to different destinations. Towards south to the city of Kaushambi and further to Deccan.

The city flourished on the south-bank of Ravati River. Which was in the shape of a crescent with the concave side facing the Kaushalan capital. Siddhartha asked Channa to drive along the river and then reach the main 'chawk', the centre of the city where all the trade routes mingled. They came to the eastern half where the common man lived among the congested bazaars. Channa after dropping his master at the perfumer's shop looked for a safe spot to park.

After buying a few vials of rare perfumes, including Kasturi (which is extracted from a doe's belly), the Prince looked for a Kashi-silk shop. It existed in another lane. Through the maze of streets he came to one, which sold saris. He was surprised to see that every street sold only one sort of item. He bought a dazzling mid-night blue sari interwoven with threads of pure gold and silver, for his wife and another one with the finest hand embroidery on pink for his mother. He couldn't think of a gift worthy of the king.

He came out of the narrow streets passing through the crowds which were being entertained by the dancing notch-girls and their musicians. A little further out of the narrow lanes was an arena where traveling wrestlers were in action. To his consolation he spotted Channa, parked under a tree.

"What are you looking at so engrossed, Channa?"

"At the pretty young girls, my master. Aren't they more fashionable than the girls at Kapilvastu?"

"I don't know friend. I am exhausted. It took such a long time, jostling through the crowd surrounding harlequins and jugglers! I wonder how much money people have here. Everybody wants to shop! Shop! Shop! Let's eat an early lunch and go to the theater."

"As you wish master! But why did you shop here for Kashi-silk when the Chinese merchants often come to the palace to sell high quality heavy silks which wrinkle less. By the way I also heard that natural silk calms the nerves. Is that true?"

"My mother believes so, besides the Chinese silk saris are beautiful yet they are not hand embroidered with silver, gold or silk skeins!" He undid his velvet pouch and handed over some coins to Channa.

"I believe some 'Natas' are performing nearby."

"Natas?"

"Yes, the wandering minstrel and dancers."

"Oh yes, those! In fact I have never seen them perform. But I am sure they can't play flute as well as you do."

"You'll see them today. But don't fall for the dancing girls they might be boys dressed up as chicks. As far as my flute is concerned, my mother plays better."

"How disappointing! For girls, I mean!"

"The young ladies however don't much care for a flickering flame like you." Siddhartha teased him with an amused grin, for his limply walk. Channa only smiled back and asked, "Can't we watch the rams fight which are trained and their pointed horns are gilded?"

"Next time friend! Otherwise we'll have to stay, yet another day."

After dinner the two friends went to the inn again to sleep so that they could start at the crack of dawn for Kapilvastu. It was the first cry of the cock that woke them up. They came to the highway and Channa started singing while beautiful strains of flute meandering through the misty valley.

*****

King Shuddhodhan had already built three palaces for the pleasure of his beloved son whom he and queen Prajapati pampered to the utmost. At the same time he was guided to inculcate values worthy of a prince by his father. Whereas his mother let him develop his own individuality according to his inborn aptitudes of justice and equality for all in spite of whatever their status in life. The prince did not know yet his own potential to become a world religious leader. Oblivious of his future destiny he had indulged in every delight laid at his feet.

Siddhartha was eager to meet his new bride soon; but he knew that he would have to go through some formal ceremonies before that could happen. Soon after he would reside with her in his new home, Vishram Bhawan. He imagined her making her auspicious entry, followed by him and others in his palace. Yashodhara would walk through a silver tray full of red lac dye and water, only then she could cross the threshold of her new life, leaving red footprints everywhere her tender feet would lead her.

"Channa," said the Master, "I long to hear the conches blown, flower petals showered on us, the married couple; and mother with other women relatives singing auspicious songs in their varied voices."

Chandak smiled "I can imagine all that and I too am looking forward to seeing you enjoying your marital bliss. I'll be forever ready to take you and my queen around with Kanthak. Besides now I'ld feel free to marry too. My mother had been pestering me forever."

They both were quiet for a stretched moment, lost in their own reveries as they gradually neared the familiar territory of their domain.

*****

The summer palace, where the Prince had spent most of his time was overlooking Rohini River on one side and the snowy Himalayan peaks on the other. One could peek through the filigreed narrow windows or a balcony that overlooked the stretched out vista where the cluster of townhouses ended in a stone boundary wall. Across which, were the scraggly bushes, sal or banyan trees and tall palmyra trees or wine palms.

The village boys climbed up the money-making palms strategically, and reached the topmost part of its trunk to tap and extract the sweet sap from the stumps of its flowers; in containers by hanging them underneath. The juice is nonalcoholic. But after reacting with yeast in the air, starts fermenting. Keeping it more than a day made it stronger.

The prince closed his eyes and saw-

Lush greenery and flowering trees on which birds warbled and sang all day long. Peacocks, deer and exotic fishes which swam in a crystal pond.

There she sat, in the bower with her beloved, sparkling with enchanted charm. And his melodies on flute floated across, the wide, green lawns.

Her heart throbbing! And His, matching its amorous rhythm.

Coming out of his dream-land Siddhartha looked around with a worried look. The fog had descended and began to curdle over the undergrowth.

There was a distant sound of howling barks of Jackals coming nearer. And nearer.He moved the curtains of windows and peered through the darkening envelop of blue mist. His hand went to his bow and sword. Channa increased the tempo of his horse and touched his dagger and looked at the javelin. A few dark speckles tore through the vapours and daubed the landscape. Channa's hair stood at their ends as he looked sideways. Kanthak too sensing the danger was eager to take his prince to the safety of Hamsavati palace. He galloped as hard as he could, along with his companion horses. The flames of the two torches on the sides of the royal coach flew backwards. Those kept the beasts at a distance. But they were in no way letting their prey escape. A loud shriek broke past the thudding sound and one of the foes went down pierced by an arrow. Like warriors the canines still crawled forward ready to pounce. Channa hit one of them with exact precision. Panic spread among the hungry beasts. All at once two weapons hit the targets, an arrow and a lance and the battle was won.

Reaching Kapilvastu they approached the South Gate where the guards on duty intercepted them. Peering at Channa and the crown prince, though without the diadem they respectfully unfastened the gates. Getting down the charioteer blurted, "That was quite a scare Prince!"

"I know, it was sad that we had to kill."

*****

The entire fort of Kapilvastu was like a village in idealistic settings. Yashodhara's and other palaces were surrounded by lush greenery and flowering trees. There she sat in the bowers with her beloved by her side, listening to melodies on flute. She was drenched in marital bliss of nine years and never realised when it came to an end. Walking through the latticed galleries and admiring the engravings on marble pillars she treaded on the cool marble floors followed by attendants or friends. She loved it even more when they had moved in the monsoon palace because during Chaumas her husband never went down from the top floor, where 'gopies'** danced. She had him all to herself.

The Princess had taken charge of Siddhartha's 'ranivas' and made sure that no one ever forgot as to who the main authority was. After seven years passed, her mother-in-law gently started reminding her now and then that

---

* Jatakas Tales no. 212, 291; Fick: 'Social Division in North Eastern India in Buddha's times.' p. 188.

** "Gopi (sanskrit) female cowherd or a milk maid. Since Lord Krishna of Vrindavan was himself a cowherd and a prankstir. He played flute so beautifully that the gopies danced with him.

it was her duty to produce a heir to the throne. Yashodhara would begrudge in her thoughts, 'Is it my fault?'

On the other hand Siddhartha too was getting restless with the monotony of his life. He often went to inspect and explore his kingdom with or without Yashodhara while Channa drove the chariot with snow white Kanthak harnessed to it. He would perform some administrative duties on the way.

Coming back the Prince would often see funeral pyres blazing away at the banks of tributary of Bhagirathi, surrounded by relatives mourning their loss. A dark shadow would skim through his perceptive heart. But Channa who had faced life without tinted glasses of royalty, would try to pacify him, "It is a part of life, Master. We all go through it."

However, one incident stuck to his memory. Away from the lighted pyres an old man was painfully howling at the top of his voice. A dead body of a young man covered with a torn shroud lay at his feet with insufficient logs of wood. Siddhartha followed by Channa slowly approaches him and asks, "Where is your priest father to perform the death ritual?"

"I can't afford one," and he started hitting his head with both hands in frustration. "I will have to feed the half-burnt body to the fishes. My son's soul would wander forever in the Neither lands."* Prince looked at his charioteer who disappeared while he tried to console the poor man. Soon the performing priest appeared and Channa came carrying extra firewood.

Siddhartha and Channa then walked the dank banks digging their feet in the cool sand and having friendly chats to divert their attention. He would tell his half-brother, "Channa I am satiated with all the luxuries, pomp and show and I feel as if the conventional ideas and stale traditions are taking my freedom of thoughts away. The rituals of animal sacrifices are abhorring. The priests have become suckers of the rich and are unaffordable to the poor. A storm is brewing in my heart and revolutionary ideas are sprouting. What should I do? I feel so hopeless! I feel torn between both the worlds of luxury and complacence, versus personal liberty. Like a lotus pond, which may bloom sweet smelling flowers but is stagnant after all, sometimes rotting deep within. I feel the society I live in needs a cataclysmic change to make the world a better place. I prefer negotiations to wars, especially wars of false honour. Where poor soldiers are sacrificed and widowed women and orphaned children live a miserable life with hardly any support

---

* 'Neither Lands'. In Hinduism, it means - his soul would not be accepted in any realm, after death. It would be lost for eternity, unless the death rituals are performed according to the rules prescribed by the Brahmans.

from the administration. Isn't there anyone who could stand up and tell the world, what is wrong with them!"

"Okay friend if your soliloquy is done, we could go around for greener pastures."

Siddhartha barely heard him and continued.

"For the same reason I never go hunting and killing animals lest I spoil the ecological balance. Besides we've no right to kill innocent animals. We do it for sport as wanton boys kill flies."

Channa stopped and took out his dried-gourd water bottle and offered to the prince. Who quietly took a few sips and said nothing.

*****

It was sometimes mentioned that Prince Siddhartha had never performed any extraordinary feats of valour as a young man. It was said that, 'He was totally enslaved by his animal passions.' Although his being a period of numerous disunited republics and kingdoms, battles and wars were persistently fought. The crown prince always participated in these by the side of King Shuddhodan. Yet the violence, bloodshed and deaths always disturbed his compassionate mind. He wanted to find a way to achieve peace for his people. Whenever he felt overwhelmed with his lifestyle, he toyed with the idea of renunciation. But was afraid of going through with it.'[1] People felt that he had stayed with the women of the seraglio for too long and was not strong enough to face the bitter-brutal realities of life. Whereas his belief was in environmental protection and safety of all life, alike. He realised that the greed of man, his anger and arrogance lead to his loss of wisdom which hurts others as well as him. Siddhartha's egalitarianism was considered unpractical by the republicans.

Channa on such occasions tried diverting his attention by taking him to the serene environment around the river bank.

"I find the rippling waves of Bagirathi soothing when my soul is thus tormented.

Don't you Master?"

Mum prince would look at him absentmindedly and then hear the calming flap-flap of the waves for the first time. He would then speak with resolve, "Let's go back through the main market just to see the hustle and bustle, to take our minds off the irrelevant emotions crawling in my head like worms."

Channa drove through a posh locality with a small shopping centre underneath some magnificent mansions. The road was buzzing with

1. "Abhinishkramana Sutra – (secondary source) (translated by Beal).

activities. A dwarf on the roadside was showing off antics to cheer the crowd. People were laughing and throwing money at him. Many ladies and children watched from their balconies. Siddhartha's gaze went up and he saw Mrigi in front of her father's house making amorous comments to the prince in a loud voice.

Many people were looking up amused. Siddhartha did not like her brazen attitude yet threw a necklace at her without giving a second glance. Mrigi felt humiliated and ignored, yet pretended the necklace was his gift of love, which "he did not want to acknowledge in public," she explained to her cousin standing next to her.

In the next broad street Channa looked up and then looked at the prince, saying, "Look up again. Maybe this is more to your taste." Siddhartha did. On a rich man's terrace stood an innocent looking girl covered modestly with a yellow shawl. The prince gestured his companion to stop and he recited a few word in her praise, standing up.

"O' beautiful Basanti, spring has come on your fair countenance. Do not hide it. Let me drink the nectar thine."

The girl blushed and ran inside throwing her fragrant veni[1] in his lap and saying, "I am Gopaaa!"

Shuddhodan's spies were prompt to inform him about the two girls. As it is, he was concerned for his son, for not becoming a father yet. So, he called Siddhartha to discuss the matter with him.

The obedient son told his father, "If I have to have a second queen then let it be Gopa." Shuddhodan laughed aloud, "That suits me fine son. First you marry your choice and then the second girl. This way I might have two grandsons." He continued. "I have already sent messages to the parents of both the girls. Gopa's father happily consented whereas Mrigi's needed time to consult his daughter for her decision as she is the kind who decides for her own actions."

"Suits me fine I would like some time to woo Gopa and find out if she really wants me for a husband. She seems to be an obedient daughter who may not go against her father's wishes."

"Good! You have one week's time for courtship."

The prince went to Yashodhra to break the news. Yashodhra listened in silence then lay down and put her head in her husband's lap. "I myself was going to suggest, something like this. After all you need to have a boy at least for the sake of your father and the kingdom. He has waited long enough as it is! My aunt sometimes subtly reminds me of my duty to produce a heir."

1. A string of flowers, usually jasmine tied in the hair.

"Aren't you jealous?"

"Love goes beyond selfishness."

*****

"Many young men had wanted Mrigi's hand in marriage because she was beautiful and the only daughter of a wealthy landlord. But she was lovesick for Siddhartha. So she ultimately became mentally prepared to become his junior queen. She wrote to him a clandestine amorous letter and confessed her undying passion for him. But the letter fell in Mangala's hands and never reached the Prince.

Her desire to be his Queen had to wait a little longer. She discussed the matter with her father who frowned, "Why father?"

"Because I have recently had three requests from the palace for your hand. If I refuse anyone of them, I would be in trouble. Shuddhodan wants you for Siddhartha, who'd been married for quite a few years, without a child. Whereas his peers Nand and Devdatta too are keen on you."

Confident Mrigi comforted her father, "Leave it to me, two weeks from now arrange a 'swayamvara' function for me. I myself will choose my husband." Relieved, Dandapani started sending invitations to all the distinguished Shakyan youth.

On the appointed day, Mrigi was going through various beauty treatments before finally getting ready after her bath. 'She started to decorated herself with the choicest jewels and the most costly robes. Around her head she wore a garland of the loveliest flowers and surrounded by a suite of maidens and accompanied by her mother, she proceeded to the place of assembly.'

She carefully scans each of the five hundred contestants and was disappointed to see that the young men were nothing but show offs in their showy perfumed clothes, heavy jewellery and flowers stuck in their hair or worn as garlands. Their eyes were lined with Kohl and lips coloured with red lac. Their effeminate self-indulgence repulsed Mrigi Gautami.

Siddhartha stood aloof, not ostentatious at all, like a solid rock; unto himself. Mrigi after consulting her mother, finally announced. "I will take Siddhartha as the husband of my choice."

There was snickering heard amongst the youngsters, yet they stayed for the dinner. Hearing the announcement no one came forward to congratulate the chosen one. Not even Devdatta or Nand. His half brother, who felt at times that due to Siddhartha he never received the love of his own mother as a child. He carried the resentment on his chest even as a grownup. However both the rejected suitors left disappointed without attending the wedding. And ended up in the 'Pleasure-House,' to drown their sorrow.

Siddhartha and Mrigi were married then and there, in the presence of rest of the young men and relatives.

She garlanded Siddhartha with a bulky garland of varied flowers, called 'Jaimala.' Then she put her hand upon the back of his head and spoke. "Siddhartha, my prince I take you to be my lord and my husband."

Then Siddhartha replied dutifully, "I take you to be my wife; you are my wife."

After garlanding, they went through the ritual of circumambulating around the sacred fire seven times. Each time they took their marriage vows. Four by the groom and three by the bride. Showered with flowers and pieces of gold, the Prince took his third wife to the winter palace and stayed with her continuously for a few weeks, as was the custom. Somehow Siddhartha and Mrigi had a relationship of resentment from the very beginning. Which was further enhanced because she knew that she could never have her son become the heir to the throne, if she had one. But her cautions were set aside once she enjoyed the unbound ecstasy of lust. She wanted her husband's virility to be her exclusive possession. But she knew she would only get her fair share, and wait for her turn.

All the three queens were settled in their palaces of winter, summer and rains. Gopa became the proud owner of the rain palace. Mrigi got married later than Gopa and was the youngest. Yashodhra was happy for Siddhartha.

Yashodhra gifted Gopa, her husband's young wife, a Sanskrit handbook on the art of love, named Kamasutra where advice was also given to the junior wives about the decorum of the Ranivas and how they were supposed to behave, towards the chief queen. Gopa got her hint. However, she would veil her face, unlike Yashodhara whenever her husband was around. She blossomed, immersed in Siddhartha's love, secretly. She knew about games of jealousy and intrigue being played in the seraglio so she never talked about her husband's love towards her, to anyone. Knowing Mrigi's temperament Yashodhara did not get too close to her. Yet the junior queens maintained their propriety of behaviour and speech.

According to the bards of those times. Mrigi was strong-willed like Yashodhara and would stress her individuality in no uncertain terms. They both would stick to their convictions and could not be easily swayed by the opinions of others. Her father lived in a grand palace and was owner of multiple lands, cattle and gold. Mrigi was his only child and very beautiful. She wanted to be her husband's favourite wife but she failed to bring the Prince, emotionally close to her.

*****

Chapter - 9

The Moot Hall Fiasco

THE SPRING WIND PASSED THROUGH THE FOREST,
AND WHISPERED LOW IN THE LEAVES.
AND CEDAR TOSSED HER HEAD AND THE (SHAKYAN) OAK
STOOD FIRM IN ITS PRIDE.*

Next meeting of the council was called on an urgent note. King Prasenjit had sent an envoy with the message that he wants to marry a Shakyani maiden.

After the meeting was called to order a small prayer was recited by all under the guidance of the court priest. Then the Prime Minister stood up to read the scroll sent by the monarch of Kaushal Kingdom.

"To chief Shuddhodan, it be known that I want my new queen to be from the Shakya clan of Ikshvaku Lineage. I hope to expect a response soon. May your principality stay safe."

There was an uproar amongst the dignitaries. The furore that followed was like an uprising.

"Everyone knows we don't marry our girls in other clans. Specially those of a lower caste". One of the nobles said defiantly.

Siddhartha stood up, raised his one hand while speaking on top of the noise. "Their caste, my honourable members is not low. They are kshatriyas, the warriors like us".

"Don't try to break centuries old traditions Prince, they are the progeny of a slave girl." A harsh voice arose.

"But didn't that happen two hundred years ago?"

"Yes, but the descendants are not as pure as the Shakyas who do not have a drop of impure blood in them. Genealogy matters."

Chief Shuddhodan now raised his hand. When everyone became quiet he addressed the important members of the assembly.

"My dear fellow members since King Mahakaushal is not alive to put some sense into his adamant head, we have no choice. Please come forward with your suggestions one by one."

Suprabuddha, the chief of Devdah stood up with his bearded chin thrust at the king while he looked into his eyes.

"How about refusing him point blank"?

"Won't it be like showing a powerful bull a red cloth?"

Suprabuddha looked at everyone for some approval. None was heard.

Dhrotodan, Devdatta's father who usually agreed with the king spoke up, "We should learn from our past mistakes." Observing everyone he continued. "Once when Kaushal kingdom was under the king of Panchal many generations ago, he had sent the same ultimatum, with the ambition of getting the pure blood of the Ikshavaku clan. But we, the caste proud Shakyans refused. As a result, we were butchered by his vast army. Only a band of people were secretly led by a noble Abhiraja[1] towards the safety of the east. Very few Shakyans were left in Kapilvastu to restart.

The Prime minister Mahanaam got up and opined. "He is right, he is right friends. How can we challenge a short tempered powerful Prasenjit? We need to find a practical, diplomatic solution."

Suprabuddha retorted impatiently, "Why don't you suggest us one?"

Mahanaam took the challenge and came up with a suggestion at the spur of the moment. "We can send a slave girl to him after teaching her royal etiquettes and dressing her up accordingly; pretending to be a Shakyan maiden."

"Do you have anyone in mind?" the king asked.

"I have a slave woman, Nagamunda. Her young beautiful daughter is called Vishabhakshattriya. She might pass for a Shakyani from a well-bred family. If we can guard the secret carefully, she can be given to Prasenjit in marriage."

---

1. Hinan Nan Yarzawin (Glass Palace Chronicles)

* From the history of royal dynasty of Myanmar- The refugee chief Abhiraja was experienced in governance so the people of the land between the rivers Chindwin and Ayeyerwady, allowed him to rule them. He founded the kingdom of Ta Guang in present Myanmar.

For a moment there were musings going on in each member's mind and eventually they all seem to agree except the young member Prince Siddhartha. He got up to have his say, All the dignitaries clamoured for him to take his seat. When he kept on standing defiantly the king intervened.

"Listen, friends I know the decisions in this republican assembly are taken on the basis of more than fifty percent of votes, yet everyone has a right to express his opinion."

The prince spoke with conviction in a calm voice. While Devdatta was trying to hide his sarcastic grin, he felt that his younger cousin was bent upon making a fool of himself.

"With due respect to our honourable prime minister, I dare to say that this idea is suicidal."

Devdatta butted in, "How so? Would you care to explain my brother."

Siddhartha's serene voice echoed in the hall. "Yes, the truth would always be out sooner or later and when it does even your myriad gods would not be able to save the Shakyan tribe. I have studied with Prasenjit for years at Takshakshila, he sure can be very vengeful when aroused. Do my respectable elders want the Shakyans to be wiped out from the face of the earth, once again?"

"So, what do you suggest son?" Suprabuddha asked.

"Cheating a powerful sovereign would not get us anywhere. Any Shakyan parents would happily give away their daughter to one of the most powerful king of the day. If Prasenjit's progeny also becomes high caste like us, what difference would it make? Why do we need to be so exclusive? I think, our 'honour and pride' statements only smell of arrogance. Diplomacy should rise above petty concerns."

Some voices arose from the ladies' section. Prajapati faced the members and spoke on behalf of the ladies with their approval.

"We agree with Siddhartha. We should not take such a big risk, when our survival is at stake."

Dhrotodan's brother-in-law the Pathoragarh chief, Tapodan answered her with a tinge of acid in his voice.

"I do not wish to contradict your wise advice O' queen but I think the majority is wiser".

Shuddhodan intervened "In fact the ladies do have a point there!"

Tapodan raised his voice, "Are you going against the majority chief? You and your family could be charged for treason and thrown out of the court and the palace!"*And he banged his fist on the arm support of his chair.

Shuddhodan lost his cool and roared. "You are my relative Tapodan yet I won't tolerate your belligerent tone in my court. Please leave now from today's session. We already have your valuable vote. We'll honour it."

"I sure will." He decried the lack of support from the Maharaja and was about to leave with a darkened face. The rage in his voice was insulting to the throne, still Siddhartha quickly came to bar his way and bent to hold his feet. Even Chief Chaturbhuj tried to console him. Like a snorting bull he refused to calm down.

"Please sir, do not leave because of me. Instead, I would leave if that pleases you."

"Nothing is pleasing to me right now", he glowered at the king and was gone.

Seeing her brother leave, Mangala dashed after him out of her seat.

"Brother, please do not go, you were going to talk about your daughter's betrothal to Devdatta after the court proceedings."

"No more relationships in this family again, forget it sister!" he responded in a loud voice.

After he left in indignation, things were quiet for a moment. Siddhartha came back after being rejected and his aunt went back fuming with fury at the king. The Prince spoke at length.

"Please gentlemen, do not drag my father into this. Yet I do not mind being the only one against this proposal. Call me a traitor if you must."

"It is not so simple son, explained uncle Dhrotodan. Treason is the crime of attacking a state. A traitor is either hanged or driven into the jungle, after being dethroned."

"Fine I will leave the city and go to aranya to find peace and sense."

Moans were heard from the ladies section. Yashodhara came out and faced everyone.

"That is most unfair, how can you dub practical wisdom as going against the republic!"

Prajapati came and stood next to her and addressed the gathering. "I apologise on behalf of the prince and his chief queen," then she turned to her son. "Please Siddhartha reconsider your decision and apologise to your elders for going against them."

"O queen mother do not insist please! I can see that our values need a drastic change! I do not mind saying 'sorry' but I wouldn't agree with the petition, even if I have to leave the council."

A wailing was heard from Yashodhara and the meeting dispersed without the usual bouts of drinking, gambling and laughing.

At night, many people saw and heard the tutelary goddess of Shakyas, Vimla Devi lamenting in the dark outside the city.*

*****

---

* Pali Canon (Trans.). During the time of Buddha, the tribal chief was unable to govern without the support of his assembly members. Although they were generally suppose to be an advisory comity. Yet if he was considered incompetent by majority of the councillors he could be deposed. 'Jatakas'(J. Aubr.).

Chapter - 10

The Midnight Flight

THE BEAUTIES DANCED FOR THE KING TO BE
OVERFLOWING HIS CUP WITH LUXURIES
SPILLED AND SPILLED ON HIS ROYAL THOUGHTS
MESSED UP AND REPULSED HE FLEE.

That night, was full of nightmares. Mahaprajapati dreamt that a white bull with a beautiful hump was charging out of Kapilvastu. Shuddhodan found himself in a wilderness along with Prajapati, his consorts and progeny.

Yashodhara found herself in the ranivas's huge courtyard in a circle along with her co-wives and dancing girls, all of them dressed in white as widows, beating their naked breasts and lamenting with mournful wailings.

Devdatta saw himself brutally stabbing Siddhartha while Yashodhara stood there with a Jaimala, the wedding garland in her hand.

The prince saw himself on top of the execution platform while the people of Kapilvastu clamoured around him with raised arms, "Prince, save us, our families, our properties and our souls."

Siddhartha woke up in a sweat and saw Yashodhara crying in her sleep. He went out in the balcony breathing hard and walked towards the dancing hall. The girls must have waited for him till late, drinking. Now they were sprawled out on the floor in ugly postures and with vulgar expressions. Some of them had their naked legs spread apart. They appeared to be dead bodies in a charnel ground.[1] The beauty in them was nowhere to be seen when their mouths were agape, slurring.

The bodhisattva pondered further on the transient nature of things and the helplessness of man who is chained to false notions of ego, greed and lust

1. Johnston- Buddhacharita (Pali).

and is unable to rise above them to a state of wisdom. Disgusted he came out again, thought over his plan to leave his attachments. The midnight chill hit his face. Ignoring it he thought of his women, his playmates who were his half brothers or cousins and above all his beloved parents. However, a fear of the unknown still lurked at the back of his mind. His perplexity was weighing upon his chest.

Next day, Shuddhodan cancelled all his meetings. Tapodan's challenge and his son's rigidness were foreboding hideous consequences. He did not realise that he himself was being short sighted like others, but did he have a choice? Siddhartha was a keen observer into the future. He was going against a decision which could wipe the Shakyan tribe for ever.

Siddhartha was discussing the matter with Yashodhara next afternoon. She locked her own feelings in a dark chamber of her mind and tried to help her husband to sort out his dilemma so that he changes his decision to leave his family. All he had to do was to apologise to Tapodan and the assembly, and accept their resolution which was passed in the council anyway. The girl Vashabhakshattriya was already undergoing training in the Mahanaam household, while the envoy from Sarasvati waited. She'll be married to Prasenjit's sword and sent to Sarasvati.

Yashodhara was saying, "My love, do you realise how much pain you would cause your family? Your parents might succumb to their grief and die a premature death. All the women of ranivas would become widows; as abandoned wives get no respect, luxuries or property, as before. Your seraglio might even be dissolved."

"I understand all that Yasho, but I think it is time, someone stood up to guide those who are going astray. It is not a question of my family alone or the people of Kapilvastu but the problem of the entire humanity, which is standing at the edge of a cliff ready to fall in a deep, dark, ravine of delusions from where only wisdom can pull them out, not anger, ego or wars".

"Do you possess that wisdom?"

"Not yet, but I intend to go and find a mentor who would guide me on the right path and teach me how to manage my own sufferings so that I could be enlightened and at peace. Then I would come to Kapilvastu. I promise, but when, I cannot say. Besides, my leaving would safeguard father's throne and his family at the seraglio, because I would never apologise to that nincompoop, Tapodan Uncle."

"Then, take me with you. Even Sita went with Rama when he was exiled for fourteen years."

"Yes, and took the risk of getting kidnapped by the evil king of Lanka. A war followed and Ravan was killed in the backdrop of his burning Kingdom. I don't believe in killings and bloodshed. There is always some other way out and I shall find it."

"Are you even condemning Krishna[1] for advising Arjun to fight a war for the sake of saving Dharma"?

"No, but Krishna or anyone is not my idol. Though I do agree that he was the best politician of the past. Now I shall find my own way by personal experience, instead of following pre-conceived ideas."

By this time Yashodhara could not hold herself any longer and burst into tears. Siddhartha placed her head lovingly on his shoulders and stroked her silky hair, pondering. At length she got up and wiped her tears and blew her nose in his top garment, and grinned mischievously. Siddhartha too laughed, "you naughty girl!" He reached out and grabbed her to make passionate love to her for the last time. Her heart throbbing she lay in ecstasy thinking, 'A lover like him cannot abandon his beloved.' And she slept blissfully in his arms.

*****

Now it was Shuddhodan's turn to entreat Siddhartha not to take the decision of leaving his home and family. He never took his son's philosophical musings seriously. He just couldn't fathom, 'Why? Oh, Why is he throwing away his beautiful luxurious life? People would die to achieve his status.'

Which shows how little he understood his son.

Mahaprajapati couldn't sleep the whole night. Her small snatches of sleep were punctuated by horrible nightmares. She was lost on the highway and couldn't find her way back home. Scared, she woke up early and after a cold bath visited the 'ranivas' with a fresh determination.

She upbraided the girls[2], "Let none of you fail to provide amusement for the prince night and day and never be without wine and burning perfumes …remember if he escapes, there will be no other pleasure within the palace. Arm yourselves! With swords and lances, bows and arrow to guard our beloved prince without him knowing about it.[3]

---

1. Krishna-The hero of the great war of Mahabharata. Arjun and Krishna were cousins. Krishna's father Vasudeva, was Kunti's brother.
2. Beal Romantic legend, p. 123. *Parables from Lotus Sutra, Chap. 3. Trans. Watson.
3. Lalitavistara -Chapt 15.

At this moment the Bodhisattva[1] was walking towards his father's chamber with thoughtful steps.

When King Shuddhodan was free from his morning commitments he stood next to the window looking at the distant snowy peaks when Siddhartha entered his room. After bowing at his father's feet he sat in a chair, wondering how to start. His father reading his mind, spoke, "What is it son?"

"I want to discuss something with you." The king settled down his sinewy body in another chair, by his bedside. But, before the prince could say something, queen Gautami entered and giving them one glance she settled herself on the bed against the bolsters. The three of them got distracted by a shrill screechy sound of a hawk who flew by their window chasing a reddish brown quail dove. The Prince went to the window to see the fate of the smaller bird and he saw that the bird had fallen and the hawk was plucking its feathers. The bird was fluttering, trying to save itself in a helpless struggle. Just then there was alarmed burbling of mynahs, doves and quails who were harassing the hunting bird to get off its prey. Sadly, the quail lost the battle and lay dead. The prince came back to his chair perturbed, not ready to see the hawk, lunch. His parents wore anxious frowns. Siddhartha cleared his throat and expressed himself.

"Father," looking at the king and he spoke, "Mother," avoiding her gaze.

"I have come to take your permission and blessings for going to the aranya."

They were horrified to realise their fears coming true. Then the king urged, "Please son, do not do that. I have worked hard to make you a worthy crown prince. Now don't leave your kingdom and us, when the time is ripe."

"Please father, try to understand. Yours and my people's welfare is topmost in my mind. That is why I challenged the council's decision. Their deception to powerful Prasenjit could cost them the lives of all Shakyans. Kaushalan King, the 'hawk' would kill us all small birds."

Prajapati had tears in her eyes. She asked, "Have you talked to Yashodhara ?"

"Yes"

"What did she say?"

"She has tremendous moral strength and character. She told me that she couldn't take away my freedom to choose, specifically since I have

1. One who strives to be a Buddha.

my clan's welfare in mind. She feels that I'll always stay with her, even if gone. She always wants me to be able to hold my head high with self pride.

'Do what you were born to do.' She had said at last crying. 'I wouldn't hold you responsible for the unbearable pain it would cause me.'"

The room atmosphere became heavy with melancholy. At length the queen answered.

"Since you two have made up your mind, my blessings are with you son."

"Thanks Ma, your response is as noble as Yashodhara's. I am counting on you to take care of her while I am gone." Then his gaze shifted to his father, who was looking far out of the window.

"Father, please don't hold me back because it is not right to obstruct a man who is trying to escape from a burning house"…*

"You are young and 'your mind is fickle'. Besides 'you are not use to solitude."**

The Prince eventually says, "I will stay, if and only if you can guarantee four things to me, that I will never die, that disease will never strike, that old age will never take my youth, and that I will never loose my fortune."***

The father was dreadfully silent. The Prince went on mercilessly.

"And promise me that none of my near and dear ones will disappear in my absence."****

The king looked at him with intensity and then lowered his eyes.

After a pause he addressed Siddhartha, "If you ever regret your decision, come back as the pastor to your flock."

Shuddhodan's heart puckered with fear and he placed his right hand on left side of his chest with a distorted expression; dragged himself towards his bed and slumped by his wife's side.

Siddhartha was promptly up and bent upon his contorted form anxiously. He asked, "Are you all right father?"

The king waved his hand for him to get away and spoke softly. "Leave me alone with your mother son."

---

* Buddhacharitra : 5: 30-31.

** Buddhacharitra : 5:35.

*** Lalitavistara: 1:301 ff.

****Beal's 'Romantic Legends.'

Siddhartha gently closed the door behind him and sent for the palace physician urgently.

*****

'Once face to face with misery, senility and death, the transcendental mind in him coiled in house of flesh and bone. Suddenly beamed and blazed and leaving the ailing world behind he took to austerity and longing for emancipation.'[1]

The king refused to see Siddhartha, after that. He was advised bed-rest. While Mahanaam was in charge. Who told him the next day.

"Our King is feeling much better. It was an anxiety attack due to which his blood pressure had shot up and maybe something he ate the night before."

It was on a full moon day when Siddhartha could not take it anymore. The blocked-up emotions broke their dam causing a destructive deluge. What his heart wanted his mind was trying to fulfill. He threw his fears aside and in the middle of the night waited for all to asleep. There was an uncanny silence all around. Yashodhara in her sleep was clinging to him with an arm over Siddhartha's body. He carefully slipped out of her grasp as not to wake her up. He put a bolster in his place leaving his wife's hand on it. Moonlight was falling on her face and limbs glowing with a golden hue. His feet were stuck to the floor but his mind goaded him to move on. He gently closed the door behind him and came down the stairs with a shawl over his shoulder. He was careful not to let it swish on the steps. Gathering it in his arms he walked towards Channa's lodgings. He knocked gently so that his wife and the two daughters were undisturbed. Channa came out rubbing his eyes.

An owl hooted. Some birds woke up and started chirping noisily on the boughs as if pleading the prince to stop.

"Quick, friend, bridle my horse and keep one for yourself.

We have a long way to go. As destiny is calling me prompt."

The guards at the eastern gate mysteriously slept. And the prince pursued the holy command. They galloped through the night and jumped over the sands. For a new dawn was awaiting its turn.

'He has seen the ills of 'sansara'* and is sickened

He jumps astride his good horse, Kanthak.

Crosses thirty leagues of wood sans deserts

---

1. Krishna Srinivas – The Buddha.

* Sansara=World.

Stop when he reaches the banks of the river.

It was a full moon night in the month of 'Asala."**

Siddhartha and Channa reached the end of their journey together; the charioteer clutching Kanthak's tail since the departure. They could see River Anomiya flowing on the side of their track. Across which was the dense and dangerous forest, full of underbrush, the Prince was suppose to cross it barefooted.

Across the river, Channa could see the thickened bushes and gnarled trees in scary shapes. He was shook up by the distressing sight but the ascetic in Siddharth discerned calm and freedom from the social shackles, under the gloomy shadows.

Channa looked around and made a last desperate attempt to dissuade the prince before alighting his horse.

"The forest would be infested with wild beasts, swamps and mosquitoes. How would you survive without any weapon?"

"Do not worry my friend I'll pick up one of the dried up branched and make it my staff and companion. I can envisage a forgotten city amongst the heavy thorny bushes. I want to build a new modern city on the ruins of the old ones."

"You mean an ideal republic?" Gautama looked at him and answered, "You are right my friend. My higher sensibility is urging me forward towards my goal."

Aghast Channa was not in the right frame of mind to delve down the depth of his step brother's superior consciousness. So, he quietly swung his other foot over his horse with his eyes full of tears and mind in a turmoil. The horses were left to graze while the two friends wiped the salty sweat streaming down their faces.

Exhausted, both of them lay down on the grassy patch under a shady Banyan Tree. Which could curtain the rising sun by its aerial roots. They slept through for a few hours without obstacles.

'Channa wakes up as the sun had brightened, to collect some fruits for breakfast. He returns to get the shock of his life. A cobra was coiled up towards Siddhartha's head, his hood spread out to protect his eyes from the sun; or so it appeared. He turns to stone while the cobra slithers away, across the path. The charioteer's still form comes to life and softly calls out, "Prince!"'

Siddharth woke up wondering, where he was!

** Asala=August.

After eating the berries Channa had collected from a shrub, he looked into his pleading eyes.

Channa was saying, "Please Prince think again!" You are trying to eradicate sufferings of the mankind yet you are letting your own family drown in the ocean of misery. All his life, King Shuddhodan waited for the moment when he would crown you as a King. He is a hardworking and selfless republican whose only selfish desire was to give the control of his people in capable and compassionate hands of his beloved son. What crime has he committed for which he is being punished?"

"None whatsoever; he had been a devoted father to me and a caring parent. He gave me all the luxuries though a warrior-prince is not suppose to get any. I know he still misses my biological mother Maya and I had been the loving link between them but I do not have a choice. Every revolution demands blood. Literally or metaphorically! Everything has a cost to it." And the prince got up with a jerk while Channa was sitting on the ground. He looked up surprised as Siddhartha flashed out his sword from its sheath. Channa trembled with fear.

Channa shaded his eyes from the sun and observed the Prince with eyes wide open. Who had stood up cutting his top-knot of hair, a distinct mark of his caste, with the sword. He jumped to his feet requesting, "Please, prince! Why are you doing this?"

"Give these princely locks and all my ornaments to my father and apologise on my behalf that I smashed his dream of seeing me on the throne. I am sorry for not being an obedient son. But my spiritual cravings and sense of justice makes me see pain everywhere. I need to learn to deal with that. I have gone too soft with all the luxuries he as a doting father provided me. I feel a deep sense of gratitude for him and my mother who sacrificed her affections for my brother and gave it to me instead."

Siddhartha hesitated before taking off his last ornament, his wedding chain. Then abruptly he jerked it down and handed over the broken chain to Channa. "For your Princess!"

Shocked Channa placed the hair and the jewels carefully inside his tunic pocket and girthed his sash tight around his waist while shedding copious tears. Siddhartha turned towards his constant companion, Kanthak.

"The animal opens his mouth and neighs aloud.

He flakes his ears, then turns his head around.

And he lovingly licks the prince's feet.

Bodhisattva pats him and says,

"Friend do not impede my path to Buddhahood".***

And then he was gone.

Chandak and Kanthak kept on looking at his receding figure, towards the forest, across the river.

Channa spoke aloud, to himself, "Now that you have left us our land will be deserted. And our hearts melancholy."****

The Prince moving towards his new life, did not look back. Chandak's last words after touching his feet were, "Please, Prince, leave now if you must and cross the dangerous forest before dusk."

Channa's concern moved the prince but he controlled himself and even resisted the impulse of embracing him before departing.

The Bodhisattva crossed the river and entered the shady forest.

*****

He started walking in the direction of The Ganga. The sky was clear blue and Gautama walked all day till he saw the evening hue; treading the path riddled with rough stones and thorns which poked at his tender soles.

He came across a strange sight. An ascetic, with a net and trapped birds, was walking towards him with a bow and arrow. As they met, they both stopped, eyeing each other. Bodhisattava asked, "Why does a sadhu need a bow and arrow"?

"I am a hunter. I dress as an ascetic just to beguile the innocent game."

"It's going against the natural law. Why don't you follow some other profession?"

"This is the only art I have learnt since childhood."

"Take my clothes. Interwoven, with the silk are, threads made of gold. Once you sell those you shall have enough money to start a new trade."

The Hunter's eyes shone with hope, while Siddhartha continued, "But I have two conditions! You give me your garb in exchange and no more killing of birds, and free the one's you have captured."

"Gladly!" Once freed, the birds flew away to their nestlings, their crops full of food for them.

The Prince moved forward. Barefoot, clad in the filthy rag, avoiding a wave of repulsion. He focused on his present goal and was wondering where to spend the night when he saw at a distance a few huts of a hermitage.

As he reached their glade, two women came out in rust saris. On seeing

***Jatakanidan.

****Hiltbeitel and Miller (1998); Walters (1994).

a tired 'sramana,' the wandering holy man, they welcomed him and offered him simple water, food and a hut to rest.

Gautama woke up with the sound of twittering birds. After another simple meal he thankfully left them to go towards the Ganga River.

After leaving his sanctuary of home, which to him had become like a prison, Siddhartha passed some more hermitages and remote hamlets; meeting and discussing religion with wandering ascetics he moved towards the north road. Hitch-hiking the passing caravans he crossed the Kaushal kingdom. Moving towards east he reached the powerful confederation of Vrijji and stopped at a village called Patali. After a short break he took a ferry from there to cross the Ganga River and go towards south to enter the rich kingdom of Magadh.

After many days of crossing hills and the rivulets of Ganga he reached Giriviraj, the capital of Magadh, ruled by king Bimbisar. The city was surrounded by many hills, a natural boundary. Its position at the Ganga River Valley provided it with access to the rich ports in Ganga -Brahamputra delta assisting in trade. Gautama rested at one of the Saptapanni caves.

*****

At Kapilvastu, Mahaprajapati was taking more care of Yashodhara than her own husband who silently performed his kingly duties. The east gate's night duty guards were imprisoned and given a sentence of twenty whips each, till further action.

Later as the king was passing Siddhartha's Ranivas, he heard wailing and lamenting, and Mangala coming out of Yashodhara's room with a smirk on her face. On seeing him she quickly wiped it off and pretended to be sad.

"Listen Mangala," Please stop that moaning and groaning. Tell the women my son is not dead, he is only absent from the palace. He might return any day if he gets tired of the hardships. Besides, I will take their full responsibility as a father.

Prajapati slept with Yashodhara for a week then left her with her childhood friends, Renu, Ganga, Rohini and her attendant, Bhanumati. They all kept her constant company and tried to calm her down.

Ganga—Devprayag in Uttrakhand is the place where two rivers, Bhagirathi and its tributary, Alakhnanda meet. Their distinct colours muddy and blue can be seen at the confluence. Alakhnanda gets its waters from the peaks of Nanda Devi and Bhagirathi rises at the foot of Gangotary Glaciers at the Himalayas. Both these rivers combine to form the Ganga or Ganges.

Source—Nitesh Shukla, Quora (eight years back).

Yashodhara told Renu when alone with her, "You know friend, my Siddhartha loves me so much, that he can't stay away from me for long. Once he gets enough, of his wandering he'll be back in my arms."

Renu looked at her tenderly like an elder sister. There was a tear still stuck under her one eye yet a corner of her lips was smiling with hope. She kissed the Princess on her brow, which she didn't mind. Though they both were unaware that they were actually half sisters.

"Shuddhodan had immediately dispatched spies in all directions to find the Prince. People of Kapilvastu were horror-struck to find their favourite prince has abandoned them for no reason. They were told that he has gone in search of God."

A little girl asked "God is everywhere so why should he go looking for him in the forest?"

The courtier smiled at her innocent question but he himself was confused.

Gautama meanwhile was often seen in the streets of Giriviraj,* begging. It was the capital of Magadha empire, founded by Shishupal of Mahabharat. It had taken him a couple of months sometimes on foot and sometimes on boats to cover the distance of twenty 'yojanas'[1] to reach this city, via Patali'.

There were certain areas in Giriviraj related to King Jarasandh and Lord Krishna of Mahabharat. But Siddhartha was single minded in his search of a spiritual teacher.

After begging, on the first day he sat under a tree for his only meal of the day. He felt like throwing up. He use to wonder how can some people eat so differently in comparison to what was cooked at their palace.'

Gautama took abode in one of the caves on Pandava Mountain of the sleepy town in a valley full of forests. One day as he was begging, a large crowd started following him. They had never seen such a handsome and dignified mendicant. Women looked at him from their terraces and windows. So did king Bimbisar from his balcony. He was impressed by his noble bearing and tranquil appearance. He sent a messenger to invite him in the palace for a meal.

Siddhartha bowed to the king as he entered. Bimbisar asked him, "Why does your face look familiar?"

"I am Siddhartha Gautama of Kapilvastu, son of King Shuddhodan."

---

1. 1 yojana=fifteen kilometers *Ancient name for Rajgrih, meaning 'the enclosure of hills.'

"Oh! Now I know. I attended your wedding about thirteen years back when you were glittering in jewels.What happened? Were you thrown out of the kingdom or did you abdicate the throne?"

"No such thing O king. I decided to become a recluse and find a good mentor to guide me in my search for the answers to my questions about life's struggles. I want to show others a path towards a happy state of mind. I am tired of being controlled by destiny and the shackles of rituals. As well the theories propounded by the powerful priestly class."

"So am I dear! So am I. Let's talk till the food is served."

Siddhartha opened up. "The Atman or the spirit is not an entity. There is no duality in life.* We and our entire environment are drawn from the same cosmic energy which seems to me the ultimate reality, and in the end everything would blend into it, like rivers in the ocean. The 'parpanch' or 'conceptual proliferation'** of the phenomenal world is unreal. There is no otherness in non-duality or other- ness-less in duality.*** My aim now is to find a way, which would liberate people, from the bondage of suffering after gaining knowledge about 'who we are'?"

Bimbisara who was a Jain practitioner answered.

"My dear son, there is not only duality but multiplicity in life. 'A substance has many aspects to it. Sometimes some of these aspects exist as contradictions in the same substance. Thus Anekanta philosophy holds that co-existence of opposites is the cardinal principle of Jain doctrine. Life thrives in contradictions, which co-exists. Duality like sorrow or joy, praise and blame, heat and cold prevail together. Is life real or not real, or is it 'Maya'?" The king paused and then continued. "I agree with Vedanta that the outer world is real and the inner world of our thoughts and memories etc. is 'Maya.' Anyway, non-absolutism is the way of life. Like nature, creation is a plurality. Hence reality is multidimensional. It is an ideology of synthesis and synchronism.'**** One positive and the other negative, always exist together. If there is no darkness we won't know what light is all about!"

---

* Paul Hacker: 'Sankara (650-780) Advaita Vedanta (1913-1979)'

** Magadh Empire was founded by Shishupal of Mahabharat.

***Drs.G.R. Krishnamurti and Chandrasekhar Murumkar: research article, A.J. Institute of Management, Mangalore.

****Conceptual proliferation— Non-dualism: Fabian Volker, 'The Encyclopedia of Philosophy and Religion'
(John Wiley and Sons inc. 2021)

"So you follow the principles propounded by Rishabhnath Tirthankara of the Licchavi Clan?"

"Yes I do! Yet, promise me one thing Siddhartha, when you find your path, come back and teach me as your disciple".

"It'll be an honour to share my 'way' with your highness."

Soon the food was placed in front of the guest. He started eating without much ado.

After the meal, Gautama was introduced to Bimbisar's chief queen Kaushala Devi, who was Prasenjit's sister and to his young son Ajathshatru meaning free of enemies.

Gautama got up and touched her feet. He told her that Prasenjit was his class mate at Takshakshila. Which pleased her.

Gautama left Giriviraj soon because he was afraid that the good king would try to make life easier for him by sending him food and gifts.

*****

Gautama walked aimlessly, not knowing were exactly to go. Soon, he met an ascetic, Bhargava Rishi, on the way. He accompanied Gautama to the spiritual center of Alar Kalam because he was going the same way. It took them nine days to reach there. He was told that the spiritual leader had four hundred disciples around his hermitage near Vaishali. Thus he became Siddhartha's first teacher.

Alar Kalam taught Gautama the technique of meditation by observing breath and the practice of 'Sankhya yoga'. It helped Siddhartha to know the nature of spirit and matter on an analytical and intellectual level but his dilemma was still not solved. He soon exhausted all the knowledge his mentor had to offer.

One day his mentor called him and said, "Sit with me Siddhartha, my dear shishya. You are my best student and I want to make an offer to you. I am very proud of you. You have mastered all your learning so quickly. Now, if you want you can become my co-teacher at this ashram."

The surprised student answered politely, "I am very grateful to you Guruji for imparting all your knowledge to me with affection and care but I need to move on in search of enlightenment."

"Do what your heart desires son, my blessings would always be with you."

Siddhartha also thanked Bhargava Rishi before leaving him.

Thus, Gautama walked back again towards the city of the five mountains, Giriviraj. His aim being the hermitage near Anupia, of the famous Acharya Uddraka Ramputra, suggested by Alar Kalam. He was teaching seven hundred students in and around the ashram. His center was sprawled in acres of land with tall trees overshadowing the tracks walked by the practitioners. The ambience suited Gautama's present state of mind. Every new student had to start with elementary techniques of meditation which Siddhartha was quick to master. When his seventy five year old mentor realised that his pupil has already achieved the realm of 'nothingness'. He was impressed. He offered him to be his spiritual heir and take charge of his center. Gautama wanted time to think. Uddraka taught him about the experienced or the felt ego, which should be negated. But the creative ego of the Upanishads has to be retained. The positive ego creates while the negative destroys.

One day while sitting in front of his hut, Rishi Uddraka was teaching Gautama. "After unraveling the ultimate mystery you'll realise that life and death are nothing but a game."

"But it is life energy which has guided me to you, yet I cannot see it."

"You saw its agitation ; the agitation of momentary. Now focus hard to see what is happening around you. What you see and what 'is' are not two. They merge perception."

"What they call life force or Atman, what drives it?

"If you are calm and focused you shall find a spot within you which does not waver under any circumstances. That is your true self or Atman. Just as in a wheel, it moves on an axel which itself stays stationary."

Gautama thanked the Acharya but was not satisfied. He did not want to stick to any principles and become a fundamentalist. That way he felt, 'he would lose his freedom of thought and he would become narrow minded and conventional. His spiritual growth would stop. And he wouldn't be able to find, why people suffer?'

Chapter - 11

Yashodhara's Affliction

'Am I walking? Was I sleeping?
Dearest are you watching yet?
Traces on my cheeks of weeping
Glitter, 'tis in vain I fret
Now beloved in one night we are torn apart
My heart is split I can do nothing but sob.'*

After leaving the prince, Channa started back to Kapilvastu with a heavy heart. Even Kanthak was dejected. The journey they had undertaken with the prince, in one night and day, became so oppressive that it took seven days for Channa to reach back home.

Everyone was waiting for him at the Hamsavati palace anxiously. After leaving the horses in the stables and putting fodder in their bins, he went to report to the king.

Shuddhodan and Mahaprajapati were sitting in their palace garden under the lengthening shadows of late evening. Their hearts heavy with grief and their minds searching for an answer as to where had they gone wrong? Two slave girls standing behind them with peacock feather fans were warding off bugs if any, as the royal couple saw Channa approach, limping. On an impulse they stood up. Sitting down again they told the girls to leave, Channa came forward and touched their feet. He then stood with his head bent in shame and hands clasped in front. The pregnant pause was nerve wrecking. If it was someone else the king would have thrashed him or worse. But knowing Channa's loyalty and Siddhartha's stubbornness he did not accuse him. Channa couldn't take the king's non-communication anymore.

He took out the packet of jewels and the lock of hair, Siddhartha had sent for him with the message that unless he finds a way to end all miseries of mankind he is not coming back. In the end Channa also gave the king his bejewelled sword.

The king asked, Where did you leave him?"

"At the bank of River Anomiya, en route to 'Uttar Path.'"

The queen spoke, "Channa, you both were such good friends, then why couldn't you have convinced him?"

"I tried my best Queen, as a friend. But I had to listen to my Master".

"Okay, you may go now but please see Yashodhara tomorrow. She would be expecting to hear from you."

*****

Seeing Yashodhara! Facing her wrath and pain, was his greatest fear. Next day he limped towards her palace. Entering her chamber he stood in a dark corner, apologetically.

"Who stands there in the dark?" Channa appeared in light. As soon as she saw him she pounced on him like a tigress.

'Then spoke Yashodhara eyes red with anger, her voice choking by the bitterness of despair, tears streaming through the depth of her grief. "Chandak, where has that joy of my heart gone leaving me as I slept helpless at night, as I see you and Kanthak return.[1] You have done me an ignoble, cruel and unfriendly act so why do you weep here today you heartless man?"'

Channa was still weeping when Prajapati, who too was in the room, poured out her own sorrow.

"Those soft feet of his, with lovely webbed toes, tender like lotus fiber or a flower petal, with concealed ankles, with whorl on the soles how will they tread on the rough forest ground."*

Channa thudded to the floor covering his face with his hands and sobbed violently. Renu and Rohini who did not interfere the Queens so far came forward and were trying to pacify them, while crying themselves. After exhausting her tears, Yashodhara got up and washed her face, helped by Rohini, wiping it she ordered Channa.

---

1. "Ashvaghasha's Buddhcharita"- "Lamenting in the seraglio"
   Mahayana monk between the 1st and 2nd CE. Canto 8 : No. 31 Vol. 32 Trans. By Patrick Olivelle Day Sanskrit Library. New York. *Rajini Obeyesekere-canto 55.

"Please leave friend, you have served my husband well. I can imagine your predicament at the last moment when you and your prince parted".

Channa got up, wiping his tears with his scarf and addressed Prajapati, "Maharani, since we have returned, Kanthak has stopped eating".

Both the regal ladies were not alarmed yet. Prajapati suggested, "Channa give him some time to get over his grief. May be he will start eating by tonight, start with goodies like butter and honey."

"Okay, my queen, I'll do that." Channa bowed and turned back towards the stairs with jerky movements.**

Prajapati then turned to Yasho's, maid-in waiting.

"Please Bhanu get something to eat for your mistress."

"Please mother, I do not feel like eating, my stomach is all wrenched up. I keep imagining my husband wandering from door to door with his begging bowl, to collect a few morsels of food, which may not be to his taste. He might have spitted them out the first time."

"Yet he would get use to it eventually, the choice was his."

"I know, so would I, with the kind of food beggars eat."

Soon Bhanumati entered with a tray full of delicacies. Yashodhara asked her to place it on a stool in front of the queen. Prajapati looked at Yasho, who sat opposite to her and they both shared the plate.

"Won't you eat anything else Yasho except the boiled rice?"

"Yes, Ma, please do not press".

Her aunt understood her pain, so she left the half finished platter and Yashodhara, with her childhood friends.

'Yashodhara started wailing and she tore off her precious pearls and gems, took off her silks and rings from her toes and sat lifeless, turned to stone'.[1] All her companions stayed with her all night trying to put her to sleep. But the queen was restless, missing her love and was mumbling in her disturbed snatches of suspended consciousness.

'Since he has gone in search of enlightenment leaving me behind. Now I too vow to renounce all worldly pleasures. Though he has left me I'll abide by the moral rules.'[2]

---

1. Translated by Ranjini Obeyesekere.
2. These are the precepts that laymen undertake to perform in order to enter the path to Nirvana.

** Channa had been injured many years ago in a fall from the horse.

From then onwards Yashodhara lost her smiles. She locked herself up in a mental cage, where nobody could enter. Her grief became her own private matter.

Next day when the Queen entered Yashodhara's room she couldn't find her on her bed which looked unused. She asked Bhanumati. Who bowed and pointed towards the floor next to her bed. Prajapati gasped. Yashodhara was wearing a cotton saree like a nun and had made her bed on the floor. When she saw her mother-in-law she touched her feet and received her blessings. Prajapati sat on the carpet, next to Yashodhara and touched her shoulder. "Why Yasho?"

"Mother, I'll walk the path in quest of enlightenment, along with my husband while living in the palace".

"Would you like to visit your parents for a change?"

"No, your son left me here and here I shall stay till he returns."

Just then the door opened and the indignant Suprabuddha entered followed by Amita and Shuddhodan. He raised is voice in anger when he saw his delicate daughter suffering thus, in a mendicant's rust robe.

"Get up my child! Let's go. I'll take care of you in my house. You shall rule my state after me."

"No father, please do not ask me to do that. This is my house now, even if my husband is not here." And she got up from the floor. She was very aware of the honour of Shuddhodan and Mahaprajapati in front of her own parents.

Her father dashed out with tears in his eyes, followed by Shuddhodan. Amita stayed back with Prajapati. Yashodhara was beginning to feel the healing power of her loved ones. The three ladies attended by girls kept sitting in Yashodhara's room on a carpet, till dinner time. They tried to converse on topics other than Siddhartha, to keep Yasho's mind away from him for a change.

The two men walked towards a sitting room where they usually played Chess-Chaturanga[1] or just had drinks while chatting. Once the drinks were served, they solemnly discussed the present situation.

Shuddhodan took a sip of wine thoughtfully and expressed, "I have

---

1. Ancient India- Jeannine Auboyer .Chess was invented by Indians. At first as a means of working out military strategy and was played by four players using two dice. With four figures, king, elephant, horse and chariot and four pawns which symbolized the 4 corps of the traditional army

*Buddhcharita and Abhinishkramana Sutra. Two ministers were sent to look for the Prince.

sent two ministers brother, to look for him. I don't know when they might bring some news."*

"Alas! Sage Asita's prophesy came true!"

"Siddhartha never believed in stars and destiny." Shuddhodan answered.

"He sure wasn't a fatalist like most people. Especially the Brahmans. He always said, 'man's destiny is in his own hands. He can change it anyway he likes."

"I do not know what to believe in, any more. I am only worried about my daughter. The way her husband has left, no one knows when he would return or if at all as a householder. What would my girl do if he has become a recluse for good?" As the news has spread, already young men are eager to have her hand in matrimony".

"I shall not object to that if Yashodhara wants it. Even our Devdatta is interested in her."

Suprabuddha sipped his drink without replying.

Before her parents left, Yashodhara had made it clear to them, "I loved my husband with the core of my heart I shall never let another man come near me.

After chief Suprabudhha and Amita were gone feeling defeated, Yashodhara couldn't contain herself. She kept on crying, telling her childhood friends,

"My eyes are full, my garments wet, tears fall, as my husband, nectar-like I recall……"[1]

They tried consoling her but to no avail.

Kanthak died a few days after his master left, due to self-starvation. Life started dragging at the palace. No music, no smiles, only sad faces. However, Dhrotodan, his wife Mangala and their son Devdatta were looking at the situation as an opportunity. In the privacy of their quarters, they plotted and planned. Devdatta since childhood had suffered from sibling rivalry.

Before Siddhartha was born, Devdatta was everyone's pet. Mahamaya and Shuddhodan doted on him because they did not have any child of their own. Even after Nanda's birth, the king's love for him was the same. But when Siddhartha came in this world and his mother Maya left for her heavenly abode, everything changed. The king in his grief, only had concern for Maya's son, whom he deeply loved. After all he might become

1. P. 51 The poem from Yashodhara, the wife of Bodhisattva (2nd part of verse 90) Translated by Ranjani Obeyesekere.

the king one day. Thus, two babies in king Shuddhodan's household took all his attention and Devdatta's childish mind was deeply hurt. He started hating the new arrival as his enemy although there were two more little ones born the same day in Shuddhodan's 'ranivasa'. One was Chandak and the other 'Kaludayin'. Even at the stables that was the day when Kanthak was born. However, Devdatta had hated Siddhartha most intensely, as he was growing up.

Mrigi in her own palace was more angry than sad, with her husband's departure. She thought she was the youngest, prettiest and the only queen who was pregnant with his child yet her husband spurned away her advances. Only did his duty to her. Now she only had the memory of his amorous companionship. Of the time she spent with him. 'His handsome face full of lust.' How could she ever forget him? However, her bitterness against him had concealed her passion underneath. So she persevered.

Mrigi at first thought of going back to her father Dandapani's house. But a glimmer of hope, like everyone else kept her where she was. She wanted to bring up his child in the palace. Just in case he returned!

Gopa was a silent sufferer. She was not as strong as Yashodhara or Mrigi but was slowly crumbling from within. Mahaprajapati often visited Mrigi, Gopa and Utpalavarna, his fourth queen, along with her niece Yashodhara who was closest to her heart.

She never forsook her duties as the chief queen of King Shuddhodan who too tried to immerse himself in his duties as an administrator. Every night he slept exhausted and disappointed because his two ministers had not returned yet with any news of his son. His love for Siddhartha was the deepest but he had never shown it. Every day as he slept in a different bedroom, which was a safety measure, he dreamt of Siddhartha as an ascetic, or starving or being attacked by a hungry leopard.

After a few months the news came that the two ministers had found Siddhartha meditating under a tree in Uravela village near Gaya. They requested him to come back home but his reply was firm.

"I am grateful to you, my elders, for coming all the way to seek me, but I shall only return after I have achieved my spiritual awakening. Please gentlemen, request my father not to worry about me. Many times I live in hermitages where food and shelter is no issue."

Thus, he bade farewell to his well-wishers and continued his meditation. The birds hopped around him unafraid; a stream gurgled nearby escaping from the Ganga, and leaves glistened under the rays of setting sun. At night he slept under the Pipal tree, in cool summer breeze.

The step that Siddhartha had taken was painful for everyone at Kapilvastu, except for Devdatta. It was as if an obstacle had been removed from his path to success. Siddhartha had known his ambition since long and he was satisfied that his absence would make his cousin brother happy.

As far as Yashodhara was concerned, she felt like a fish out of water, thrashing about painfully and trying to survive the breathlessness. Her mind became numb, suddenly trapped in an emotional vacuum, with no husband or child for support. Only elderly in-laws who needed her care and love, to put a balm on their bleeding hearts. For a few days she lost touch with reality. Every morning she expected Siddhartha to be lying next to her. She felt as if she was dead. At least psychologically and was only going through the motions of living.

Mahaprajapati had tactfully removed everything from her room which would remind her of her beloved.

As the time crawled she started confronting the reality head-on. When her own parents had come to take her back with them, her refusal to go made her realise that she needs to find some way to cope with her loss, rather than letting herself drown in a deep dark hole of non-existence. She was thinking, 'This is a time to test my moral strength and perseverance. I have had great happiness with my husband in the past. I will cherish those memories and live by them. We both truly loved each other. But now he has expanded his horizons to include the entire humanity in his love. Can I blame him for that? Neither can I blame myself for it. I was always a devoted and loving wife. Then why? Oh, why did it happen?'

Yashodhara's very foundation was in pieces. She felt that she, now was in another lifetime. As if reborn as a woman whose sole purpose is to look after others. The emptiness inside was there to stay, except a sneaky glimmer of hope; a tiny, flickering flame of her love for Siddhartha which guided her in the dark alleys of her low moments to give her strength.

She was gradually learning to share her grief with the other inmates of the seraglio, with Mahaprajapati always the beacon showing the path. The ladies at first sat in a circle, on carpets, in the inner courtyard and discussed their common sufferings. Children would be playing about as the mothers were learning to cope. Excerpts from Vedas and stories from the Upanishads were shared and 'Bhajans', religious songs were sung together in chorus. The girls who loved to dance often performed on the theme of Radha and Krishna, the divine couple. They fasted on special days of their goddess and refrained from drinking wine and eating onion or garlic which were suppose to be stimulants for the body. Thus, they found emotional support in their religious practices and healing power in each other's company.

Yet Siddhartha's many queens were pining for their prince though angry. They would sometimes go on religious excursions with the inmates of 'ranivasa,' or played games, like 'chaupad' with each other.

During one of the excursion departures Yashodhara saw Devdatta in his breaches and boots standing near the gate. He was equipped with bow and arrows, javelin, and a dagger to embark on a hunting spree followed by a few courtiers. 'Beaters armed with nets and traps, together with a pack of hunting-dogs,' to help them kill lion, deer or wild boar.

She ignored him yet he came towards her and whispered with a piercing look and a quirky smile, which twisted one end of his lips.

"Your husband is not coming back, why don't you marry me. Then we shall rule the kingdom together after Shuddhodan."

Yashodhara's face puckered with loathing and vicious anger. She spat out her words in disgust.

"Are you crazy? I find your very presence repulsive. I would rather die than let anyone, above all you, dare to touch me."

"Have it your way for now. But one day I am determined to possess you. You are Siddhartha's pride and that is something I would love to crush under my boots," and he rubbed his one boot viciously in the soil. Laughing sinisterly, he galloped on his stallion.

Yashodhara felt as if the fading sound of the horse's hooves was stomping her heart. Humiliated she started crying. Renu, Rohini, Surma and Ganga her companions, all consoled her.

"You don't need to worry about that nasty creature. He cannot put his finger on you. Our quarters are so well guarded by our little army of brave strong women armed with bows, lances and axes on a spike.* Who keep constant vigil on the ramparts and on all the gates. Inside, the strong eunuchen keep their eyes peeled off to watch for any unauthorised person entering your palace. So far, the only men who can visit you apart from the King, are Chandak and Kaludayin, who treat you with respect and a brotherly affection."

Yashodhara shook her head, as the file of covered chariots with horse-riding escorts started moving. They proceeded to pray to their fertility goddess Abhaya Devi at the Rummindei Park where Mahamaya gave birth to her son Siddhartha and possibly she herself was born there. Yashodhara had a soft corner in her heart in connection with the birthplace of her husband.

*****

Rummindei grove felt like a sanctuary to Yashodhara, with its serene and quiet surroundings. Absence of men gave her youth, a sense of freedom. This was one place where she could let her hair down and think of her grief in peace. She moved to the spot where it was believed that Queen Mahamaya gave birth to her son, while holding the branch of a Sal Tree and assisted by her sister Prajapati.

Yashodhara was thinking, 'Today my husband turned thirty one, I wonder what were the constellations like at the moment when one life was ready to leave one body and another was entering the world. Siddhartha's life had started with a sad beginning. Maybe the inborn loss made him the way he is.' She wondered, 'What he might be doing at the moment!' Her thoughts continued flowing like an unbound river.

'In the shadows of the forest you now walk,
There is no resting place for you in that dark
Unceasing burns the fire that sears in my heart
My hand on my heart I beat my breast and weep.'

Yashodhara quickly wiped the tears from her eyes as she heard foot-steps.

Rohini and Surma stopped near her.

"Why such a long face Princess? Come let's go and pray to the goddess for our Prince's safety. Renu is preparing the plate for worship with offerings. Let's go and light the sacred lamp!"

Yashodhara went to the nearby pond known as 'Pushkarni' to wash her hands and feet before the prayer. She could visualise Mayadevi taking a dip there before going to the spot of her delivery. Even her husband as a baby must have been given his first bath in this pond. Musing, she walked to the Bodhigara, the tree-shrine where under the shade was a carved-in-black-stone, statue of the mother goddess of fertility. It was small and kept on a circular wooden bench around the tree. Smeared with sacred vermilion and decorated with fresh flowers. The goddess was supposed to reside in the ancient tree. Women went around the tree circling it with a yellow and red holy thread, a few times and prayed with folded hands, bowed head and closed eyes.*

*****

Alar Kalam and Uddraka Ramputra, did not believe in arguments over traditional religious theories. They believed in gaining knowledge from

* Old custom of Tree-worship. Darlington (2012). Lewis and Tuladhar trans in 'Ancient India,' by Auboyer : p. 276.

meditation and personal experience. Uddraka advised Gautama how to sit like a Yogi as suggested in Gita, "Sit still with your back and shoulders straight with tongue sticking the roof of your mouth. Let your thoughts flow freely, with closed eyes, till they are exhausted. Try to rid your mind of past, present and future. Now focus your mind on its emptiness while breathing with lungs full and belly stuck in. Practice this till all your anxieties cool down. You are afloat in immense calm."

"Let the light enter your vacant mind. Do not let the environmental sounds and conditions distract you. Leave your mind open to new thoughts and sensations. Breathe through your entire body and go deeper within to soak yourself in your very being. Stop breathing and see what happens next. Breathe out with your entire body and open your palms to receive your brand new, original thoughts, fearlessly. That's the unique 'you'. You are now in touch with yourself."

"Dwell in the present moment to experience the supreme truth of that moment alone. Unpolluted by any previously set notion. Be original. Be creative on your own, instead of following the beaten path. The entire universe lies within each cell of your body."

Siddhartha was still in a dilemma. "If you say only eternity is permanent! Then what about the present moment?"

"One is reality and the other, perception. Your choices create your perception. When reality combines with perception, 'ultimate reality' is realised."

"How can this ultimate truth eradicate poverty and sufferings from this earth, down here, where I am standing?"

"Once your agitations of the momentary die out what you see is reality. Where there is no birth, life or death. It is all just a game played by emotional energy. You are happy or sad due to its agitations."

Gautama became silent.

"Go, sit under a shady tree and meditate, watching your breath. You'll find your answers," advised the Rishi.

Gautama soon learnt to control his body and his feelings through practicing meditation. His attachments started dissolving into nothingness and his mind was moving towards a state of extreme peace and equanimity. Small, little irritations and anxieties of the palace life and the constraints of a crown prince, were exuding out of his system. He felt light and free. Yet, his target still was, to learn to teach people to overcome the griefs of sickness, old age and death,* in the simplest possible terms.

He knew that it wasn't possible for everyone to leave home and come out and dwell in the forest, to stay away from the problems of everyday life. It'll be escapism. He also wanted to devise concepts which could bring forth wisdom and happiness while going through various obstacles in life itself.

He was beginning to realise that the problems of life cannot disappear in thin air but our understanding and correct perception, can teach us to override the pain and deal with the situation wisely.

While the Buddha's rules later on established for monks were strict, it was not so for the lay disciples; the householders. Who could help the Sangha in their own way while attending Buddha's sermons.

*****

After learning from his two famous teachers, Alar and Uddraka, Gautama still was at a loss to come to terms with the sufferings of sickness, old age and death. He had met many other religious preachers and 'sramanas'; wandering sadhus in search of the truth of life but failed. From the Magadh Capital, he walked and walked; over the hills, down the valley and across the rivers towards Gaya where his ancestor Rama with Sita and Laxman had offered pind-daan** for their late father Dashratha. It was only half a day's walk away from a beautiful spot at the bank of Niranjan river, in the district of Uruvilva, generally called Uruvila.

Buddha later described to his disciples:

"I saw woods that were delightful, lovely, secluded, sequestered, remote from turmoil, remote from men, and growing in seclusion amid charming lakes. Round about were herd-men's villages, not too far away not yet too near, but accessible; a level tract and the River Niranjan with its pure water flowing still and clear between the beautiful banks." **

There was a cave on Uruvilva hill close-by. Near its base, a shady Peepal tree grew full of lush green leaves. A narrow dirt track passing from near the tree headed for the village temple. A few times, people passed by early in the morning without disturbing the 'Yogi Maharaj,' ascetic in his meditation.

Gautama continued meditating for three years, under the benign tree. He would beg for food from one household of the village and survive on that. Sometimes an irritable housewife would only splash water in his bowl which he drank for the day.

** Pind daan is a ritual which is suppose to detach the soul from its worldly attachments so that it is freed from the cycle of rebirths and attains 'nirvana' or everlasting peace.

He later recalled, "I only took a handful of each meal, whether of bean soup or lentil soup or vetch soup or pea soup….My limbs became like the jointed segments of bamboo; my backside became like a camel's hoof; my ribs jutted out as gaunt as the crazy rafters on an old roofless barn; the gleam of my eyes sank far down in their sockets; My scalp shriveled and withered; my belly adhered to the backbone; if I defecated or urinated, I fell over my face; if I tried to ease my body by rubbing my limbs with my hands, the hair rotted at the roots, fell off." ***

At times his eyes became moist but he was getting used to hunger and was losing weight. Self-awakening was nowhere in sight. He did not want his senses to hinder his thoughts. Although he had experienced great peace in a state of 'emptiness or void of the mind' yet his target was not achieved, with this concept. Gradually Siddhartha ate only one 'jujube' fruit a day. The severity of his fast turned his body into a skeleton. A secret spy of Shuddhodan who always kept a watch on the prince, dressed as a villager, sent a message to the king through the express mail of a hired horse.

'Our prince remains sitting cross-legged, most of the time since I have come. I have never seen him defecating or urinating, spitting or blowing his nose. Neither he bends his limbs or stretch them out. He never lay down on his belly or back. He has turned black! The colour of Madgura fish.'**

Even the villagers who saw Gautama often wondered, "Why has the sage turned black?"

Shuddhodan immediately dispatched five men to take care of his son. He could have sent more and so would have Suprabuddha but they were afraid that Siddhartha would never like being chaperoned. The three men from the King and two from Yashodhara's father went to their prince dressed as ascetics and served the Bodhisattava as his first five disciples, near the Niranjan River. The messenger who was stationed there earlier went back to Kapilvastu to report.

Kaundinya one of the five, was in charge of Siddhartha's education at the palace when he had been younger. Later he was replaced by Vishvamittra, the court priest. Rest of the four spies too were Brahamans.

The messenger who left Uruvilva, on reaching home gave his report,

---

* 'The story of the four sights which is told by traditional Buddhism where the Buddha sees- a sick person, an aging person, a corpse and a wandering monk is not Siddhartha Gautama's story. It forms part of a mythical tale about another Buddha called Vipassi, who lived in the distant past. The story has nothing to do with Gautama himself.

*** These were Budda's own words to his disciples.

in private, to King Shuddhodan and Queen Prajapati, when they were together.

"Your Majesty, the prince is almost dead as a result of his severe austerities and meager diet. He no longer inhaled and exhaled but lay like a log of wood. However, he was revived before I left."

Prajapati started crying. The king dismissed the messenger and took Prajapati in his arms and stroked her hair. "Our five men are wise and responsible. They won't let anything happen to your son. Besides Acharya Kaundinya was always fond of Siddhartha. With him next to the prince, I am relieved."

The queen sat straight and wiped her tears, "Let's not tell Yasho about it." "Okay but give her the news that Siddhartha's whereabouts have been located. But he may not be coming back soon so she can re-evaluate her situation." "Alright, but she has already chosen her path of relief work for the needy and organising religious discourses called 'Satsang' with the ladies of seraglio. Mrigi with her son Anand as you know, has gone back to her father, Dandpani."

*****

Thus, a painful routine was set for the hundreds of widows of Siddhartha. Previously their entire day use to be spent in their beauty treatments and bedecking of themselves for the moment when Siddhartha might appear. But now since no one was there to appreciate their charms, beauty treatments, jewellery, makeup and good clothes, all luxuries became a thing of past.

Mrigi's son Ananda was born at Siddhartha's palace. But because his 'Ranivas' was closed down, his women lived under Shuddhodan's protection, as widows. They had no right to any property.

Jealous Mrigi could not stand living close to Yashodhara. So she had left for her father's household, to bring her son up within familiar surroundings. She was also having thoughts of a second marriage but wanted to wait.

Siddhartha's progeny was growing up at the women's quarters. But the children had no hereditary rights or confirmed future. He, in one stroke had left hundreds of women without any self-respect or major benefits. They had shelter and food and their basic needs were met. That's all! They became like empty shells strewn about on the beach without any life residing inside. Many of them, from good families chose to remarry and left with King's or Queen's permission.

King Shuddhodan and chief Suprabuddha were very worried to know that Siddhartha's health is badly affected by his severe practice to expiate his negative thoughts. So they had sent the five men; to take care of the Bodhisattva. One of them Acharya Kaundiya had left Kapilvastu, when Siddhartha was still under his tutelage, due to some palace intrigue by other priests.

The five Brahamans reached near the Niranjan River, after a long travel dressed as common villagers. They could see from a distance that Prince Gautama, was bathing in the river, although barely recognisable. They waited behind a clump of trees to assess his condition. When he was done, he couldn't climb up the bank due to weakness. With great effort he grabbed the overhanging branch of a tree and pulled himself up, and fell on the sand, breathless.

At that moment two village girls were passing by, towards the temple with a bowl full of rice-pudding offering for the Gods of the forest. The girl-servant Purna pointed out the fallen man. Nandbala quickly went to him and poured some milk on his dried up lips. Siddhartha licked it and with an effort sat up. "Sister, I had given up food till I achieve self-realisation."

Nandbala scolded him like a mother, "Don't be so ignorant. A healthy mind resides in a healthy body. Unless your body is strong how can you achieve anything, spiritual or otherwise?" and she fed him the entire bowl of 'kheer,' slowly. That uneducated village girl taught Gautama a lesson. From then onwards he did not starve himself. He chose the "middle path", instead of extremes.

As soon as Nandbala and Purna left, Gautama sat on a big rounded boulder to dry his long hair. He noticed five men in rustic attires approaching him. He looked at them and recognised Acharya Kaundinya. He had been with Siddhartha even at the hermitage of Uddraka Ramputra. Although he had looked different in a long beard and long hair, in a background of hermitage rather than a palace.

Gautama heaved himself up and touched his feet. Kaundinya said, "No need for that Bodhisattva, I have come here to serve you as your disciple. Please oblige me and my friends, Dasbal Kashyap, also known as Vappa; Bhadrika, Assaji and Mahanaam."

Gautama requested them humbly, "Please be seated next to me, after freshening up.

After washing their faces and dusty feet, they sat around the Bodhisattva. Kaundinya started, "Acharya Uddraka, Asita and Alar Kalam are no more. Before their passing away they had told me that they did not have any more knowledge to impart to me; and that I should seek you, because you might have attained self-realisation by now!"

"Not yet Acharya. But we can all stay here, at Dangshiri mountain and practice meditation sitting in different caves. One of us, each day would go to the village to beg from one house and share the food." Thus, one handful of rice each day, kept them lean and thin. At times Nandbala brought food for all of them to share.

It had already been three years since Gautama had left home. Yet his goal still was nowhere in sight. Undeterred, he continued staying under the same Peepal tree and meditated. During his sixth year, Kaundinya realised that Siddhartha was nearing his target so he told rest of the four followers to leave him alone for that special moment. After giving Gautama some excuse they moved to a village near Kashi and constructed a small hermitage, at the Deer Park.

*****

Gautama's one target now was to overcome all fears. He gradually overcame the dread of wild animals. Of tigers, pythons or snakes! Yet his concern for human suffering remained. He practiced holding his breath for long periods of time till his lungs felt ready to burst, and he would start sweating. This increased his threshold of pain. But he soon realised that one need not torture one's body in order to open up his mind. If body is relaxed so will the mind be. He saw the oneness of body and mind; that each and every cell of the body along with the brain contained all the wisdom of the universe. And when body and mind become one with the universe one starts living in his present moment. He hears the chirping of the birds, the blossoming sound of opening-up of buds into a flower or the breaking away of a butterfly from its pupa.

Gautama now realised that a person is not an individual. He is a part of a whole. There is nothing like the atman of the Vedas. 'Non-self or 'anatman' was nature of all things.' One day, while he was pondering over these serious ideas. He opened his eyes and saw a little boy standing in front of him with a handful of Kusha grass. Gautama asked him, "Who are you?"

"I am Swasti, an untouchable. I tend water-buffaloes for my master. I would like you to sit on a cushion of this grass if you may. This would make you more comfortable. My mother recently passed away and I have three younger siblings to take care of." The child introduced himself in one breath.

Siddhartha was touched by the eleven year old's statement. 'Forgetting about his own miseries he was thinking of a stranger's comfort.' This kind of selflessness, Bodhisattava wanted people to cultivate. When one is drowning in his own problems, thinking of other's, would make them forget their own and that is when compassion rises from one's heart and gives one contentment.

Siddhartha smiled at Swasti, as no one had ever smiled at him before. He then got up and touched his head, blessing him. He took the grass as if it was very precious and spread it on his spot under the tree.

"Thank you my child, you are very caring," said the dignified sage.

Swasti's face shone. His self-esteem increased his confidence in himself. Overwhelmed, he ran away, not knowing what else to do. He never felt so elated.

Soon after Nandbala and Purna arrived with some food. They bowed to the sitting yogi who opened his eyes. Nandbala spoke hesitantly, "Please excuse me for the last occasion when I fed you food without telling you that I am a low caste. My father Senayana is a cowherd, of ahir caste but the Village Head as well."

"You cannot be a low caste as you saved a life. From now onwards I'll call you 'Sujata' meaning, the high born. Come give me what you brought for me to eat."

*****

At Uruvilva village Mara, like the Satan never stopped torturing Bodhisattva's mind. He came in different forms to beguile his thoughts. Once he pretended to rape Yashodhara but when Siddhartha looked closely, his face transformed into Devdatta's. Gautama realised that although his attachments were fading away, yet his fears are still haunting him. He was concerned about his other wives too.

That night was a moonless night. Siddhartha went deep into the jungle to get away from his fears. He barely escaped stepping on a cobra. He imagined he saw a python wrapped around a deer's inert body. For a moment he felt that the deer was Yashodhara and the python Devdatta. To make sure he poked the twenty feet long reptile with a twig. Caught by surprise it loosened it's coils and wreathed away and the deer scampered off to safety. From a distance he heard a lion's roar and the birds twittering away in flight. His hair stood at their ends as he continued walking and came back to his cave before dawn. Feeling that something was amiss.

The same night at the ladies quarters, at Shuddhodan's palace. All was quiet. It was autumn. The dry fallen leaves were rolling on the ground, rustling away in the wind. A figure dressed in dark, was crunching the leaves with his boots. A woman guard on the rampart shouted, "Who goes there?" She tried to look in the faint light of the night lamps. Since the silhouette of a man had stopped against a thick tree trunk, she couldn't see anything. The intruder threw a pebble at a distance. The guards ran that side to check while the shadow crept over a sturdy creeper and jumped inside the balcony in front of Yashodhara's quarters. A light thud did not alarm anyone. Yashodhara's window had vertical iron bars but its flaps were unfastened. The man who was said to have the strength of an elephant, pulled out a few bars after bending them. And placed them on the floor softly. He skidded his lean body through the gap, head on and landed inside on his hands. Standing erect he looked around with his red intoxicated eyes and saw Renu and Rohini sleeping on one side on the floor. He pulled out a bunch of flowers from his sash and one by one, let the sleeping girls sniff it. Next he came to Yasodhara and did the same. She opened her woozy eyes for a moment and saw faintly Devdatta's face hovering over hers as if in a dream. Before she could scream, she lost her awareness.*

Next morning when the three women woke up, they noticed the broken window. Yet nothing of value was missing from the room. Their dizziness soon wore off. After her bath, the full impact of what had happened during the night, hit Yashodhara. She had found one of the gold earrings with a drop of emerald hanging from it, lying near her bed. Ganga exclaimed, "This belongs to Prince Devdatta!"

Yashodhara urgently sent Rohini to call Channa to her presence. Once he came, she pointed him to the damaged window and with a finger on her lips, conveyed not to let anyone know about it. The secret was kept and the window repaired.

*****

After one month, Yashodhara called Channa again. "Here is a letter Channa, for you to deliver only in the hands of my husband. Let Kaludayin accompany you on this secret mission."

Siddhartha had stopped going to the village to beg for food everyday since his five disciples went instead, turn by turn. Nandbala who use to call herself Sujata now, would always bring something to eat for her 'God-of-forest.' She even released Purna, from slavery but kept her in her house, as a part of the family.

Gautama was slowly gaining health as he took a reasonably small diet. One day as he was about to close his eyes sitting under the Peepal tree. He saw Swasti coming his way followed by two horse-riders, walking by his side. As they came nearer the Shakya Muni was happy to see his friends Kaludayin and Chandak. The buffalo-boy ran away after finishing his errand and the Bodhisattava embraced his friends. After catching up with each other, Kalu went to meet Gautama's five disciples, who were meditating in their individual caves. Siddhartha looked at Channa meaningfully, who extended a letter towards him, and stood up to leave him to his privacy. The prince read,

"Arya,

Without your protection I stayed safe and pure for more than five years. Then one night a storm blew and broke through my window, to destroy my chastity and pride. I am broken into bits accused of being unfaithful to my lord and master. Show me the way, please!*

Yours Yasho"

Siddhartha borrowed some ink and a feather to write on a palm-leaf 'parna' from Sujata's father and wrote a letter to King Suddhodan.

"Father,

Yashodhara is perfectly pure and innocent. She is carrying my child; your grandson. Please take care of her.

Siddhartha."

Siddhartha's friends took leave from him and his disciples, next morning. Chandak had kept the letter to the king, safe in the secret pocket.

Suddhodan, who was planning to punish Yashodhara severely once she had delivered the child, calmed down after receiving the letter from his son. Everyone was told about the paternity of Yashodhara's child. Suprabuddha and Amita too, were informed.

As Yashodhara's child grew, inside her, Siddhartha's vision cleared day by day. She waited her confinement and he his liberation. Dhrotodan and Mangala knew the misdeed of their son, the very night, he had disappeared for a couple of hours in the gloom of the dark, and lay down drunk in his bedroom, later. Chanting, "Yashodhara, Yasho, I love you."

They were shocked and full of dread. "What if the king finds out! If not beheaded he would rot in the prison for the rest of his life." They, both waited for the impending doom. But, Siddhartha's claim of the

* Mara-in Hinduism the god of death, sometimes seen as one aspect of a god whose other aspect is Kama, or the erotic desire.

child's paternity cooled their anxiety and their hunger for power returned. Suddhodan was no fool, he had misgivings.

*****

Dawn was breaking up on the horizon. Gautama had been fighting with Mara the wicked god of delusions and attachments, all night. His worst fears were crawling like worms inside his head. That, Devdatta had usurped the throne by force and imprisoned his father. He had also taken over his ranivasa and his queens were being raped. Mara urged Siddhartha to get up and go to Kapilvastu to safeguard his family. But Mara lost his battle of all kind of temptations, like beautiful women and imagined threats. A moment came when all anxieties oozed out of Siddhartha's being. It was exactly as Sage Ashtavakra had told king Janak. Where he says in "Ashtavakra Geeta," "O king as soon as you put your one foot in the stirrup of your horse and heave your body to swing your other foot, to reach the other stirrup and straddle the horse, enlightened stage of consciousness, can be achieved. It is only a moment. A ripe moment. Like a fruit bursting forth to disperse its seeds far and wide."

Siddhartha, at that moment, was glowing within and without with inexpressible joy and peace. He felt awakened from a deep slumber, all refreshed. There was a bright aura around his persona and a faint halo about his face.

"Of might magnificent explosion
Revealed to Him a throne of reality-
Wisdomed and illumed –
A movement of glorified Revelation."

At the same moment Yashodhara started having her pains. And a beautiful boy was delivered. She spent her spare time in her old habit of reading. These days she was going through 'Astavakra' Gita song. It was based on Sankyayog Darshan, philosophy as dialogues between sage Ashtavakra and King Janak of Mithila or Videh where it was suggested that the "Absolute is not subject to birth, change and death. It is unborn and eternal." Siddhartha focused on the absolute under a peepal tree, as Yashodhara read about it. Gautama was having his final battle with Mara, who was trying to distract him, when Yashodhara started having her pains. Many women got busy taking care of her and the baby. Mahaprajapati took charge of everything as a mother. Shuddhodan was not thrilled but once he saw the face of the child, he picked him up and blessed him for the benefit of his mother and others.

*****

Gautama went for a dip in the river, and washed his two garments while he donned the hemp rag his washerwoman Gava had respectfully given him, as a gift. His own clothes were all tattered and torn. When they dried up he sat down to mend them as Sujata, Purna and Swasti approached him under the tree. They marveled at the sacred fig tree because it had started dropping ripe figs in the month of Vaisakh whereas in the normal course the figs ripened one month later.

A fragrant wind had started blowing from the Niranjan river. Soon there was a slight drizzle, soaking the dry earth as if commemorating the awakening of the fourth Buddha.** The children were surprised to witness a shower before its due time. When they looked at Buddha as he sat there, eating the porridge, kheer they felt all their tensions leaving their bodies. They felt psyched up yet calm. When Buddha finished eating, Sujata asked, "It appears as if you have changed somehow. You are shining bright."

Before the Buddha could answer, Swasti questioned "Have you found what you were looking for?"

"Yes", Buddha answered with a divine smile.

"Would you share it with us?"

"Sure! You would be my first followers, I would be sharing my spiritual or psychological findings with! Come tomorrow with other children and we shall talk about mindfulness."

Buddha's five discipled who had not gone too far after leaving him had established their own hermitage under Acharya Kondinya. They had kept a tab on Gautama's progress. When they came to know about his enlightenment, the news was immediately dispatched to King Shuddhodan, his father. There was jubilation at Kapilvastu and Yashodhara's hopes of seeing Siddhartha were soon revived. She kept herself busy taking care of her child and waited for further news from her husband, though he was an ascetic now.

No news came for a long time. She would cry herself to sleep, on the floor clinging to Siddhartha's flute. Next to her baby in the crib, who was named Rahul because of configuration of stars at the time of his birth.

Gautama was found, as usual under the peepal tree mending his torn garments when the children from the village approached him. There were two new girls and a few boys along with Swasti's three siblings. Sujata offered the rice she had brought for the Buddha on a banana leaf, along with sesame salt. He made small balls of rice before dipping them in the salt. Bhima, Subhash and Rupak, all watched his graceful demeanour as he

** Siddhartha Gautam was the 4th Buddha of the later period.

ate, relishing his every bite. There were also green coconuts to be enjoyed with their cream and water within, along with palm sugar. In the end Sujata uncovered a basket of tangerines. All of them had one each. Buddha looked at the orange fruit admiringly and started peeling it.

"Thank you Sujata for all the food you and other children brought to share with me. Thank you all! Now lets eat this tangerine with complete mindfulness. We shall enjoy it's beautiful colour with our eyes; it's soft feel with our fingers and palms and it's aroma through our nose. After peeling, see how many sections it has! Take each juicy chunk and place it on your tongue and squeeze the pulp. The delicious sap fills your mouth. All your senses – of touch, smell, taste and feel are gratified and your mind is fully aware of what you have accomplished just now. During these moments your mind was perfectly attuned to the fruit. You were one with it and enjoyed the moment of eating it, to the utmost. There were no other thoughts distracting you. This is doing something with full awareness and living fully in the present moment. When fickle minded people have their thoughts flitting from present to past and future constantly they get to lose even their present. An aware person looking at a tangerine, can imagine its tree, leaves and flowers which bloom in spring and transform themselves into juicy wholesome fruits with seeds. The sun and rain nourished the tree, the winds and humans helped in the dispersal of the seeds for the new plant to grow. Thus we see we are a part of the lifecycle of things in this universe. When we experience that tangerine in real that means the person eating it is real too. Those, who do not live their life in mindfulness, for them nothing is real. Nothing is worthwhile not even they themselves. Such people are lost and unhappy. They can even become self-destructive. We should never forget the interconnectedness of all things and live each moment in awareness."

Buddha asked, "Swasti what do you think?"

"You are right teacher if I am distracted I make more mistakes. If I won't wash my water-buffaloes with attention, I might overlook a wound which may become worse by next day and cause more problem for me as well as the animal."

Little Bhima spoke in her childish lisp, "Yes teacher. Even I loose a game with my friends if my mind is elsewhere. When I focus my awareness on the game I always win."

"Good girl, Bhima. If you can understand this, so can everyone else! An aware person is in complete touch with life. He sometimes understands others more than they understand themselves. Understanding develops patience and compassion."

Swasti told everyone about a past experience. "Once Bhima started crying in the middle of the night. Older sister Bala got irritated and hit her. When I went to console her, I realised she was feverish, to my touch. Understanding her condition, Bala lovingly picked her up and took care of her till morning."

Sujata folded her hands and asked, "Can we call this, the path of mindfulness."

"Sure you can! The path of awareness towards yourself and your surroundings leads to spiritual awakening."

Subhash asked, "Can we call you the awakened one?"

"Of course you may!"

"In Sanskrit they call it Prabuddha", Bala informed, who was somewhat educated.

"We shall all follow this lesson even if you are not with us." Sujata said with tearful eyes.

"Buddham Sharnam Gacchami" recited Jatalekha, the girl with curly hair and brown eyes.

Buddha smiled, "I am very happy with you children. You are all intelligent and responsive."

"When are you leaving, to spread your teachings, from Uruvila mount?" asked Sujata.

"In a few days. Till then we can meet every day. And please Sujata arrange for me a razor so that I can remove my hair."

"Sure 'Buddha Dev'."

And he smiled.

Next day, Buddha shaved his tousled hair on the scalp and his scraggly beard. Sujata collected the discarded fluff considering them sacred. He had repaired his robe with many square patches here and there and wore it. When the children looked fascinated, he explained, "My robe now looks like square patches of fields, where your food is grown." Children smiled.

After a few days, once again, Buddha with shaved head and beard walked towards Giriviraj. To fulfill his promise to king Bimbisar. On the way he stopped at the hermitage of Acharya Kondinya.

*****

Since Rahul was born, Yashodhara's painful journey, in the absence of her husband became worse. Shuddhodan had compromised with the situation but gave little affection or sympathy to his daughter-in-law.

There was an uproar among the chiefs of smaller republics. Tapodana, of Pithoragarh requested a meeting of the assembly to thrash out the issue. They were afraid that the king might accept the bastard as his grandson and the heir to the throne, after Siddhartha. Tapodana and Dhrotodan were hoping that after the king, Devdatta would ascend the chief's throne.

On the appointed day of the assembly, the moot-hall was buzzing once again, with activity. That particular day the buzz was even louder. A royal lady's sanctity was in question.

The king in his bedroom was feeling out of sorts since last few days. Prajapati, formally dressed up entered the chamber. She came near his bed and touched his forehead.

"You don't seem to have cold or fever, why are you still in bed?"

"I don't know Praja I just feel listless."

"You can't afford to, my dear. Nand is waiting outside at your door, and the councillors, you know some of them… "

On her insistence, he got up to get ready. Nand, who had come back to Kapilvastu after finishing his studies, waited outside to escort his father to the moot hall.

Meanwhile, Suprabuddha, Dhrotodan and Tapodan, kept complaining that the meeting should start, they were getting late. The king may not be interested in coming out of shame. The minister Mahanaam requested them to be patient. But Tapodan continued, "Since Siddhartha has left, Shuddhodan is becoming less and less attentive towards his administrative responsibilities."

"That's not true!" contradicted Mahanaam, "I am always there by his side. His work is his balm for his wounded heart. He is never slack in his duties."

"Maybe then, age is catching up with him. If we have a younger chief…."

Someone asked, "Do you have someone in mind?"

Tapodan replied, "My sister's son Devdatta is a good candidate!"

There was a lull in the meeting. Only Mahanaam and Devdatta kept standing. One annoyed and the other pleased. Just then the crier announced, "The honourable Chief of the Shakyas is about to arrive." Everyone stood up. Some happily others upset. As soon as the king sat on the throne he motioned everyone to be seated. "I am sorry for the delay. What was going on Mahanaam?"

Mahanaam hesitantly replied, "The members are suggesting, maybe you need to retire now and put the heavy load of administration on some young shoulders."

"Like who?"

"Maybe prince Devdatta or Nand!"

"I am not dead yet. These children haven't been exposed to the kingly duties so far. Let them gain some more experience, then we can decide on this issue. For the time being we shall discuss the question of my grandson Rahul's paternity."

Everyone nodded and shifted somewhat in their chairs, for the mysterious drama to unfold. Shuddhodan spoke again.

"I personally believe in queen Yashodhara's chastity. If any of you thinks otherwise, go ahead and explain, why?"

Chatuma chief said, indignantly.

"Your so called grandson, Rahul was born six years after Siddhartha left. How would you explain that?"

"I would. But first you tell me, what do you think?"

"I think, she has gone astray and should be severely punished for that! So that other ladies should not behave thus, in the absence of their husbands. We all know that they have a choice to remarry, open to them, after being abandoned."

"Yashodhara is not only pure, she is also well educated and knows her rights fully well. She has been emulating her husband's austere lifestyle right in her room under my Queen's watchful eye. She dresses like a nun and eats only a handful of rice everyday, like her husband. Many offers of young nobles have come her way, but she rejected them all."

"So you're telling us that her pregnancy lasted six years, coinciding the child's birth with Siddhartha's enlightenment?"questioned the prince of Khomadussa, scornfully.

"I am not suggesting anything. I have a proof of her innocence."

"Before that let Yashodhara come in the assembly with the child and take an oath that Bodhisattva is the father of that child." Demanded the chief of Ulumpa.

Now Mahaprajapati came out to speak, "The honourable members of the sabha, association have always held me in high regards. You were the very elders who had chosen me for the role of a loving mother for Maya's son."

The queen addressed the members again after a pause, "I am going to release a secret about the 'Ranivas', where Yashodhara has her accommodations, in front of all of you."

Suddhodan stopped her.

"No need for that Praja, let me give them the proof."

The king handed a letter, written on dried palm leaves, by his son Siddhartha, during the rainy month of sawan, when many months before his enlightenment, Mara was still tormenting him and he was greatly disturbed.

Shuddhodan handed over the letter to Mahanaam, to read aloud. On hearing the confession of Siddhartha that he is Rahul's father, everyone became quiet and Suprabuddha heaved a sigh of relief.

Tapodan's dream of seeing Yashodhara being whipped and executed went down the drain. The letter was being passed around for all to read. Yashodhara entered the conference room dressed as a nun, with shaved head, from the side gallery of the king's throne, infant Rahul in her arms. She placed the child at the feet of the chief and declared in a weak voice, "Anyone who thinks my child is a bastard, should spill his blood right away."

Suprabuddha shouted concerned, "You can't do that my child!"

Drotodan, looked at everyone worried. When no one came forward he picked up the child carefully and gave it to Yashodhara.

"Thank you gentlemen and ladies for not making me walk like queen Sita, through the fire for Agni-pariksha, to prove my innocence. Why is it that only women are demanded to prove their chastity and not men?" saying that she turned away towards the ladies quarters from the back door.

The king looked at everyone and announced, "Now there is one thing more I need to say to all of you. If any of you have objection please raise your hand. Should anything suddenly happen to me, Yashodhara will rule the kingdom after me."

No hands were raised in denial. The king clapped and some serving girls appeared with drinks and snacks on trays. Boards of chess, or chauppad were laid up in the adjoining room.

Yashodhara, trembling left the court followed by Bhanumati, who held the baby now. They reached her royal chamber together. She ordered, "Please leave me alone for some time."

Her maid gently placed Rahul in his cot and left the chamber. Yashodhara sat by his side, trying to gather some strength from the little fellow. The child seemed disturbed, not understanding the recent happenings. His mother lured him back to sleep by singing softly.

"Let storm winds eddy, and scream, and hurl…

Sleep sound on my breast fair and ample,
Dull brain, dim eyes, and deaf ears,
Feel not the cold touch on your temple…
Let thyself sleep in the night- watch."
'I shall keep awake to guard over you.'

Gordon's Poems.

*****

Chapter - 12

Amrapali

'NIGHT BLACK AND CHILL, WIND GATHERING STILL,
WITH ITS WAIL IN THE (VILLAGE SMALL)...
AND ITS HEADLONG BLAST LIKE CATAPULT CAST,
ON THE CREST OF THE OUTER WALL,
AND ITS HAIL AND RAIN ON THE CRASHING PANE
TILL THE GLOSSY SPLINTERS FALL'[1]
MY PRIDE AND INNOCENCE; MY FAMILY AND LOVE,
I LOSE IT ALL! I LOSE IT ALL!

In the north east of Himalayan Gangetic region the most ancient republic of Jambudwipa+ was the archaic metropolis, Vrijji. It was one of the Janpada** confederacies, a union of eight Kshatriya kings presided over by one chief. The Chief was chosen after their voting and called Maharaj. The capital of the Licchchavi clan was at a city called Vaishali, named after King Vishal during the period of Mahabharat. In Vishnupuran a Hindu scripture, records of thirty four kings of Vaishali exist. The last was King Sumati who was contemporary of King Dashrath of Ayodhya. At a little distance from the capital, there was a small hamlet, named Ambra, because of abundance of mango orchards. It was situated near the tributary of Ganga River called the Hiranyavan River.

It was a summer month. No rains in sight yet. The mountains surrounding, however were cool to the eye. In a hut at a farm, sat the farmer Raman waiting for his breakfast. His wife Mamta placed two sweet balls or laddoos made from sautéed wheat flour, sugar and ghee and a tumbler full of cow's milk, kept warm by his side. She was about to place two bananas as well on a banana-leaf when her husband motioned her to remove it with the impatient gesture of his hand.

---

1. Anonymous Sinhalese Poem – Trans – Paul Caurus.

"Please dear, I always tell you that kadali I can eat anytime while working."

"Okay! Okay. You can, since they have started ripening."

"Yes and mangoes have been ripe since quite some time. If you have some raw ones please make 'Aam-chutney' today with rice."

"Sure!" and she started fanning the flies away with a palm-leaf fan.

Finishing his food, his wife helped him wash his hands from a bucket full of water. He wiped his hands on his cotton stole, hand-woven with white and red threads and threw it back on his shoulder, before going out to work on his modest-sized farm, in a 'dhoti' and hand stitched vest.

"Please get some ripe mangoes for me", he heard his wife's request from a distance.

Mamta, her cotton sari tucked high soon came out; carrying a metal pail and went towards the cow-shed to milk her cow. The aroma of ripe mangoes hit her nostrils. She let the calf loose, who ran to its mother for a feed. After he had enough Mamta tied him again to a stump. She sat folding her legs and digging her toes in the soft ground with a bucket stuck between her legs and squeezed the cow's udder one by one with her thumb and fingers. The strong spray of milk hit the metal-bottom of the bucket, 'Ting, Zing! Ting, Zing!' It went on. Before she could finish her job she heard the faint sound of a baby crying. Her obsession to have a child was so strong, that she thought, 'It's all in my head.'

Finishing her chore she got up and was about to leave when the cries became louder. She left the bucket in the hut and mesmerized walked towards the infant- sound. Under a mango tree she found a wriggling bundle of white muslin. She quickly went forward and exposed the pink face of a newly born girl. Gently picking her up she placed her next to her bosom. The baby on an instinct, started moving her mouth to find a source of milk. Mamta went inside and taking some cotton wool started squeezing cow's milk, drop by drop in the pink pout. Once satiated, the infant dropped off to sleep.

Mamta wiped her rosy lips with the edge of her sari. Her heart felt wobbly. Leaving the child, safely in bed she went out excitedly looking for her husband who was watering, the banana patch.

"Ramana! Ramana! Swami, come quickly. I need to show you something!" Mamta couldn't conceal her exhilaration. Her eyes were shiny and smile broad.

"Mamta, I need your help, rather than your exuberance, right now."

"I know! I know!" and she took the huge bunch of green bananas he was holding, from him, put it aside and almost dragged him to their one room residence. He came inside and heard a low whimpering still wondering, as to what is the surprise?

"A kitten! A puppy! Or …" he couldn't think beyond that. Mamta tenderly picked the bundle up and turned the tiny miracle towards him. Raman's heart fluttered with joy. "Where did you find it?"

"Under the mango tree near our gate."

He warned Mamta, "We'll have to take the child to the village administrative 'Panchayat' tomorrow, and see what they have to say. I won't tolerate an accusation from someone for stealing their newly born!"

"You are right, let's go to the 'Mukhia', the Village-Head today, but only after I feed her some more milk with the help of a wad of cotton wool." She said possessively.

After listening to their story and taking a payment from them, the village-chief let a drummer announce in the entire village about the episode and that a meeting would be held at four p.m. at the village 'chaupal', the informal center for meetings.

The five 'Panchas' or judges sat under the hundred years old shady banyan tree, on a round stone-platform encircling the thick tree trunk. Villagers sat facing them in a semicircle, squatting or sitting cross legged. Raman and Mamta stood in the centre facing the judges.

"Are you the mother of this baby?"

"No Sir, I found her under a mango tree at our small farm."

Then he looked at the crowd, "Does this child belong to any of you?" Nobody got up to claim her.

"In that case we could send it to the orphanage in the city of Vaishali."

Mamta looked at everyone, her eyes pleading, "Please brothers and sisters let this child stay with us. I am childless. I'll bring her up lovingly under the eyes of the Panchas." Her husband too shook his head, in affirmation with folded hands.

The judges discussed the matter among themselves and proclaimed, "Villagers, we shall wait for forty-five days. If no one comes to claim the girl, she would be known as Ramana's daughter."

A chorus rose from the villagers, "We all agree."

Raman soon had to hire a man to help him with his orchard, since his wife was happily busy with the newly-born. The crop of mangoes was good that year which fetched him more cash. He thought, 'My girl is lucky.'

The help, named Gynaeshwar was a decent man, who chiseled stones to make troughs for animals, to drink water from. He had had a son recently, Pushpkumar, so he eagerly accepted the part time work to earn some more.

Slowly and gradually as the two children were growing up the boy started accompanying his father to Raman's farm. The children played together as their fathers worked and became close friends. They had passed more than a decade seeing each other every single day. They shared laughter and tears; childish fights and making up to become friends again.

Amba was fond of dancing and singing so her father put her under the guidance of Mahanaman, dance tutor, after school. Pushp, her friend started learning to make statues of gods and goddesses of burnished clay. At a young age, he earned well and helped his father financially. He soon graduated to sculpting stone statues.

By the time Amba or Amrapali, the 'mango-girl' and Pushp Kumar were nearing the age of sixteen, they were deeply in love. Their parents decided to marry the lovers together. But before that, destiny played her finicky game. A crier from the city came with his drums and announced that a dance competition was going to be held during the 'nine holy days', of Navratras at the court of the king.

Amba was adamant to participate. So Pushp was given the responsibility of escorting her and other dancers, along with their teacher Kulpati Mahanaman. He had been a feudal lord from a nearby village who too had gotten besotted by Amrapali's beauty when she was only eleven years old. He was a great classical dancer. He left his territory and moved to Ambra village and became her dance teacher.

On the appointed day, his girl students and the Guruji reached the court of king Manudev of Vaishali on a bullock-cart and waited along with other participants from the city who were much more richly dressed than the girls from Ambra and other villages. However, Amba was the most ravishing beauty amongst them.

Kulpati Mahanaman was given a seat along with the judges and Pushpkumar was allowed to come inside as their escort. Beautiful classical dances were performed by young talents while the courtiers watched fascinated. All through the quarter and semi-finals people's eyes were glued to Amrapali. No one could beat her expertise and grace, except for Kadambini of the Vaishali city. The final competition was full of energy between the two. As Mahanaman beat his mridang- drum, with both hands faster and faster; Amba's feet went flying in the air and anklets saying 'tir-kut-dhoom, tir-kut-dhoom, ta, tha.'

Kadambini too, matched the rhythm of her teacher's drum beats. The ambience became taut with the jingling of Amba's anklet bells and jangling of Kadambini's. The crescendo was getting higher and higher when Kadambini gave up, sitting down exhausted. Amba kept on reveling with vigour and charm, around the entire floor in circles. Then she stopped in front of her mentor and touched his feet, breathless. Going to the king, she bent slightly with folded hands.

The applause was deafening. The judges were consulting the king, who was so enamoured of Amrapali that he wanted to keep her for himself. She was announced as court dancer of Vaishali and bestowed upon her, was the coveted title of 'Young Miss Sovereign citizen' or 'Vaishali Janpad Kalyani' for seven years, as the most beautiful and talented girl of the confederacy.

Amrapali was sprinkled with the water from Abhishake Pushkarni, the coronation tank. The Ganga water stored in it was considered sacred and sprinkled on every new monarch of Licchavi clan before his coronation.

The prime minister then asked the winner, "Amrapali, everyone is impressed by your beauty, grace and talent. If you love your country then come and stay at the King's palace and become a dance teacher to the girls of the king's pleasure house. You would become rich and famous and move amongst the elite gentry."

Amrapali grasped the situation and replied demurely, "Sir it is an honour to be selected for such a high position but I need to go back home for the last time to meet my family and explain everything to them personally."

"Do that and be back by tomorrow or at the most day after tomorrow evening," the Maharaja ordered.

Amrapali and party left for their village late at night. Jostling in their bullock-cart under the stars, afraid of interlopers. Her friends were happy for her achievement and all the perks that would go with it.

Her best friend, Malu looked at her concerned, "Why aren't you happy? What is there to be sad about? And why are you sulking, Pushp?"

Just then a jackal howled at a distance. All became stiff and quiet. Only the lanterns at the back and front were dangling. Kulpati Mahanaman spoke at length, "They have bought her body and soul; snatched away her life. She shall almost be a puppet in their hands. I am glad that, I probably would always be allowed to stay with her as her 'Guru.'" Pushp Kumar was pale and silent as a dead man.

On reaching the village Kulpati Mahanaman dropped Pushp Kumar and Amrapali, near her gate and continued with the other students down the street. They walked and heard foot-steps following them. But couldn't see anyone due to the dull moon. The nocturnal sounds became frightening. They were happy to see Shera, the street dog, guarding their gate. Both of them went inside, locking the rickety gate behind them.

They woke her parents up and told them the bad news disguised as good. Pushp Kumar said, "She'll be rich and famous if she goes to the city. I do not want to impede her progress."

"Don't be naïve Pushp. You know what they'll do to me. I could see lust in the king's eyes. He wants me as an asset to his throne. I do not want to share his plan. I don't want fortunes and power, I only want your love, and be a mother to your children. Let's run away tonight before the King could destroy us for his greed and use me as an utility item."

The parents were thoughtful and sad. Raman spoke, "It is impossible to go against the king, Amba. He'll get us all killed. Or throw us in a dungeon and abduct you anyway." He then turned to Pushp, "You go home and discuss with your parents. If they agree we can perform the wedding ceremony secretly tomorrow night. And assist you both to elope towards south after the marriage. Though that would jeopardise their own and other children's lives."

Pushp left with a heavy mind, hardly noticing Shera wagging his tail.

Next night was ominous. Ignoring the omens Mamta coloured Amba's hands with henna. Her heart was struggling with ill-boding shadows. Her hand quivered and she ruined the design.

The couple was planning to run away the same night towards south taking a boat on the Hiranyavan river.

Pushp Kumar was walking fast towards the priest's house, to escort him to Raman's farm for the marriage ceremony. To save time he took a short cut through the harvested fields, with heaps of debris at intervals. It was late evening. The weary sun was setting, spreading its last rays on the burnt stumps of the uncleared land. There were hardly any trees around. When Pushp found a babool tree, he stood against it catching his breath. Two sturdy arms came from behind the thick tree-trunk and held his neck, dragging him down while his accomplice, another thug came in front and pulled his feet, to make his slim body fall flat on the ground. The first villain came forward and straddled his torso and started squeezing his throat with his powerful hands. Within five minutes the victim's face and lips turned blue and his eyeballs bulged out. His violently thrashing body became still as his feet were firmly pinned down.

The would-be-groom while loosing his consciousness amidst indescribably dreadful pain, envisions Amba's beautiful sad face in front of his unseeing open eyes, as he lay still, legs apart. High above, birds were flying home but the dead man had no home to go to.

*****

Amrapali and Malu, her friend who was darker in complexion, were cooking dinner while the grownups were preparing the fire pit and collecting wood, waiting for Pushp to return with the priest. Suddenly Sheru, outside the gate, barked ferociously. Mamta said, "How could Pushp come back so soon!"

"It is someone else!" As Raman and Gyaneshvar, were getting up to check, four guards from the palace, trundled along aggressively and dragged Amba and Malu from their cooking and tied their arms behind their backs. The men tried to pull them away, but were no match for the trained soldiers. Amrapali screamed like thundering clouds while her eyes became flame red. "How dare you touch me!" The guards stepped back.

"Lady, you do not know that you have been announced, by the king, the 'Nagar Vadhu', the bride of the city. You would be free to choose your paramours but you shall never belong to any one man from now on. You can never marry." And they looked at the sacred fire pit and the other marriage preparations. One soldier poured water on it in derision.

"You'll have to wait till my would-be groom returns from wherever he has gone. I would need to explain the situation to him."

"I am sorry," spoke the superior. "You do not need to do any such thing. King's order! We must leave right away. Your unlucky groom can follow later, if he must."

The women were all wailing. Mamta screamed, "What kind of degraded king do we have, who forces young innocent girls into prostitution! He is a curse on the noble Licchavi clan. I cuss him with all my heart. He shall roll in dust and die a pitiful death. He would be degraded and humiliated before he perishes." And she howled, loud beating her chest with both hands.

"I don't know all that madam. I am only suppose to follow the orders. Quick girls, the palanquin is waiting outside."

Mamta told Malu still weeping, "Please go with your friend now. Pushp would come tomorrow and fetch you both, if possible!" and she sobbed violently, all over again, shaking like a dried up leaf. As the soldiers were forcing the handcuffed girls Malu shouted back, "Please let my parents know."

The whole tragical drama was over in no time. Turning the tide of destiny against the beauty of her times, Amrapali.

*****

The two thugs in the lonely field were looking at the young body of a sixteen year old, lying on the burnt bristly stubs of the crop, with his bruised back and stiff limbs sprawled out. They tied his feet and hands and wrapped him in a white shroud, fastened with a rope. Pulling the light corpse with one end, one by one, they finally reached the sandy bank of the river, where it was dumped like a log. Finding a heavy stone, they tied it carefully to his cold feet and dragged him further towards the middle of the rivulet as far as their necks were above the water. Letting it go down with the heavy weight slowly into oblivion. Satisfied with their project the assassins turned back to the village where they had left their horses.

The village was silent as death. The temple gong had long stopped echoing. The cattle were already home and safe in their enclosures. People were preparing for bed after early dinner, snuffing out the lights.

Raman, Mamta and Pushp's parents waited for him, their eyes glued to the gate, throughout the devil's night out. No one came except Malu's father to take her back home but left empty handed grieving like the other two families.

By the time the two girls, reached the city gate, dawn was breaking up behind the walled city. Their cheeks were salty with dried up tears. They didn't remember being ushered in a room and thrown on the bed.

Next night was the darkest night of their lives. Along with their bodies, their souls too were torn to shreds. Pushp Kumar never turned up. Off and on during the day they cried. By evening, they were decked up and taken to the pleasure house where Amba was forced to dance and Malu to sing. They were put under the training of the most experienced lady in the art of love. She gave the distraught girls some motherly affection. At the same time, taught Amrapali alone, the sixty four, tricks of the trade of lust. So that she could talk to her clients on any topic of the world and other things.

Amba was also learning the art of spying to help the kingdom by getting important information as the undercover spy. Her cover, still was that of a courtesan. Her charms became too hard to resist, by any man. The only satisfaction, she had from her new life was that she was able to serve her country, one way or the other. Secondly, she could send money to her own, Pushp Kumar's and Malu's family. She had already heard whispers about her beloved's murder. A fire for revenge burnt in her heart, day and night. Her mother's curse for chief Manu resounded in her ears.

*****

Amrapali soon was given a palace of her own which was constructed outside the city for peace and privacy. At a small distance she could See the Holy Ganga flowing in all its glory. It was a ritual for her to go and bathe there every morning to absolve her sins. On those occasions Malu and Mahanaman would accompany her. Next to her home was a mango grove, Ambavan, presented to her by the king. Her price for one night had gone up to fifity Karshapanas. She became richer than some kings. And paid heavy taxes to the kingdom's treasury, increasing Vaishali's wealth.

One evening, before one of her regular admirers came, she was talking to her friend. "Malu deep down in my heart, I loath myself. My beauty killed my lover. My elderly parents need my care, but I am not allowed to go to my village because plague has engulfed a cluster of villages. The city has self-isolated itself but what about the infected rats? They do not need to enter Vaishali, through the guarded gates. The drains are good enough for them!"

"That is true. I heard, I hope, it is a rumour. That the plague cases are increasing in the city too. It is a natural calamity for which we have no remedy yet!"

"I wish the king to suffer from plague and die!" Amba cursed.

Malu got up and brought her veena in the chamber and tightened its strings while Amrapali started talking to her parrot in the golden cage. She was saying lovey-dovey; sweet nothings, for the benefit of her expected guest, in case he eavesdrops. Just then the great monarch entered, and Amrapali embraced him passionately and then offered him to sit next to her in a love-seat. Malu, touched the Veena strings ever so slightly. The resonance was soft yet touching the heart.

King Bimbisar asked, "How have you been Amba?"

"Not so good in your absence O'most powerful one!"

Amba got up and brought two silver cups of the best imported wine, from Athens.

Bimbisar took one sip and looked at her with passionate eyes.

"I need you to be there for me, whenever I want."

"Am I not?" Amba fluttered her eyelids and signaled Malu to leave. "Yet what's so special about you?" she said teasing him.

"Since I met you, at prince Siddhartha's wedding so long ago I've been crazy about you. For me you are worth your weight in gold." He paused and took another sip. "I shall always keep you in style! You should have more jewels, servants and carriages. Silken and brocaded clothes from Kashi. Exotic perfumes and beautiful chandeliers and velvet curtains."

"You've already given me all that. But what about your three wives, one from Vaishali itself. Don't you love them?"

"They were liaisons, which helped me in the expansion of my empire. You are the love of my life." He winked and added, "As well as lust."

Amrapali filled up the cups again and sat down.

"How is our son?" she asked.

"A good physician and surgeon working at my court, so that I can see him everyday."

"I am so glad to know that he is under his father's protection."

"Somehow Ajatshattru is envious of him as well as of his other half-brothers."

"Why?"

"His greed for power, I guess! He doesn't even like my joining the Buddha's following! He thinks that I am too influenced by him and throw away money, for his Sangha's benefits."

"Has Jeevak met the Buddha again?"

"I don't think so! You took him once to see the sage when he was twelve while you were staying at your palace, outside the city of Giriviraj."

"I remember. Also that the palace was a gift from you."

"Don't even mention it. We have only two days, so let's not waste any time. I can never have enough of you."

"Is beautiful queen Chellana going back with you?"

"Yes! She is exceptionally beautiful I agree, but doesn't love go beyond that? If you look from a man eyes no one can beat you in charm, intelligence and…"

He stood up with his cup of wine and moved towards the luxurious bedroom followed by his paramour.

After King Bimbisar left with his wife Chellana for Magadh, Amrapali resumed her social work along with Malu and a few servants. She spent good amount of money on charities. She had founded schools, hospitals, temples and other institutions as well as spent money on the construction of roads. Specially the one going to Amra village. Due to her fame, Vaishali city too became famous. She had setup a welfare organisation for the soldiers of her country. During a war she would nurse them and encourage other young men to join the army. She was also famous for her patriotism.

Amrapali now wanted to do something for the plague victims. She would educate people about the disease. About how quarantine and social-distancing could help. And provide them with Ayurvedic medicinal herbs.

People were dying like flies and their close ones were fleeing their homes, leaving them behind. It was heart wrenching to imagine, villages full of rotting dead bodies. The king had ordered her to stay in her palace since she was a valuable commodity.

One day, Amba heard that Tathagat was visiting Vaishali. She was worried for him. But the day Buddha entered the city it rained and rained, and the contamination of the kingdom was washed off completely. Everyone noticed the miracle. Amrapali herself went to visit Buddha and invited him to stay in the mango grove, near her house along with his hundreds of followers. She also provided them with meals. Before she came to talk to Buddha the new disciples were told to close their eyes in her presence otherwise they might get influenced by her powerful charm.

Shariputtra asked, "My Master didn't Amrapali's beauty ever move you?"

"Bhikshus the true nature of all 'dharmas' transcends beauty and ugliness… if one is obsessed with a woman's beauty he can lose his way.

One day Buddha was sitting under a tree in Amrapali's mango orchard when a group of monkeys came and surrounded him. Watching him encircled by the unpredictable animals, his senior disciples came running to save him. On reaching the spot, they saw the monkeys were feeding Buddha honey, with their cupped hands. This miracle too was long remembered by the people of Vaishali.

King Manudev who was a Jain follower invited Buddha to a sumptuous meal at his palace, followed by a sermon. After which a forest outside the city was gifted to him for the Sangha.

Kulpati Mahanaman, the dance teacher was still with Amrapali. Although he had always kept his feelings to himself. He still hoped to win her someday with his silent love. He never left her side and was a constant solace to her. He and Malu were her family.

*****

Chapter - 13

Yashodhara's Dharma and Sangha

'You are no false ideal
Something is left of you.
Present perceptible, real palpable
Tangible true.
On shred of your broken necklace
One tress of your (raven) hair[1]
And the heart so reckless,
That the worst it would gladly dare.'

'Man is a gregarious animal, yet in order to achieve enlightenment or the state of self-awareness, he needs to sit alone and meditate under the guidance of some teacher.' Or so the Acharyas believed.

According to Yashodhara's observation, after Siddhartha left her for no fault of hers, she learnt to find solace and healing, first from Parajapati then other ladies of the seraglio. She realised, 'We are not many. We are all one. Sharing the same pain and problems. When we sit in a circle exchanging our experiences and thoughts about building a new life for ourselves we feel reborn with a different purpose in life. Once our children grow up and get settled, our role would change again. What then?' the question haunted her. She felt a transformation in her. She no longer resented the emotionally fragile Gopa. Instead she started treating her like her younger sister. With her support Gopa too felt stronger and self-reliant.

Buddha's teachings were reaching the palace through messengers and spies. But Yashodhara did not accept them right away. She used her own spiritual insight to analyse them first. One day she was telling everyone about Buddha's four noble truths and eight-fold path – right view, right speech, right action, right meditation and so on. But she questioned everyone, "Why not right relationship? Unless we live with others in

1. A. L. Gordon – p. 115 – 'Gordon Poems.'

harmony we cannot learn that we are all drops of the same ocean. This understanding would give rise to compassion and we can move together by dialogue to reach the state of wisdom and shed our ignorance like an old torn garment." She stopped to see whether she was making any sense to others.

Queen Gautami's understood the originality in her ideas. She encouraged her, "Yashodhara please continue."

"Now if we forget about the torn and old ignorant habits we can come to a new point in our thinking process. We have thoughts! We all have innumerable thoughts throughout the day. A deed is the result of an idea. That is why our religion says that a wrong thought is as bad as a wrong action. Cleanse your mind of all the accumulated erroneous ideas so that you can instead, practice the four noble truths which over time lead you to the right behaviour. A conduct which would not contradict your moral values. A Buddha is an ordinary person, minus the delusions. He can perceive the true nature of things which are happening at the present moment or could happen in the future due to our wrong or right actions. In simple words first practice morality, then meditate to gain wisdom; which would lead to enlightenment. Isn't that simple enough equation!"

The afternoon meeting of the palace women was about to end when some maids brought out in the garden, trays full of snacks and a hot drink made from spices along with cane juice and drinks of fermented barley.

The soft wind was slowly gathering momentum. Queen Gautami applauded Yasho for her wise understanding of Buddha's precepts. While everyone clapped and started enjoying the hot beverage and light snacks. A question- answer session followed.

Yashodhara was trying to get over the humiliation at the confederation meeting. She was practicing to rise above the accusations of infidelity because she believed in her own innocence. Yet she still harboured grudge against the powerful members of the council demeaning her for their own gratification.

Apart from taking care of her child, she practiced Buddha's preachings as they reached the palace, and did social work.

As Buddha gave talks in different cities she practiced at home, with other women of the seraglio or the servants. They would all sit in a circle in the palace garden, along with Mahaprajapati when she was free and discussed Buddhist concepts or their own thoughts. This use to be one occasion where all were treated equal, whatever their designation. She was asked to, but she never sat on a higher stool, as Buddha did. Even Mangala aunt was also beginning to mellow down. No one knew, but she had stopped encouraging her son, Devdatta with his evil designs, who was becoming more rowdy and indisciplined each day. Once when contradicted by his father, he pushed him aside rudely, before he stormed out of their sitting room. That was the last straw, for his ambitious parents. They had started fearing their own son, who still believed that Siddhartha was the root cause of all his troubles. He wanted to destroy everything he cherished. He hated to hear that his cousin has gathered a large following of disciples even in the forest.

*****

After leaving the beautiful surroundings of Niranjan River, the Buddha walked with a begging bowl in his hand to find his five disciples who had abandoned him, and settled in a hermitage at Isipatana. They were happily surprised to see, the great change that had come over Gautama. They bowed to him and made him relax under a tree with a bowl full of clean drinking water and some rice. After which he washed his hands and feet and described to them his experience of enlightenment and his newly understood philosophy, in simple terms.

"Friends according to me there are four noble truths we need to accept and challenge. First, that suffering in life exists. Second, ignorance is the cause of this suffering. Third, by applying 'mindfulness' in our lives, we can know the ultimate truth about ourselves. Fourth, when we have full self-awareness, sufferings are eradicated, or rather understood and dealt with. For instance some people imagine that the only way to please God is by rolling in the dust, self-mortifications, sacrifices and torturing of flesh…the irrational dependency on the distorted Hindu rituals and rites emphasised by greedy Brahmans, have made me deny the authority of Vedas… and the theory of divine creation."

"I believe that a practitioner should live a simple life, following the 'middle path'. Neither too austere, nor too indulgent. Hindus have been trapped and confused for centuries by religious dogmas. Due to their faith, they can hardly comprehend the true identity of things anymore. Even the educated ones have become puppets in the hands of 'pundits.' Spending money to save their souls from sins they might have committed. People should get out of these set ideas. Experience for themselves and formulate their own beliefs. Go through a human revolution. Exchange greed, anger, ignorance or revenge for love, compassion, patience, calm and forgiveness."

As the Buddha continued his discourse he noticed Kaundinya's countenance brightening up. He looked at his beaming smile and addressed him, "Kaundinya please tell everyone, what you went through just now."

"Yes master! I suddenly felt a flash of lightening go through my mind. A radiant energy surged through my body which made it feel light as a feather. Your each word started making more sense!" Kaundinya's enthusiasm kept flowing like a stream down the mountain. "My heart felt like a Kumudini lotus opening up with the morning rays of the sun. The clarity in my mind increased manifold."

When he stopped Buddha added, "If one practices each day with mindfulness, within three months he could experience spiritual awakening and become 'Arahant' or a 'Buddha'. His listeners became captivated by Buddha's words and fell at his feet.

*****

Buddha was teaching his followers at the Deer Park named Mrigadavana at Isipatana. One day as usual, he was having his morning walk when he saw a young man in stylish clothes, sitting by himself on a frost-ridden rock and crying loudly. He was so engrossed in his grief that he didn't even notice Buddha nearing him.

"What ails you my friend?"

With a jolt the young man stood up.

"Who are you?"

"People call me 'Tathagat.' Why are you in this wilderness, so early?"

"I am Yash. My father is a rich merchant in Vaishali. We are here on a business trip. I have everything yet I am miserable. I have no aim in life. It is meaningless. I want to kill myself."

"Don't even think about it." Buddha said exhaling warm air mixing with the mist. He continued, "Life is so beautiful. Can't you see the lush greenery around or twittering of the morning birds? When they are living life to the fullest, why can't you?"

"I don't know. Nothing seems to give me happiness anymore."

"Because of your wrong approach to life. Waiting for a desire to be fulfilled is more pleasure than its fulfillment. In the end you feel its futility, and do not receive the joy you were expecting. Because happiness is a state of mind. It cannot be found in materialistic things."

Buddha then sat on a stone while Yasha sat on another, opposite to him. He was told by the enlightened one, "Close your eyes and take a few deep breaths.Now open your eyes and look around."

The sun was gliding up the crown of a dense green tree as an orangish hew coloured the sky. Birds were chirping as a deer darted at a distance. Rays of rising sun were filtering through the glistening leaves, to cut through the mist in diverging slants. Yash's face was losing its tense expression. He felt a cloud of gloom lift up from his heart and he prostrated, at the enlightened one's feet and requested, "Please make me your disciple, Tathagat."

"Think twice. Because you won't be getting any of the luxuries you are use to. You would need to beg your food and eat only one meal a day. You would have to construct your own hut wherever we go; meditate in seclusion, and be in touch with other followers to learn the 'way'."

Yash folded his hands and spoke eagerly, "I am ready for all your conditions. The charisma of your personality is so captivating and…and divine."

Just then Buddha's five devotees appeared looking for him. Buddha introduced Yash to all of them and asked Kaundinya, "Please take charge of the new Bhikshu. Teach him how to dress, eat, beg and sleep. Tomorrow he can learn to watch his breath and start meditating."

Soon his hair were removed with a razor. He was given three brownish garments and a wooden bowl.

By afternoon, Yash's father came searching for him. Finding him with the monks he looked at his altered appearance with astonishment. He noticed the gleam of satisfaction in his eyes, which he had never seen before; like a person, who's shackles had just been removed. The father was relieved to see his child safe and sound. Yash touched his feet and explained, "I am sorry father, I couldn't take your permission before becoming a recluse. I was meaning to commit suicide when the enlightened one found me. He saved my life as well as my soul."

Yash's father turned to the Buddha and touched his feet.

"I'll be forever indebted to you O' sage. Please accept an invitation to the house, where we are staying temporarily, for a meal with your disciples. So that his mother can also see him. She has been crying since he disappeared."

The invitation was gracefully accepted. After Yash, many of his friends too joined Buddha's group of followers which was now called 'Sangha' organisation. Soon there were sixty disciples under Buddha and Kaundinya. By this time the rest of the four original followers who also had become awakened were told by the Buddha to travel in different directions and bring happiness to all sections of society.

****

Yashodhara had started her own 'Sangha', parallel to Buddha's at the palace. Although she had her limitations. Some of the children too sat with their mothers and participated in the spiritual discussions. Rahul was seriously trying to understand his father's principles as he heard about them. He had stopped playing war games with his friends and did not like to behead his enemy toys like other children. He preferred to pretend to be a mendicant asking for alms.

Once king Shuddhodan reminded Yashodhara that Rahul would be trained to become a warrior, so bring him up accordingly. To which she replied, “Father, I do not want him to learn marshal arts. Because his father wouldn’t wish that for him.”

The king said, “As you desire. After my experience with Siddhartha, I believe it is better to leave children to different exposures as long as they are not unsafe, and leave them to find out their true purpose in life.”

Mahaprajapati was becoming fond of Rahul and even Mangala aunt liked to play with him. That was something which annoyed his mother. Yahsodhara had given Devdatta’s earring to his mother, soon after she had found it in her bedroom. From then onwards Mangala could never face Yashodhara, without guilt. She had tried hard for Devdatta to marry, but he always retorted, “What is the need for it? I have all the women, I want at my disposal. If you want to play with a grandson, go play with Rahul or other kids of the seraglio.”

Devdatta’s father had stopped talking to him since long.

*****

Buddha during his travels, also started taking lay disciples. The monks took the vow of serving the society by teaching them how to ride over their sufferings. The lay followers just had to follow a few simple conditions.

Not to kill, steal, or practice sexual misconduct; lie or take stimulants like alcohol because that makes the mind dull.

Yasha’s friends were Vimal, Subahu, Purnaji and Gavampati, who were all sons of rich merchants. They were being taught the practice under Acharya Kaundinya. The next fifty young men who followed these four also belonged to their circles. Soon hundreds of men and women became Buddha’s followers as lay disciples and would never miss his discourses when he was in the vicinity of their town.

Many people from Kashi heard about the prince, from Shakya clan, who has attained enlightenment or Nirvana and had a big following whom he taught his ‘path.’

Buddha’s period was one of prosperity. Which led to the development of a powerful middle class of wealthy merchants and bankers. Due to the economic growth the rulers could afford vast armies needed to expand their empires. This, also helped them to nourish the unprofitable class of priests and monks.

After training them, Buddha sent his bhikshus far and wide to explain his precepts so that people could attain the state of supreme joy. Only twenty members of the community were left at the Deer Park. But those who had gone, brought back many more men who wanted to join the 'Sangha' community. Thus, the net of followers kept on expanding.

As the number of Bhikshus swelled, Buddha told Kaundinya, "Please Acharya, take the responsibility of the Sangha. I need to travel."

Buddha started walking on the road, from Kashi to, Giriviraj towards east and then south. By afternoon he reached a small village where he begged for food. After that he started his meditation, sitting on a stone under a tree. Soon he was disturbed by a group of 'dandy' young men, called 'nagarakas', or the urbanites. They were clean shaved, and their eyes were still smeared with black kohl, and their lips coloured with red lac. Surprisingly they wore no jewels.

"Sage, have you seen a girl, go by, from here," one of them asked anxiously.

"Why do you ask?"

"We are from Kashi. We came to the forest for a moonlight picnic and brought a girl along to entertain us. When we dozed off she bolted with our ornaments."

"As you all were sloshed after the party!"

They looked at their feet.

"She robbed you in the past. She will keep on robbing you of your future. Because you would keep on imagining where you might find her if you followed."

The young men became thoughtful. Buddha continued, "Are your ornaments worth loosing your past, present and future. In other words, loosing yourselves?"

"What do you suggest?" one of them asked.

"This is a moment which gives you two choices. Either go find the girl or sit here to find yourselves."

All of them sat on stones. Buddha suggested, "Close your eyes, and take a few deep breaths. Now open your eyes and look at the natural beauty around you. Feel the touch of breeze on your face; hear the rustle of leaves and see the sun beams caressing your body. We waste our lives regretting our past or dreaming about future. Thus, missing the present moment. Which means we are not living at all and become unhappy. The moment you learn to live in the present, you are awakened to your true self."

Buddha saw a flute held by one of the boys. A shade of memory floated through his mind. He said, “Why don’t you play something for us?”

The young man played a sad tune, probably expressing his mood. Then he offered the flute to Buddha.

“Please teacher, now you play something for us.”

Gautama remembered how sometimes he use to play in the palace garden at night in company of his friend Aniruddha while Yashodhara would bring an incense burner to improve the ambience and sit with them.

Everybody was enchanted to hear Buddha play a divine tune, which drifted through the thinning fog, and hung in the air. He told the boys, “I am amazed that although I was out of practice for seven years yet due to my recently acquired, mindfulness my performance was better than before.”

The impressed young men became his followers. He told them, “Proceed to Isipatana at the Deer Park and meet Sage Kaundinya. I would see you sometime, as my Bhikshus.”

Tathagat again proceeded on his journey alone. He reached Uruvilva village by evening. Spending the night, he woke up to find Swasti at the bank of Niranjan river, busy cutting the Kusha grass for buffaloes. Buddha talked to him while helping him cut the grass. He told him, “Please inform the other children to come and see me tomorrow.”

Buddha had finished eating from his begging bowl, when children appeared all cheerful and elated. After chatting for some time, Sujata gave him the latest news, “Tathagat a new hermitage has been established at some distance from our village at Gayasiras hamlet, by a Sage Kashyap. He is a ‘fire worshipper.’ They keep the holy fire burning in their hermitage all the time.”

“Thanks for the information Sujata, I would like to go and meet the Guru at his Ashram, who thinks that by worshipping fire they can attain ‘Nirvana.’

The sage welcomed the Buddha and had long discussions with him privately. Gautama answered all his queries and impressed his intellect. Kashyapa understood the doctrine of ‘no-self’ and ‘mutual- inter-dependence’ along with the four truths and eight-point path. The middle-path made sense to him. The fire worshippers dropped all devices used for fire rituals, in the river and decided to follow Buddha on his path. His disciples too readily agreed.

Sage Kashyap had two brothers in the same fire-worshipping practice. When they learned about the change of faith in their older brother, they too followed on his footsteps. The three brothers had following of nine hundred disciples who all joined their masters to Magadh.

Buddha and his new following left Gayasiras and walked towards Giriviraj to meet King Seniya Bimbisar. He was quite unaware that the 'pundas' or the priests and Brahmans who considered themselves custodians of the Hindu communities were planning to uproot the young tree of Buddhism, which had started giving shade to humanity, even before it became strong like a banyan tree.

At the court, the royal chaplain Gyaniji was talking to his subordinates, while they waited for the king's arrival. He whispered, "Let us talk to the king about this new upstart who is going against the eternal Hindu religion, 'Sanatan Dharma.' He does not believe in gods or the Vedas. This is sacrilege." Even the chief-minister agreed with Gyaniji, who continued, "We should request Maharaj, to crush this movement in infancy before it turns the Hindus into heretics. Besides if all young men became Bhikshus, who would fight the wars?"

Just then a messenger came and informed the minister that the king has gone to meet someone important and would come later. The minister continued, "I have heard, that this Shakyamuni is well-versed in the Vedas. He can explain with ease even the most profound passages given in Rig-Veda and other scriptures. He also has deep knowledge of history, philosophy and rituals, we brahmans perform. I also heard that he can play flute very well."

"What kind of religious preacher is he who loves music?" asked one of the priests.

"He just might be a social reformer, who is out to topple the society upside down", said another courtier.

"And what would he get out of it?"

"Power, I guess!"

Just then the call of the crier was heard, "His majesty, King Seniya Bimbisar is entering the court."

Before he finished, the king was already on his throne. Everyone got up and the king waved them to be seated.

"So what was the discussion going on?"

"Maharaj, we were talking about Shakya Muni", spoke the chief priest.

"I heard the last sentence. So you think he is greedy for power! For your information he is the son of King Shuddhodan, of Kapilvastu. He would have ascended the throne after his father. He left all the luxuries and power in order to remove the sufferings of mankind. All of you should go and listen to him preach. Only then you shall understand his wisdom. Many scholars and renowned sages have been ordained by him."

Gyaniji requested, "Your majesty why don't you organise a debate between him and your most learned Brahman?"

*****

When the Buddha had reached Giriviraj with his following of twelve hundred and fifty Bhikshus, along with Sage Kashyap, King Bimbisar was already prepared to welcome his guests. They were invited to the palace and served a delicious vegetarian meal. There was a pin-drop silence as more than a thousand Bhikshus ate with mindfulness and calm faces.

Afterwards, the children of nobles and rich merchants in fancy clothes were given a sermon by the Buddha. He related a story to them with a moral to learn. In simple words he explained the concept of cause and effect. He said, "When you help others you help yourselves; when you protect others, you protect yourself."

The king was so impressed by Buddha that he became then and there his disciple. In 'dakshina' his Sangha, was given the much needed gift, 'Venuvan,' the bamboo forest. It was two miles away from the city secluded as well as near. King Bimbisar took some water in his hand from a silver jug and took a vow, "From now onwards the forest belongs to you and your Sangha. I shall help you build a monastery there, especially when during 'Chaumas', you have to stay in one place for four rainy months."

That was the first donation of land to the Buddhist community. The king's son Ajatshattru and the priests had smoke rising from their swollen heads. They criticized the king later, among themselves.

Sage Kashyapa's disciples knew how to build and organise an 'ashram,' hermitage. Shariputra helped them. One of the bhikshu built a platform of bamboos for Buddha to sleep on. This stout young man, named Nagasamal became voluntarily his personal attendant. In the centre of the hermitage was a lovely lake named Kalandaka where the bikshus bathed and washed. A rich disciple donated a big bell on Shariputra's request. He hung it on a sturdy branch of a tree. The bell use to ring when it was time for sitting and observing their breaths called the Vipassana Practice.

One day as the Buddha was busy in walking meditation. He saw three familiar figures approaching him. He calmly moved towards his cousin, his half brother and his friend, to welcome them. They followed him to his hut and sat outside it on bamboo stools. Devdatta and his two companions were looking around with awe, at the serene, hushed and holy silence. Surrounded by leafy bamboos and punctuated by shanties for bhikshus.

Buddha spoke, "Brother it is time for the evening discourse. Would you like to hear it or rest?"

Devdatta answered, "We'll stay here tonight and go tomorrow to meet the king. By the way your father sent me as a messenger, with an invitation for you and your followers to visit his kingdom. He would organise a large dwelling for your 'honourable' disciples." He said with a twist of his lips.

The jab was lost on Buddha, like the water slips down an oily pot. He answered, "Please inform my father, I shall see him after the rainy season is over."

After the religious discourse, everyone shared the dinner, contributed to them by the house holders. Each one of the bhikshus sat down to meditate, at different spot.

Buddha gave his own hut and the bamboo platform to Devdatta for the night. Channa shared Maudgalyana's hut and Kaludayin, Shariputra's.

"Where will you sleep?" asked Devdatta.

"I shall be comfortable under any of the trees." Buddha replied. "The summer breeze is very pleasant. Specially next to the lake."

It was a dark night of Krishna Paksha. The waning moon was not visible yet. Buddha meditated late into the night then lay down under a mango tree to sleep covering himself with a hand dyed cotton cloth. The man known to have the strength of an elephant was nearing him, crouching and sniffing like a rat. Gautama who once use to be strong and muscular had turned quite lean due to a frugal diet. He would have been no match to Devdatta if they wrestled today. However, his sensitivity to his environment had increased many-fold. He could sense the slight crackling of dry leaves, around him. But he didn't stir. The shady character became more confident and extended his powerful hands towards Buddha's delicate neck. Instead, he found his own torso in the powerful grip of strong muscular arms.

Buddha sat up and conveyed, "It's okay Nagasamal, he is my cousin, maybe he came to talk to me in private."

"Good for him! I thought otherwise."

"Please go and sleep while I talk to my cousin."

Devdatta peered at Gautama in the dark with shame. While he lay down again turning his back towards him. The villain had no choice but to go back to the hut to sleep. Where he overslept as usual.

After the morning prayers the bhikshus were ready to go to the city with their begging bowls. That is when Buddha's two friends found a chance to talk to him alone. "We don't want to go back. Please accept us as your disciples."

Buddha smiled, "Not yet my friends. Let me come to Kapilvastu first."

After getting ready Devdatta told his companions, "We'll stay here for a few days before leaving."

After he was dropped at the palace he ordered them, "Park the chariot under the tree at the palace gate, and go back on foot. I'll come on my own."

Reaching the palace, Devdatta wanted to send inside a message for the prince but he saw Ajatshatru himself coming out with some courtiers dressed up for hunting. On seeing him, he welcomed him from his high horse, "Ha look what the wind blew in!"

There was a snickering among the courtiers. Ignoring it the Shakyan Prince said, "Prince Ajatshatru I need to discuss something with you."

"Sure, come along with us for a hunt and while taking a break, we can talk."

Trapped in the situation, Devdatta had no choice, but to follow him. He was offered an extra horse.

By lunch time, they had killed a few deers and pheasants. Fresh meat was being cooked on fire as both the princes, relaxed under a tree, with wine goblets in their hands.

Ajatshatru asked, "So what's your problem friend?"

"We both are facing the same problem. If we help each other, it'll be mutually beneficial."

Ajatshatru raised his eyebrows in amusement, and smiled sarcastically.

Ignoring his expression, Devdatta continued, "We both are eager to sit on our thrones. But your father Bimbisar and my uncle Shuddhodan are in no hurry to die."

"I know", answered the Magadhan prince. "I hate my father for his domineering attitude and now he has become a disciple of the Buddha. Without consulting anyone he gave away acres of land to him, and built a hermitage too, for the rainy season. Besides I also dislike him because of his liaison with the Licchavi courtesan, Amrapali. Isn't that an insult to my mother and his other queens? He has built for her, on the outskirts of our capital, a beautiful palace too, where she visits. She owns it."

"Everyone knows about that affair!" retorted Devdatta.

"So what do you have in mind?"

"I have cultivated a private army of soldiers, without the king's knowledge. He admires my efforts to increase the size of our warrior units.

Specially after many young men have taken refuge in the Buddha and his Sangha. Anyway, whenever you are ready to overthrow your father's power, I'll secretly send my soldiers to help your loyal ones. But your success would depend on the element of surprise. King Bimbisar has a large number of loyal followers. It may not be easy to beat them!"

"Don't I know that ! And what do you expect in return?"

"Magadh is one of the most powerful kingdoms in the north. You could use your influence to put me on throne of Kapilvastu."

Ajatshatru, took a sip of wine, before answering, "Okay! If I manage to capture my father and imprison him, with your help, I'll do what you want. After usurping my father's throne I'll starve him to death."

"I too, would have to manage the assassination of the ruling king of my clan, somehow."

By the time, the aroma of roasted deer meat on the open flames, spread around, Ajatshatru was starving. Whereas Devdatta's mind was focused on his own ambition. When the Magadhan Prince started enjoying the delectable dinner served to them, the latter started expressing what was on his mind.

"Look Prince! We are both in a similar quandary."

"You already said that!"

"Your father is too young to give up his throne yet. His people love him. So a revolt is out of the question. Same thing goes for my uncle Shuddhodan."

Ajatshattru, for a moment, stopped tearing flesh from a piece of bone. Showering some spittle on his own beard and answered, "I have accumulated about three hundred soldiers, who have come to my side without, my father's knowledge. But in the face of an army of thousands, it won't be enough." And he started sucking marrow from a bone making loud noises. Devdatta was not really relishing his dining mannerisms. He answered.

"I too, have succeeded in assembling more than two hundred loyal men and my maternal uncle, who hates the king's self-pride, has promised to help, if it comes to usurping the throne. Besides if I am the chief of the confederation, he too would benefit. Hence, the help."

"What's his name, and how many men he would offer?"

"He is Tapodan, the chief of Pithoragarh, a part of Shakyan republic. He can give us five hundred soldiers in secrecy."

"If we use the right strategy and the element of surprise, it might work."

"Let me know when you are ready. About seven hundred soldiers would reach, in the uniform of your Army, at a rendezvous. No one would know the difference. After you imprison your father. Your enhanced political clout and military might can attack and kill Shuddhodan. With his crown prince gone to the forest there won't be any claimant left to defy me."

"Good idea", and prince Ajatshattru extended his messy hand for Devdatta to shake, enjoying his discomfiture with a smile.

Devdatta shook his hand and thought, 'In time of need there is no harm in claiming a jackass as your father!' And he tried to focus on his lunch, yet couldn't taste anything in particular because his mind was stuffed with his ego, more than anything else.

*****

Yashodhara by now had understood in depth, the importance of relationships in the community. Whereas Siddhartha in the past had been overwhelmed by too many relationships. Half of them he found meaningless or lacking in depth. This fact hit him hard after he had come back from Takshakshila. Many of his cousins considered him haughty and spoilt because he was the chief's son. Devdatta's greed; the 'Ranivas's intrigues, as told by Yashodhara; and his father's ambitious demands; everything made him feel like a fly trapped in a spider's web. Above all he was always worried about the outcome of the deceitful game which had been played against King Prasenjit. He had had his fill of the opulent luxuries afforded to him. His pleasure house of sexy dancing girls had become nauseating. He felt that he doesn't know who he is, anymore. His problem of existentialism was clouding his thoughts about relationships. He had no faith in gods; neither in ancient Shiva-Shakti nor in later creations by the Aryans of Vishnu and Brahma at his navel. So to find 'his own uniqueness as a self-determining individual' he had gone forth towards his search. But Yashodhara had stayed behind, at Hamsavati to fulfill her duties towards her relations.

*****

One day, the news came from Devdah, that queen Amita, Yashodhara's mother was very sick. Her husband had died many years back. One foggy evening he had mounted an elephant with a white parasol on top and gone just outside his palace for inspection of the mint where silver and copper coins were punch-marked. The place was just around the corner, yet when he reached the narrow gate of the mint with two guards on two sides, a horse who's rider wasn't able to control his animal got struck between the elephant and the gate. Both animals were trying to get free of each other. With a jerk they both untangled themselves and barged in opposite directions. The king lost his balance and fell on the paved floor. His head split opened and thick, red blood gushed out. He was quickly gone. His body was taken to the palace by his guards and soldiers.

After getting the news of his sister being very ill, king Shuddhodan invited her to come to Hamsavati where Yashodhara, his daughter and Mahaprajapati could attend to her.

Amita was more than willing. Once she came, Yashodhara was constantly by her mother's side. She found her slipping away every day. It was painful. But she would hold her hand and talk about Buddha's philosophy on transient-ness of life. She was very alert and mindful in her care of her. She recited to her 'the eightfold –path, the four noble-truths and the middle path'. Sometimes she would just sit in silence holding her hand feeling intensely the journey of sorrow she was sharing with her. This seemed to comfort her yet she could notice her countenance changing with each passing day. She also smiled at times and blessed her daughter with a raised hand. Siddhartha's teachings were leading her towards understanding of the self and it's relationship with the environment.

Sometimes Prajapati spent the night with Amita, her sister-in-law while Yashodhara slept for a few hours. When Amita couldn't sleep, Praja would try to enlighten her about life and death, based on, Tathagat's philosophy. She would say, "Dear Amita, non of us has a separate self; we are nothing but flesh and bones, plus our memories. If we can get rid of the extra baggage of attachments we'll be more at peace while leaving the mortal cage. Our life energy would diffuse into the vast cosmic one. We have in us all that is around us. We are a part of the whole where we are all inter-dependent on each other and the phenomena. When you leave this world, you would still be alive. In Yashodhara and in Rahul. How your five year old grandson comes to his maternal grandmother, to sit with her for a chat, whom he had hardly seen before!"

A smile spread over Amita's ninety year old pale face, at her grandson's mention. Stretching her wrinkles to make her look younger. Just then Yashodhara entered. She addressed her mother-in-law, "Now you go and get some sleep mother."

"Okay, just let me feed some spoonfuls of water to my sister who is looking at you so adoringly."

"Of course Ma". But both of them watched with horror as the water trickled out of the corner of her mouth and her eyes kept on staring at Yashodhara, without blinking.

*****

Yashodhara always gave priority to community over an individualistic approach towards mankind. She felt that close connections, heal a person engulfed by sorrow; can prevent suicides and share not only thoughts, but others', concrete, day-to-day issues. Man, being a social being needs to communicate. He cannot be 'an island unto himself.' Her mother's loss was heart breaking. Rahul could not understand why suddenly his grandmother has disappeared and his mother is very sad. He had no idea. That she was trying hard to forget her memories of the past, to be wholly aware in the present.

For forty five days, mourning and rituals went on before the usual routine commenced at the seraglio.

It was about three, in the afternoon when the ladies from the women's quarters started trickling out, in the garden. The ponds here and there still had pink and blue lotuses blooming. The rest of the flower beds were somewhat barren. Yashodhara, who loved flowers before, had lost interest in all things of beauty. She got use to looking at the intrinsic beauty of everything. She was waiting for everyone to gather when she glimpsed at her forty one year old withered face as a reflection in the water. She sighed, hopelessly. She threw a pebble among the lotuses and dissolved the image.

Soon, their circle was formed. Everybody had a ray of hope shining on their faces. They expected Devdatta, Kaludayin and Chandak to return soon from Magadh, after inviting Buddha to come to Kapilvastu.

It was the last phase of monsoons, and Buddha and many of his monks were residing in the Bamboo Forest at Giriviraj. For their welcome at Kapilvastu, the king was getting bamboo huts constructed in the Nigrodh-van park.

The city was being decorated with colourful banners. The dried up fountains of palace gardens were, once again happily ejecting forth. And the ladies in the circle talked about the happenings going on in the palace and at the city. Over the last twelve years, their sense of interconnectedness had become very strong. Like a close knit family. Sitting on the garden floor, they all became one entity. Sharing the same ground, wind, sun or sky. Drinking the same water from the earthen pitcher when, thirsty. Except the ladies from the king's seraglio, everyone was dressed in saffron saris. Some young men, like Chandak or Kaludayin were allowed to join their group. They all waited for the queen while chatting in soft tones.

Though Siddhartha and Yashodhara were a long distance apart, they were treading the same noble path, of how to remove the suffering of others. Gautama focused on the role of mind in achieving happiness;

whereas Yashodhara was trying to give the less fortunate, moral support, financial help and other practical services as a social worker.

After the queen arrived gliding gracefully in a gold trimmed lemon sari and took her place on the cotton-spread, she asked Yashodhara, "Please address the congregation Yasho."

The princess started, "My friends your belief in sound reasoning is the best way to find out what is right. Logic and independent experience only, can lead to wisdom. Do not believe in what others say, find out for yourself." She further explained the theory of Karma, as 'cause and effect', "What you sow, thou shalt you reap."

"To improve one's state of mind, one must avoid gas." Everyone snickered. "What do you mean princess?" asked Gopa, one of the junior wives, innocently.

The princess smiled. "Greed, anger and stupidity or ignorance. These three poisons must be avoided all the time. Life is a mirror. You see your own face in it. You only find fault with others if you yourself are guilty of the same. If you are of pure mind you can't feel malice for other people. We were born pure. But as we immerse deeper and deeper in the mire of wrong notions we learn deception. Our original pure thoughts become impure and lead us not only to our own misery but of others' as well. As Yashodhara stopped talking Mahaprajapati took over.

"All of you know that we might see our dear Shakyamuni, soon." She smiled, "I assume the news has spread far and wide." The young ladies smiled back. "But just remember one thing girls, we are still clinging to our fond memories of him, of the past. But he had left his history behind, at Kapilvastu, when he detached himself from all of us. Do we, in our hearts blame him? And why? Let's discuss our love and grudges for him today."

Gopa said, "Maybe he went looking for god!"

"I don't think so" replied Utpalvarna. "I think he realised that his luxurious life at the palace was hollow and meaningless. There were so many crafty intrigues going on in the republic that he got fed up and left to find mental peace; a 'path' by which he could put some sense into people's thinking.

Mahaprajapati responded, "You are right, Utpalvarna. But I feel that what disturbed him the most was the plight of the poor and the downtrodden, like those of the lower caste plus the great disparity between the rich and the poor. On top of everything the issue of war. He believed that wars start in the minds of the kings. If they would use wisdom and dialogue with their enemies, half the wars could be averted. Arrogance and stupidity are reason for wars. During the last meeting of the council he had attended, he was against sending a slave girl to king Prasenjit in marriage. That being a big deceit. Gautama felt that truth cannot stay hidden forever. The far reaching consequences could annihilate the Shakya Tribe."

Prajapati looked at Mangala. "What is your opinion? Say something." "I think Gautama had left all emotional baggage behind him, never looking back. To seek, 'The deathless supreme security from bondage'. Actually it appears more than just that. He underwent a personal crisis of some kind and was seized by 'existential questions. Or perhaps his war experiences disturbed him to the extreme, as you had mentioned."

"Beautifully expressed Mangala. You've hit the nail on the head. Death is constantly stalking us. Our deepest fear is of being annihilated. Siddhartha wanted to find a way by which people could come out of their bubbles of these fears and live their lives without dread and at ease! But at times a thought occurs in my mind..." and she looked at Yashodhara before completing her sentence. "...that because of the conflict in opinion at the council before he left, he was disturbed at the thought that if he does not agree with the members, he might put in jeopardy the security of his father's throne."

"At the same time he might have felt that more than his family he would be doing injustice to his people and clan, by dashing their hopes of a secure future under his fair governance. He would rather have led a monarchy like Rama's Ayodhya than an ignorant and arrogant republican-oligarchy. He must have been torn between his two choices."

At last one of Yashodhara's companions spoke, "I feel the main factor for his disenchantment might have been his abhorrence towards the bloodshed and preference for sanctity of life. Which must be valued."

"True Ganga, 'Bodhisattva rejected animal sacrifice. He perfects himself not through sacrificing another in place, but by sacrificing himself for the sake of others.' He felt, that the self-sacrificial ritual is a 'bloodless path to Buddha-hood.'"*

*****

Parallel to the ladies. Buddha was busy in his discourse to his disciples, "Brahamans have instilled a fear in the hearts of people regarding their next life. If anyone has sinned knowingly or unknowingly, his next birth could be of some lowly creature. A cat, dog or even a worm. However, if they want to absolve their sins they need to make charitable causes to eradicate

* 'Sacrificial Sutras': Natalie D. Gummer.

their negative karmas by giving gold, silver or clothes to a Brahman. And why not to a needy person? May I ask?"

The monks only shook their heads in agreement.

It is believed by the scholars that Buddha's philosophy was targeted towards the urban populace. He wanted to re-educate the educated ones who may become the leaders one day and then with their wisdom and compassion, could take care of the uneducated poor masses. He could see that those unfortunate men and women were so tied up in their everyday grind that they may not even understand his theories in depth. However, they would eventually get the trickled down residual philosophy anyway. Yet they needed the governance of the wise.

*****

The Buddha had won Mara, the evil god in his final battle. But His prophecy that Devdatta would take advantage of his wives seem to be coming true.

It was a dark moonless night! Murky and foggy. Yashodhara slept with her son and her personal maid Bhanumati in her room. Mrigi was at her father Dandpani's house bringing up her son Anand. Gopa and Utpalvarna were in their own bedrooms.

Shuddhodan's Palace was at peace yet the guards were alert. A shadow was creeping up the steps of ladies quarters stealthily, looking this way and that cautiously. Reaching upper floor balcony of the king's seraglio, the dark-clothed man was slowly shuffling against the wall till he reached Gopa's chamber. Dim light and warmth were oozing out of the cracks of her window. It was past midnight when a gong sounded at one end of the palace and a guard announced loudly, "Second watch of the night is over."

The shadow stood still.

That evening Gopa's lady-in-waiting needed a leave. She had asked the Queen if a replacement should be sent to her. Gopa replied, "Don't worry Kunti it is only a question of one night. I'll manage. I may look fragile but I am strong."

"Thanks Queen! I hope you won't need to use your strength tonight." And she left. Gopa, before going to bed kept a sharp dragger under her pillow, just in case. In the third watch of the night, she heard a scratching at her door as if someone was trying to pry it open with a scimitar blade held between the two doors. She was suddenly fully awake. In anger she grabbed the weapon from under her pillow, and surprised the intruder by flash opening the door and shutting it back again hard against his hand which got squeezed between the two wooden panels. Blood started dripping and he stifled a scream.

The snooper, with the strength of an elephant thrust his full weight against the door and barged in. But Gopa's dragger pinned him to the now closed door while evil one's weapon had dropped when his hand got crushed. Devdatta in excruciating pain fell on her bed. The queen, overpowered him. Standing across his body with one foot on his heart and the other on his ankles, she prepared to kill him, but before that taunted him with the words,

"You have not heard it said, O wretched man that the lotus which a wild elephant in rut has once uprooted, trampling it in mud and water, still preserves its virgin freshness. Other elephants do not wanton there!"

The intruder apologised profusely and promised, "You are just like a sister to me from now onwards but please let me go this once." While begging for his life, he was in constant fear of her dragger which was advancing towards his neck. The queen spoke jumping off his body, "Your worse punishment would be to humiliate you and let the king decide your retribution." Before she pardoned him an image had flashed through her mind of her ex-husband who believed in non-violence.

She let the villain get off the bed, at the point of her dragger and made him go out in the balcony, next to the railing. Suddenly she pushed him hard. The guards came running when they heard a splash in the pond below and arrested his drenched and wounded pride. Water trailing down his pathetic locks he was handcuffed like a criminal and caged behind bars till the morning.

*****

Giriviraj at that time was a trade centre with large population. The natural boundary of the hills had walls built in between them. There were beautiful springs pouring down the mountains. Some of those being hot, had their advantages. The place had iron and copper mines which made it rich. To protect all the riches the city had a heavily guarded military base.

In the bamboo forest, Buddha had found a sense of tremendous freedom. He still remembered how he had reached there twelve years ago. 'Sometimes joining slow-moving caravans of bullock-carts, covering little more than one yojana a day. The jungles on the way were infested with dangerous animals like rhinos, tigers, lions, bears or bands of dark jungle tribes, ready to kill for loot. Now he was planning to go back the same way to Kapilvastu after the rainy season, when swarms of mosquitoes was another threat. Many could suffer from risky 'Swamp- Fever'. To avoid that they had sacks full of green bitter oranges containing quinine from Cinchona tree. He knew it won't be easy as the boggy ground with muddy potholes would be hard on the wooden wheels of the wagons. One or the other of which could get struck, on the way. Sometimes he and his train would stay in some park or a village and next day move again heading for Ganga which would be overflowing with water. This time however he had three hundred bhikshus with him and was given oxen-carts by king Bimbisar as a help.

Buddha with his group reached Nalanda village by late evening. The sun was setting, so the bhikshus, all calm and saffron-clad stayed in a mango grove at night near the Nalanda Mahavihara after their late evening meditation. Next morning was crisp and full of sunshine. They saw that a group of villagers were coming towards the trees where 'Kokilas' were cooing a sweet melody of welcome. Each of the men was holding a banana leaf or a dona-bowl made up of dry leaves, filled with food. One by one they placed the food in front of each bhikshu with folded hands, politely. Buddha was amazed about their source of information and generosity. The Bhikshus chanted in unison and began eating.

After lunch Buddha sat on a boulder, facing the villagers and the Bhikshus. He thanked and praised the locals, before starting his sermon for the day. The lay people had never heard such enlightening ideas. There was nothing mystic about them. Buddha's words were crystal clear, light and logical in regards to day-to-day life. Some village folks whispered to one another, "He does not fear god as the brahman sages have told us to do. His religion does not scare us with god's wrath and punishment. There is no sword of fear hanging over our heads." Another one whispered, "But he tells us to cleanse our minds of all negative emotions like greed, anger, ignorance or guilt. Our only possession worth keeping is a sound mind with compassionate fellowship." Soon they focused again on the Buddha's words.

Leaving Nalanda the Buddha's followers reached the southern bank of River Ganga. From there the bullock carts were sent back to Giriviraj. Villagers could see a file of ferries crossing the river, while the saffron stoles, flitted in the breeze.

On the northern bank, they reached the village of Pataliputra, under the jurisdiction of Licchavi Janapad. The capital of this ancient republic was Vaishali, famous for Amrapali more than anything else. The state was governed by a parliament of many members, called the kings and their head was addressed as 'Maharaj.'

Resting at the monastery of the forest gifted by Chief of Vaishali, they planned to stay there for another day.

Next morning an elegant chariot was racing towards the Buddha's retreat. A shimmering ladies stole was flying out of the window. When she stepped out to go and invite the Buddha the new adherents were amazed at her beauty. She reached the Buddha's hut, he invited her to sit. His countenance was perfectly calm, unaffected by her charms. Amrapali requested Buddha to come to her house with his disciples and give her the opportunity to serve them food. Buddha agreed. On her way back she saw two chariots, fancy and rich looking coming headlong on the narrow track, she was passing. There were young boys from noble families dressed like princes, riding in it.

"Hey man," one of them shouted at her driver, "Move aside, we are going to invite the Buddha."

Hearing this Amprapali also put her head out of the window and answered,

"In that case you better return. Because he has already accepted my invitation for tomorrow."

"So, that's the 'mango-girl'. Why don't you invite us instead you shall have fun, as well as money. What would that sage give?"

"You won't know unless you meet him!"

With careful maneuvering the chariots passed each other.

At the Buddha's hut, they were told nicely by him, "I am sorry boys I have already accepted another invitation."

"Do you prefer an invitation from a lowly courtesan than from high officials of the kingdom?"

"In our sangha no one is high or low. We treat all alike! Now friends since you are here you may listen to the preaching before you leave."

They all agreed. When the meeting was over they fell at the Buddha's feet. Shedding salty tears through which their arrogance came pouring out.

"See", Buddha said. "Her tears are as salty as yours, so what's the difference!"

*****

Chapter - 14

The Home Coming

'OH MY BELOVED RAHUL, YOU WERE A MISFORTUNE FOR
YOUR FATHER FROM THE VERY BEGINNING ...,
EVERYONE ACCUSES YOU OF BEING ILLEGITIMATE;
AND PEOPLE LOOK DOWN AT ME AS A WIDOW.
MY SUFFERING BRINGS ONLY TEARS.[1]

King Shuddhodan was getting news about Buddha's approach, every day through his spies. As he reached Sarasvati city in the Kaushala kingdom, they all had settled at the Jetavan, a retreat he had been gifted by a rich banker and trader. Due to his charities for the needy and helpless he was generally known as 'Anathpindica'. Whereas his name was Suddatta. He had become an ardent follower of the Buddha when he had visited Giriviraj on business. He bought this land from Prince Jeta, younger brother of Prasenjit, at exorbitant price in gold. However, later Jeta too was greatly influenced by the Buddha and helped in building a monastery along with Shariputra and Suddatta.

Suddatta had taken one year to collect the amount of gold Jeta demanded. He went through dangerous forests, crossing tumulus rivers, and travelling long distance to reach the Magadhan port, with his caravan. Then boarding a sea faring vessel he sailed with his cargo to foreign lands to sell and purchase. Exhausted yet jubilant he came back with silver and gold to fulfill Prince Jeta's demand.

After they were about to reach Sarasvati, the bhikshus had rested in the cool forests along the banks of Aciravati River at night before reaching township. The first group of about hundred Bhikshus arrived, led by the Buddha. Followed by a second group after a few hours led by Assaji. And

1. Obeyesekere – 'Yashodhara'; 'Stars at Dawn' – W. Garling, p. 210.

the third group, under the supervision of Maudgalyana reached as the sun was just setting.

A reception organised by Prince Jeta was in progress. Many local people came to welcome the monks, and to hear Buddha's 'Dharma Talks.'

Prasenjit's palace was just a mile away. He came in a procession riding his well decorated elephant followed by his queen Mallika, his younger sister Suman and his sixteen years old daughter Princess Vajiri, in their fancy chariot. They were followed by his General and friend Bandula with his devoted wife Mallika along with other nobles.

The Buddha was grateful to Anathapindika and before starting the Dharma Talk he expressed his thanks for the gift of Jetavan, saying –

"They ward off cold and heat and beast of prey
And creeping things and gnats and rains
The hot wind arising is warded off,
To meditate and obtain insight in a shelter such."

Buddha was also obliged to the King for the gifts and food donated by him for entire congregation. Forty year old practical Gautama knew now the importance of the elites for the safety and survival of his Sangha since they were a non-productive part of the society.

It is said that Anathpindika bought the land for eighteen crores* and spent another fifty – four crores for its building, toilets and wells dug up for water. Prince Jeta constructed the great entrance archway of magnificent façade on top of which a room was built for guards.

The function was attended by the very rich as well as the common folks, with great pomp and show. This retreat became Buddha's favourite spot for most of his preachings. The ground was covered with lush green trees and many ponds. In front of the gateway was planted a Peepal Bodhi tree.

However, some bad incidents also had taken place near the vihara later on. One was the murder of Sundarika brahaman and the false allegations of a woman that Buddha had made her pregnant. Also Devdatta's attempt to poison Tathagat.

*****

ANGULIMAL

Buddha kept on travelling after leaving hundreds of Bhikshus at

* 180 million Rupiah.

Jetavan, as he had done at the Bamboo forest. He was dispersing the seeds of his accumulated knowledge on his path, believing them to sprout some day and bear the fruit of wisdom for the laymen and elite alike. He was however, warned by Prasenjit not to walk alone through the Jalini forest as a serial killer called Angulimal waylays unguarded travellers and kills them. His patrolmen were not able to trace him. He comes like a flash of lightening and disappears among the mountain bushes leaving a dead body minus his little finger, yet pockets full. He has to be caught and apprehended. Buddha had thanked the king for his advice yet he did not alter his route.

When he reached the notorious forest much ahead of his followers, the sun was setting. From the corner of his eye Buddha could see the dreaded one dashing down the mountain. But he neither stopped nor wavered his calm walk.

The shocked culprit shouted after him in a thunderous voice to scare him. "Oy, can't you hear me? Stop! I said stop!"

Buddha ignored him and continued walking. Angulimal was perplexed at his undaunted attitude. While Buddha answered back, "I have stopped since long, it is you who has to stop now."

The killer jumped in front of him barring his way," What do you mean? "I mean I have stopped my wrong doings long time back Ahinsak, now it is your turn to stop." Ahinsak now flabbergasted, peered at him closely. "Who are you? How do you know my real name which I myself have forgotten. Are you the king's spy?" He gave Tathagat a threatening look.

"I was at Takshakshila with you where you were studying Tantra Science.* I am Siddhartha Gautama. Only you have a bushy growth of hair now while I have none."And the Buddha had a divine smile on his face. A sudden realisation of who he actually was, jolted him back to reality and he fell at the Buddha's feet washing them with his long dried-up tears saying, "What have I become trying to oblige my Acharya!"

The Buddha advised him,"Never go by words of people. Hear, think and thrash out the essence behind and intention of conveying behind them. With your misguided understanding you have not only killed so many people but also killed yourself."

Angulimal crumbled to the ground and held his forehead with both hands in despair. "I am sunk in the mire of sins till my neck. I was one

* Richard. Gombrich suggested that in Tantric Science those days, ritual sex and even human sacrifices were advised to arouse innate divine power or Shakti. The earliest evidence of human sacrifice was found during bronze age of ancient India.

finger short and was going to kill my own mother for it. When you came my way and prevented me.Take me in your refuge Gautama. Save me! I beseech you O Savior! Give me a new life." He said crying.

"Tathatsu"! Buddha blessed and led him to a nearest monastery where his disciples were waiting for him. In secrecy the notorious dacoit was ordained into a bhikshu. He was told to proceed to Jeta Van and meet Modgalyana.

*****

Monk Kaludayin who had been a messenger between king Shuddhodan and the Buddha soon gave the news to the king and the queen that Tathagat was on his way. He then walked back with his begging bowl to meet him en route, who would have travelled for sixty days to reach Kapilvastu.

On their arrival at Kapilvastu, they divided themselves into groups and begged in different localities. Those who saw the Buddha were amazed at the change in him. He, like all the others had turned dark due to walking in the sun many times. People were gawking at the Prince's transformation and Mrigi was showing her son Anand his father. "Look son at his handsome face and dignified bearing.

King Shuddhodan left the palace in his carriage along with the queen and prince Rahul, to welcome his son, turned sage. When he reached the eastern part of the city he saw him begging from a poor, old woman's hut. He felt so humiliated and repulsed that instead of meeting him he headed towards the Nigrodhvan forest, which he had prepared for him and his followers. He was sad as well as furious. Sad to see his son the crown prince, a beggar and angry because he had tarnished the name of his proud ancestors.

Queen Gautami consoled her husband, "Arya, your son now does not belong to any clan. He has severed all ties. His relatives now are, according to his belief. For him, Virtue of truth is his mother; the (virtue of) wisdom is his father; his knowledge of (the dharma) must be his assisting brother; his virtue of kindness must be to him most excellent friends; and his firm faith might be his wives; his (virtue) of patient endurance must be as a helping son. These six relatives have continually preserved him until now. Besides he is not a beggar he is a sharer of the society. The almsman is differentiated from an ordinary beggar by the sacramental character of his begging. He is a recluse yet integrally involved in society. He is not one of those renunciate who go to the Himalayas and even after enlightenment never get in touch with the ordinary people."

The king was focused at what Prajapati was saying. By this time the hustle-bustle of the city had disappeared and the road became uneven. Among jerks and jostles they were approaching the forest where water resources were already available due to digging of 'sink wells' in order to reach deep flowing waters of the rivers. Shuddhodan looked at his wife as if for the first time.

"How could you explain Siddhartha's ideology in such depth?"

She only smiled. "This is merely the tiniest particle of his philosophy. You shall hear when he speaks."

"Hmm!"

Their chariot entered the tall entrance to the Nigrodh-Van where Nigrodh trees were in abundance. There was written on a horizontal flat beam, on top of the two pillars, in Sanskrit 'Buddham Sharnam Gacchami!' …I take refuge at the Buddha's feet.

The king got down and helped the queen by holding her delicate hand. Immediately a man came running with a white parasol and shaded them while they walked to an old Banyan tree under which a bamboo bench was waiting. The secluded spot was peaceful. Some monks were busy fixing things here and there for the Buddha's arrival. When they saw them. They went to wish and offer them drinking water. The king spoke to his queen.

"Doesn't it look barren and reticent?"

"It won't, when your son arrives. The birds would start singing, the breeze would blow, the gongs in the distant temples would be heard and the surroundings would turn joyful."

"So be it!"

There was commotion at the main gate when the Buddha entered the grove and was told about the king's arrival. Gautama straightaway reached his parents who were still in conversation under the tree curtained by aerial roots.

He came forward and touched their feet with reverence. The king blessed him and the queen got up and faced him while she observed him like only a mother could. Once satisfied she put her head on his shoulder and cried out the tears she had been holding back for last twelve years. Like queen Kaushalya might have done when Prince Rama returned after fourteen years of forest-dwelling. Except that this time 'Dashratha'* was sitting on the bench moist-eyed. He too got up and embraced his son,

---

* Kaushalya and Dashratha were King Rama's parents. Dashratha had died pining for his favourite son Rama before he came back from the exile after fourteen years.

forgetting his resolve not to become emotional. The bhikshus left them in privacy and started making preparations for a collective dinner of the food given to them by the householders.

After the emotional reunion, the family sat on the same bench exchanging news. Siddhartha, who sat on the ground near their feet asked, "How is everyone at the palace?"

"All is good except…."

"Why did you stop father?"

"Devdatta tried to invade the privacy of Gopa at midnight. But the brave girl…" The whole episode was explained to Gautama. "And now he is in jail. We thought that since you were coming you should decide his punishment."

Buddha thought for a moment then faced the king, "Free him father! His pot of sins is about to be full. When it breaks, he would go through hellish mental torture. And that would be enough punishment for him. I hope, that'll change him."

"I trust your wisdom, O' Buddha. I have a request though, come to the palace with your followers and dine with us."

"Sure father. We shall have our afternoon meal at the palace tomorrow but the first evening Dharma-discussion should be done at the Nigrodh Van, once you formally offer it to the Sangha along with queen Gautami."

And he looked at his mother for her approval. Mahaprajapati who was listening to their conversation silently, nodded her head with a smile and the king and the queen of the Shakyas got up to leave.

*****

At Samsavati Palace preparations were going on to welcome the Shakya Muni, after an absence of twelve years. By mid-morning the Buddha leading a large group of bhikshus left the Jeta retreat for the palace. At the same time the rest of the monks proceeded in smaller groups to the city to request for food by singing in Sanskrit – "Devam Bhikshami."

Their breathing, speech, and walk were calm and well-controlled, and commanded respect.

When the Buddha with his orange clad bhikshus with shaved heads reached the palace, king Shuddhodan who was waiting for him along with queen Gautami came down the steps excitedly and walked forward to welcome him near the ornate entrance. Then the king conducted the Buddha inside the palace.

Yashodhara goes to the balcony to have a glimpse of her husband, with Rahul.

As the Buddha enters the palace gates Yashodhara is overwhelmed with emotions seeing her husband after twelve years dressed in a 'hempen robe of a mendicant'. When Rahul saw her crying he asked, "Why are you sad mother?"

"Nothing my child, except that I see your father after a long time."

"Really? Where is my father?" He asked eagerly.

"The very tall sage in the front, whose face is shining like gold."

Rahul got so excited on seeing his father that he ran downstairs to greet him. King Shuddhodan had warned everyone not to tell Rahul that the Buddha was his father. When the little prince reached the exalted one he stood in front of him spellbound and looked and looked at his serene demeanor.

In his closeness, every pore of his being tingled and his hair stood on end.

He was overwhelmed and perspiring,

His body thrilled.*

He wanted to say 'father'. But his mother had told him not to, unless he is introduced as such by the king, his grandfather, who asks Tathagat openly, "Is it true or not that this is your son?"

To which the king heard him say, "Yashodhara is perfectly pure and innocent. This is my son." Thus, any doubts regarding Rahul's paternity melted away just as the nightly frost evaporates when the sun shines. However, Gautama also knew that the shrewd king would not be easily convinced. So when Rahul clung to the Buddha saying, "....If he is my father, I will go forth from home to homeless state and follow the way of my father."

Rahul then ran back to his mother upstairs and told her about his desire. To which she answered, after holding him in her lap, inside her chamber.

"Rahul, my son, do not go forth to the religious life. What you have in mind my son, is hard to achieve... Your fine garments, magnificent beds and delicate food to eat, would not be available. You will lie on straw on the ground...sit under a tree; you will have to go begging for alms... and look at the snorting mouths of angry men, and eat cast-off morsels of food; ... wear discarded rags of a slave-girl from the cemetery ... And dwell in forest

* Trans. From Pali Text.

tracts. There you will hear dreadful cries...of lions, tigers and jackals... Surely you would overcome this delusion...What then?" "Nothing! I will learn to be joyful under my father's guidance. He seems to be a great sage, he'll give me a heritage of happiness for life."

Yashodhara was amazed at his six year old's mature answer. The argument was over but for King Shuddhodan, it wasn't.

After the meal, the Buddha introduces his disciples one by one. When the king realised that most of them were of Brahman caste, he was furious. As it is, he was in a disturbed state of mind after seeing his son who 'wore no royal headdress but was close shaved and clad in a poor...robe.' But he retained his anger for the time being. Mahaprajapati, watched him from a distance and hurried to his side, giving him a calm sense of sharing his feelings.

Soon the ladies of the women's quarters arrived to honour the Buddha and receive his blessings except Yashodhara. The king sends a maid to ask Yashodhara to come. She thinks, 'First my husband leaves me in search of truth while I wait for him. I have done nothing wrong. I faithfully performed my wifely duties towards him. I must be a person of little merit. I can accept being abandoned, but the Buddha should have sympathy for his son Rahul. He is lovable and innocent... we have suffered greatly as if crushed by a mountain. My son's, princely childhood ceremonies were never performed; his horoscope was not prepared by the court 'purohit'. His hair were never braided in a ritual or earrings given to him as the heir to the throne. The priest was never present for him. Why?' At last she told the maid, "Please apologise on my behalf and tell my father-in-law, if I am worthy, let the Buddha come and see me at my apartment."

When the answer from Yashodhara was given by the young maid, the king looked helplessly at the Buddha who said, "Never mind father I'll visit her, while you, Maudgalyana and Shariputra would come with me."

When he entered her chamber Yasho was hiding in a dark corner behind the door, crying silently. As she heard the approaching footsteps her heart missed a beat. She scrunched her body further back the dark crook and held her breath.

On the way Buddha had told his disciples,"From not having seen me for so long a time, she is exceedingly sorrowful; unless this sorrow be allowed its course, her breast will cleave; she will take hold of my feet, but as the result will be that she and the other queens will embrace the priesthood, you must not prevent her."

Yashodhara had asked Channa to take care of Rahul in his room so that he is not disturbed by the drama that might unfold when she is alone with her husband.

Tathagat entered while the king and his two disciples stayed behind. He was standing against the sunlight in the doorway till his eyes adjusted to the gloom in the room. Yashodhara slowly peered out of her hideout when all became quiet. All at once she found herself face to face with her long lost husband. She couldn't discern the change in him as his anterior was in the shadow. Yet, overwhelmed with his very presence she fell on his feet sobbing uncontrollably; ** her body shaking violently, never realising who all stood at the door.

'Her eyes are blinded by tears; her body heaves and quivers. That was the first time Maudgalyana and Shariputra saw, a tear roll down Buddha's cheek.'**

The king then came forward and spoke to his son, "Please do not mind her loss of self-control. She had been a loyal wife to you, bearing her sorrow alone, with dignity so far. I'll see you downstairs."

Yashodhara stood up with a sigh and looked at Siddhartha's radiant calm and unwavering eyes. Her heart tightened into a painful knot. The moment came to a standstill and she stared at him in shock; she heard a sharp sound; cracking of her hopes into fragile fragments like dried lava. Her head covering slipped from her bald scalp as she perceived that he was not Siddhartha who abandoned her but was The Tathagat, a realised soul who teaches people how to purge their sufferings. She quickly covered her bare head. After that she half heard whatever anyone or The Buddha was saying while her heart and mind crawled away to her lonely world of disillusioned love.

Maudgalyana and Shariputra heard from outside, Tathagat's deep-throated monotone:

'You've wept more tears for me, than the seas can hold water.

Does this wide world hold a woman, as good as you.'

He paused and went on, "I am sorry I couldn't come earlier. Begging food in the streets is looked down upon by the proud Shakya clan, probably that is why we were never invited by the King. I did not want to humiliate him or his people."

"Rightly said Enlightened One," and she was quiet.

Yashodhara was unaffected by his words. They were hollow and meaningless to her, in her present state. She didn't want to be praised but needed to be remembered and loved.

**'Yashodharavata', Trans. Obeyesekere (2009).

Yashodhara was trying to find her mental balance after the earthquake, for a second time, which shook her very existence. Wiping her tears unobtrusively, she at last composed herself saying, "Please Tathagat, I'll be honoured if you could come to my dwellings with your retinue and share a meal with us."

"I will be happy to do so but tomorrow I shall be dining at the queen's palace. She already gave us an invitation."

"It's fine Tathagat, I shall see you the day after tomorrow then." And she bowed reverently in front of him.

At night she dreamt Siddhartha and herself dressed as the bride and the groom, moving happily towards their summer palace. Suddenly there was thunder and lightening in the sky and all went dark. Afraid to death, she wandered hither and thither looking for him throughout the night. Through the stairs, streets, buildings and the dreadful forests, without even a dirt-road. When the first ray of dawn filtered through the Sal trees, her husband, transformed into a bedraggled bhikshu was walking away from her holding Rahul's hand. She heard his receding call, "Follow me Yashodhara! Follow me!"

Day after the next, she was hostess to the Buddha and his followers. She along with Queen Gautami and the helpers served them food, with their own hands. Little Rahul was feeding only his father as he looked at him adoringly and sat in front of him and watched while he ate with perfect calm like the others.

After the meal, the ladies of the seraglio came to hear the Buddha who spoke on charity, morality, heaven, merit and the discourse on fruition of merit.

While the dharma-talk was going on the six year old prince sat clinging to the Buddha. Maudgalyana and Shariputra tried to separate him but Buddha stopped them with a gesture of his hand. Rahul got hold of the edge of Buddha's upper garment, 'sanghati' and covered his head and face with it. He rested his head against the lean body of his father and fell asleep. After the sermon, Yashodhara asked his maid to take him to his bed.

"I am sorry Tathagat." She said with lowered eyes. Before Buddha could say anything Shariputra answered gently, folding his hands.

"Actually O' Queen, no one is supposed to touch the enlightened one."

Buddha raised his hand again. "You mean well Shariputra but he is only a child, let him be. If he is ordained as he wishes, I'll put him under your care and guidance."

When Shariputra walked two steps backwards, Yashodhara spoke once again, “Please Arya, let me join your Sangha as a nun.”

Gautama looked at Queen Prajapati and said, “The first right of a woman to join our Sangha goes to my reverend mother.”

Queen Gautami came forward and answered, “Sorry teacher, I would like to be a lay practitioner because I have responsibility towards my husband, who needs me more than ever since you left.”

“Do not feel bad mother, when the time is right you shall find yourself at the Sangha door.”

Gautama looked at Yashodhara to take his leave when she said, “I apologise Enlightened one I own nothing worthy of offering you as a gift, so I donate to your Sangha what is still mine. My solace, our son Rahul.” Queen Gautami looked at her rigid, blank expression with shocked disapproval but said nothing. Yashodhara’s eyes were cast low.

*****

Every evening since Buddha had come, there use to be Dharma Talks attended by his adherents, at the Nigrodh park. His family and the people of Kapilvastu entered the ‘Hall’ constructed by the king for such gatherings. Everybody sat on the floor. The Royalty in the front and the rest after that. The princes from the palace never liked to touch Siddharth, their cousin’s feet. Because they still thought ‘He is the same impudent prince of the past.’ But after King Shuddhodan touched Thathagat’s feet, they had to follow. After listening to him, they realised the depth of his intellect and bowed to him willingly. Mrigi and her twelve year old son were also sitting in the ladies sections with the other queens.

In the first meeting with his people the Buddha explained, “Listen my friends and listen carefully. I am not propounding any new religion. I only want to change the values of our society so that a new civilisation could emerge out of the old one where the vast difference between the rich and the poor could be narrowed down. Gratification of the basic needs of every man should be his birthright. To the kings and chiefs, I suggest, if people are above the poverty line, there would be hardly any criminals left. To be jailed or punished. The judiciary should be impartial and kind.*

The political ruler acting as the head of the state should be concerned to establish a Buddhist style of public life, with appropriate institutions for the public welfare, in conjunction with the Sangha.” He insisted that morality and politics should be wedded together. Corruption would lead a country nowhere.”

Buddha further dispelled the notion of divine beings, "Who would never come to one's help even if one prayed to them day and night, so stop depending on gods or demigods who may or may not exist. Has anyone seen them? If not then simply rely on your own intelligence and efforts. Your choices in life make or mar your future. Your destiny is in your own hands. Trust yourself, know yourself and be constantly aware of your surroundings by observing mindfulness. By inculcating high morals and strong mental discipline, you would be able to bring out your true potential. Remove complex religious rituals from your routine and learn to lead a simple life devised by nature for us. There are no demons or angels. It is all in your imagination. Cleanse your mind by watching your breath and meditation. Learn to pursue the right path to salvation. Meaning peace of mind. An unagitated mind without any sense of guilt or regret is the way to follow. Make logic and reasoning your gods and compassion and universal love, your goddesses."

Although Yashodhara's name had been cleared in connection to Rahul's paternity and she had reclaimed some of her dignity, yet she wanted to hear straight from the Buddha about it. So on the next occasion of his visit to the palace she told Rahul, "Go on son, ask your father for your inheritance." Because she wondered that since Prince Siddhartha had abdicated his right to the throne, is Rahul still the rightful claimant for the succession?

Rahul went to the Buddha and tugged at his sleeve,"Father, please give me my inheritance." The Buddha who was busy talking to his uncle did not pay heed. His son tugged at his other sleeve. Gautama excused himself and told the child, "Come to the retreat tomorrow and I'll give you your inheritance."**

"I'll go with you today and come back tomorrow with my mother after your preachings."

"All right son, now go and play. I am talking to my uncle."

Next day when Gautama's family visited the Nigrodh van they were shocked to see little Rahul with Shariputra. His head shaven, his clothes orange coloured and he was holding a wooden begging bowl awkwardly, not knowing 'what to do with it'! Prajapati and Yashodhara had tears in their eyes while agitated king went to see Siddhartha.

"Love for our children, Lord, is too deep to explain,... it would be good if the venerable ones did not give the going forth without the parent's consent. It is enough that the Exalted One himself renounced his sovereignty...please order Rahul not to go forth so that the royal family be not made extinct."

"Rahul has chosen his path himself, your majesty, even though he is of such tender age. We don't take bhikshus in our Sangha before the age of twenty. He could still change his mind if he wants to."

"Okay, but please make a rule, that no more than one son would be ordained from one family."

Gautama turned to Maudgalyana and spoke, "Please make sure that our king's command is followed."

Slowly and gradually the crowd dispersed. When Mrigi with Anand approached Tathagat he looked at her questioningly. She said to Anand, "Son, wish your father." The twelve year old bowed and touched Tathagat's feet. Despite the Buddha's attendants being there. This time they did not object.

After coming home Anand argued with his mother, "Why can't I be ordained like Rahul?"

"Because I don't want you to!" She turned her back and went to her room crying. She was still resentful towards Siddhartha who left her so soon after her marriage. She still craved to be with him. But everyone in Kapilvastu now knew that he was never coming back as a householder.

Buddha wanted to settle Devdatta's fate as quickly as possible. He suggested to the king, "His punishment for his misdeed towards Gopa should be to ordain him, Your Highness. He might learn some discipline by the austere lifestyle of the Sangha."

King answered, "I would need to talk to his parents first. Though he himself won't be willing."

Drotodan and Mangala agreed with Siddhartha's choice.

Nand, Gautama's half-brother was also suggested by the Buddha to do the same and in an unguarded moment he agreed too and was ordained with the king's permission. Who had responded to the Buddha's request saying, "He is good at heart but does not have enough strength of character to be a successful king. He is somewhat whimsical and gets carried away with his feelings."

"Don't worry your majesty, I'll keep him with me for a few months to build up his ethical and moral discipline as well as his will power. After that he can make up his mind."+

Nanamoli: Life of the Buddha. ~~Abhishkramana Suttra.

+Going to Sangha was considered by the elites as an educational and disciplinarian opportunity.

Nanda was engaged to a girl at the palace, Janapada Kalyani who was very beautiful, and Nanda loved her passionately. But at the monastery he never got a chance to see her. Because Gautama made sure of that. He realised that the time has come to choose between the Sangha life and his Kalyani. The Buddha asked him, "Do you want to be able to control your mind and serve the humanity or do you want to live an ordinary, self-centered life with your beloved?"

Nand who loved Tathagat, his half-brother and the relaxed monastery's life, agreed to stay. However, it took him a long time to forget Kalyani.

Thus, the family, the Buddha had left behind was slowly and gradually coming to him.

After ordaining many new disciples the Buddha and a few hundred of his followers after six months, moved back the same way they had come, leaving the rest behind.

*****

Chapter - 15

Support of the Elites

BUDDHA SOUGHT TO BUILD AN EMPIRE,
OF SAGES AND MEN OF COMPASSION.
THE HELP WAS NIGH OF KINGS AND ESQUIRES,
AND EXPERIENCED HERMITS AND SAINTS.

In the hierarchy of castes, after the Brahmans, and warrior class, come the Vaishyas or the traders. They were allowed to study the Vedas yet were considered inferior to the first two. Some of them initially farmers became rich landlords. Others chose to pursue varied money-making ventures. They would not only move in caravans by road but also used the sea routes to their advantage, accumulating great fortunes. This new bourgeoisie class set up guilds. They were given high posts at the court and were much needed by the non-productive Brahmans and Buddhist monks, who were dependent on the society for their survival. With their help and that of the royalty, number of the Buddha's lay disciples became innumerable. This business class even helped the king with financial help during war or famine.

The former summer palace of Siddhartha where he had spent maximum of his time as a young man was also donated by King Shuddhodan to the Buddhist Sangha along with its extensive lawns and lotus ponds. Shariputtra was given the responsibility of turning the property fit for a monastic living. Thus, due to support of many wealthy followers, Sangha was established in the major cities of the north-east and west of Jambudvipa. Now Kapilvastu too became an important center for the Buddha's philosophies.

Other significant monasteries were established due to the generosity of people like Sudatta who established Jetavan. King Prasenjit was always helping the Buddha. The Magadh retreat at the Bamboo forest or 'Venuvan', the Buddha's cave at the vulture peak on Grdhrakuta mountain was used by the Buddha due to king Bimbisar's generosity. Who had made steps for him to climb up.

Buddhism flourished in Isipatana because of kings and wealthy mercantile class, of Kashi. King Manu of Vaishali had given a forest for the Sangha monastery, Kutagarahshala. Amrapali donated the mango grove. Lady Vishaka too was a great benefactress of the Sangha, though a lay disciple.

Buddha's relationship, however, with King Prasenjit and lady Vishakha was of special importance.

Lady Vishakha was a married woman from a rich family. She had sixteen children and eight grandchildren yet when one of her grandchildren died she was grief-stricken. She came to Buddha for solace who asked, "How old was your grandchild Vishakha?"

She replied with tears in her eyes. "He was only three Tathagat. He died of typhoid."

"That is very sad. I can understand your loss. Do you like to have many grandchildren?"

"Oh yes, the enlightened one; I would like to have as many children and grandchildren as the people of Sarasvati!"

"In that case, be prepared to cry constantly. Because if your family became so large one or the other death would occur every day. What will you do then?"

Vishakha was thoughtful for a moment then bowed her head to the Buddha. "I understand my Lord. The many the attachments the more the suffering."

Lady Vishakha had been a lay disciple of the Buddha since long. She too being a wealthy patron like Amrapali had donated, lands, got monasteries built and parks donated as the teaching centers and sanctuaries for the rainy season.

One day she observed, "Tathagat, usually people give left overs to bhikshus. I noticed that the food they eat is not healthy enough. Please allow me to offer them food everyday as long as they are in my city."

She was often seen coming to Buddha's retreat with cartfuls of clothings for thousands of monks. Even gave packets of food to those monks who were ready to embark on a journey to spread the Buddha's 'way'. She provided medicines to the sick and extra clothing to the women to wrap around while having a bath in the river.

Buddha realised that she is not only a valuable asset to the Sangha but is intelligent and sharp. He asked her one day, "Vishakha, I find your suggestions about the Practice very useful. I want to appoint you as one of my trusted advisers."

She helped the Buddha during the early stages of development of the Sangha, and protected his mission, to the utmost of her ability.

Tathagat believed that the two women who understood his 'Dharma' the most were MahaPrajapati and Lady Vishakha. Like Sujata, she only believed in serving the Buddha, not joining the Sangha. Like her, she was motherly towards Gautama and his religion.

*****

King Prasenjit one day, came for a visit to see the Buddha at Jetavan. He was led by Maudgalyana to his 'Sugandhi Kuti' covered by a fragrant and cool grass.

Buddha got up from his bamboo seat and offered him another one. The king was obese, with fears and demons fighting in his head yet proud of his intellectual prowess. After polite talk at first, Prasenjit suddenly questioned him.

"So Master Gautama, how can you, who are still so young and have only recently left home, possibly say that you are a sage?"*

"There are four things Your Majesty, one should not meddle with, a fire, a snake, a warrior, and a monk…you tamper with them you will either die or remain childless or hairless like a Palmyra tree."*

Prasenjit's fear that his brother Jeta might try to overthrow him because he had not produced a heir yet, was hinted at, by the enlightened one.The King, instead of getting angry became thoughtful and asked Gautama, "Please accept me as your disciple Master."

The King, however was not impressed by the Buddha's teachings in any way but he valued his wisdom as a friend. On Tathagat's advice he altered his diet. From eating bucketfuls of rice and curry he came to small portions and lost weight.

*****

Buddha had stirred the stagnant, soiled waters of the prevalent society. People who milked the ignorant masses got worried of his popularity and started conniving against him and his Sangha. Because the new philosophy, with clarity and ease was gaining strength, making the priestly class afraid of losing power. Although majority of the monks, too were of Brahaman origin.

The orthodox religion was like a big, many centuries old banyan tree, which did not let the sapling growing under its shade, flourish. Gautama

---

* 'Confessions of a Buddhist Atheist' by Stephen Bachelor. There is pun on 'hair'. Since prosenjeet was heir less.

did not care to subdue or compete with any religion. All he wanted was to let his 'way' eradicate wrong and harmful practices of Hinduism, which were like placebo rather than the bitter pill to cure. He wanted his practical wisdom to enter the realm of politics. Where an ideal monarch like Rama should rule with compassion and provide equal rights to the rich and the poor. Thus, a monarchist democratically non-partisan governance. He felt that the workers who perform the labour do not get their fair share of the produce because the owners of the land and businesses get away with most of the profits and social benefits. So, the poor despite working hard always remained poor. Now the problem was to find the ideal monarch. For which Tathagat groomed young educated men from influential families to understand his philosophy or 'practical wisdome' in depth and become uncorrupt future rulers.

*****

An example of an individual going against the Buddha was Sunakkhata. He had been his disciple who had attended on him, at Vaishali.

One day when everyone went to the city with their alms-bowls, Anand, who had been ordained when he had turned twenty, followed Sunakkhata who instead of begging for food went sunakkata towards the palace. Anand hid himself behind a pillar as the brahaman talked to the guard. An elite, who looked like one of the important members of the court came out. They both started talking in whispers near the thick pillar. Sunakkhata told the noble, "Sir the so-called Buddha is just an ordinary person. I have stayed close to him to find out. He has no divine insight into things. His teachings are only for individual benefit, not for benefit of the society."

"Good, now leave the Sangha and give lectures here and there, turning people against Gautama and his Sangha, and confuse them regarding his teachings. Our number of soldiers is reducing because young men are becoming his disciples instead. It seems that he is trying to change the course of political systems everywhere."

The courtier then gave a small pouch filled with jingling coins to the informer and left, to tell the king to reduce or forfeit the benefits awarded to the Sangha."

At the Sangha Anand confided in Shariputra about Sunakkhata. They both came to Buddha who listened to them calmly and advised, "Do not worry. A lie does not have legs, it'll fall sooner or later."

*****

Chapter - 16

The King's Demise

'Long is the road you have travelled O King,
And always did you strive to do good.
You know nothing of evil desires;
Your heart was innocent of hatred ...
Your mind is pure O King, and your death
As calm as close of a lovely day.'[1]

Yashodhara who by now had learned to follow Buddha's precepts, had started educating all the women and servants of the Seraglio, in her spare time. Channa who provided her 'Tathagat's' concepts time to time also studied from her in gratitude. Buddha's sutras, Yashodhara realised that Buddha's teachings were not merely philosophical theories but were a way of life. 'Unless those were practiced in day-to-day routine what use was the theoretical knowledge!' The Buddha wanted everyone to undergo a human revolution on personal level. Breaking the bonds of old habits and erroneous beliefs. Yashodhara still thought of Siddhartha as her husband and followed his beliefs, after scrutinising them.

The only difference was that while Gautama started with enlightenment then Dharma and eventually Sangha, Yashodhara started with Sangha, then Dharma and in the end, after being an Arahat, striving for a state of Buddha-hood, before reaching, Mahaparinirvana or the tranquil-extinction.

Buddha, for the sake of delusional people once explained the difference between nirvana and Buddha-hood to his disciple, Shariputra.

'I for their sake established expedient means,

1. 'The Life of Buddha' – A. Ferdinand – p. 206.
Tr. By Paul C. Blum (1922).

Preaching the way that ends all suffering.
And showing them nirvana but although I teach nirvana,
This is not a true extinction.
All phenomena from the very first
Have of themselves constantly borne the marks of
Tranquil Extinction.
Once the sons (and daughters) of the Buddha have carried out this path,
Then in a future existence they will be able to become Buddhas.'*
The Buddha-hood is transcendental to nirvana. It is Tranquil Extinction.

Channa after the meeting one day, informed Queen Yashodhara, "The Buddha' these days is at an important monastery in a large forest, owned by a lay disciple by the name of Ghosira and the location is also named after the owner. There, as well as at other monasteries, bhikshus with good memories are given the task of memorising the sutras and are called sutra-masters. Important sutras are recited by all the monks twice a month. Apart from these, there are precept-masters who explain Buddha's tenets to the newly ordained members. So O'Queen, do you think if we also did some thing like that in our group, we'll be helping Buddha's cause?"

Yashodhara became thoughtful and then answered, "It's a good thought Channa but we are all lay disciples. We all have other responsibilities apart from building up our moral strength and making our minds disciplined. Yes one day when Buddha accepts us women as nuns we can ask for his guidance on this matter.

Just then a maid came running. "O'Queen come quick, the king is not well I had sent someone to get the royal physician, who is right now checking his pulse.

Yashodhara and Channa briskly walked towards the king's chambers with long strides.

The vaidya doctor was bent upon the king looking into his eyes with a light, while queen Prajapati was standing with a worried expression. No other relative was told about his condition yet. King Shuddhodan called Yashodhara with a gesture and whispered in her ear when she bent low, "Send for Siddhartha." Yashodhara nodded her head and asked Channa to follow her.

"What is it doctor?" The Queen asked at length.

---

* Excerpt from the second chapt. Of Lotus Suttra.

"His brain seems sound. It could be his heart. I'll check further."

*****

Channa was driving fast his four-horse chariot while an attendant sat by his side. It was as if they were flying towards Vaishali where Gautama's sojourn was expected. They had to cross the Rohini River* at a ford, and bypass the Koliyas territory to reach the North Road to go towards east. They exchanged their horses at many places and drove alternately non-stop for many days taking all kinds of shortcuts through the various forests till they reached Kutagarshala hermitage near Vaishali.

Channa and his companion from the palace another charioteer, reached the monastery exhausted and disheveled. It was midnight. There was a hushed peace spread out in the faint mist. Hearing the chariot wheels crunching on the gravel, Nagasamala came to investigate, and immediately took them to Gautam Muni's hut. The bhikshus after their night meditation had gone off to sleep. Only the crickets were trilling. Buddha woke up and so did Shariputra and Maudgalyana. They all talked together and a decision was reached. Shariputra went to Anniruddh hut and woke him up to get instructions from the master while he would be away to check on his father along with the three of them.

The Buddha told everyone, "Get ready quick."

Then he turned to Annuruddha one of his favourite disciples, "Please take care of the Sangha while we are away. I need to fulfill my last obligations to my father." "Sure master," replied his cousin.

Gautam along with his close disciples left for Kapilvastu.* On the way he talked to them,"Thank you all for following me, without questioning. I know it is against the rules those I had propounded for my Bhikshus, to use any transportation for moving about. But to fulfill the last desire of my dying father, as my filial duty I will have to sacrifice many of my accumulated merits or 'Punyas.' You three would not be sharing my demerits." Everybody nodded but no one spoke.

It was a dark night and there were darker clouds in the sky, ready to burst any moment. No one spoke anything except the thudding hooves of the horses. Channa and his companions reined the horses turn by turn. They felt as if they were soaring on the winds. Which whooshed and buzzed past their ears. They had left the heavy clouds behind them. That is when they again resorted to the shortcuts through the jungles, crossing the rivers at fords and begging food at some hamlets to barely survive. Gautama told everyone, "Do not worry my brothers. I know my strong-willed father. He won't go away unless he sees me, in his last moments."

They entered the Hamsavati palace, at the crack of the dawn. All drenched in the heavy rain. An elderly guard, with an umbrella opened the gigantic gate and peered at Channa, astonished. Channa put his finger on his lips and gave him a stern look. He got the message. Leaving his passengers at the palace steps he and the other carriage-driver went back to their dwellings after leaving the horses at the stable along with the coach.

There was a stir inside the palace as an eunuch led them to the king's chamber. Where Prajapati was sitting next to the king touching his frail hand gently. As the attendants looked on concerned, the royal physician administered some medication.

The king's eyes were closed. His face gaunt and pale and his white hair, beard and proud mustaches were reflecting the yellow light of his bedchamber. A mild fire was burning in an alcove.

*****

"Siddhartha! Come my son!" He mumbled.

Gautama, who had reached his bedside by now answered, after wiping his hands on a small towel offered to him. "Did you recognise my footsteps father?" And he touched his father's head and forehead saying, "I give up all my accumulated merits in order to eradicate your pain."

Soon King Shuddhodan's head was devoid of all pain. Hearing him, Rahula, who had fallen asleep at the feet of his grandfather, woke up and looked at Gautama with amazed eyes. Anand who had come with his mother Mrigi, had gone to get more towels for Gautama and his bhikshus, to dry themselves up, more thoroughly.

At one side of the room, four ex-queens of Siddhartha were sitting on the carpeted floor. While Gautama was helping his father in relieving his pain. The same was being done by, Maudgalyana, Shariputra and Nagasamala on his both arms and one leg. Watching them Rahul got up and did the same with his grandfather's other leg and said, "I give up all my merits..." Gautama was amazed to see that the young prince with his innocent love and pure compassion also achieved the same results as seasoned practitioners did.

Shuddhodan opened his eyes, "As you came, my aches and pains left me son." Siddhartha nodded his head. "Now your mental agony shall

* The Theragatha Commentary informs that as Rohini river flows southwards, it separates Shakya and Koliya Kingdoms. With Koliyas being towards east. According to Rhys Davids Kapilvastu was 450 miles from Vaishali.

go too." The Buddha then talked about the impermanence of the entire phenomena.

"Life is change. Not only you my father, your entire generation is walking towards the gate of eternity. We are nothing but energy trapped in a shell of flesh and bones along with our attachments."

The king who was hardly listening, had other things on his mind. About the welfare of his people. He knew that without a competent and firm ruler his kingdom would go to a waste. As soon as he would die the vulturous enemies would kill a weak ruler. Then he spoke feebly, through Buddha's discourse, "Son my crown is lying behind you on a tall table. Tell me who is fit enough to wear it?"

Hearing this fourteen year old Rahul hid behind Gautama. Who now looked at Anand, who returned his gaze and bowed at the Buddha's feet. "My lord, I am twenty now, I take refuge in your guidance. I have selected my future as a Sutra-Master at your Sangha. I am good at memorising words!"

At this point Mrigi got up from the floor, angry and looked at her son accusingly.

"No mother. Don't say anything. I am mature enough to know my mind. I'll get trained by the Buddha and serve him and his community. He is no less than a king, who rules over a large number of population in north, west, east and towards the southern part of the entire Jambudvipa. The sangha does not go to wars to expand His Kingdom. It needs young people like me to spread his word."

As he became quiet, the silence in the dying king's chamber became heavy. Despite the 'Vaidya's' efforts, the king's breathing had become erratic. Gopa, the most tender soul was stifling her sobs in her sari and Yashodhara's consoling hand was upon her back, while they sat with other queens. The rest of the ladies were waiting outside in the courtyard, hoping to get some good sign from the king's room. Young princes were morose while they stood against a wall. Gautama looked at them one by one then gently requested the king, "Please your highness perform your last duty with grace. Who do you wan't to appoint to the throne?" He pointed at the crown which Siddhartha brought to him. He then motioned to Yashodhara to come near him with his fingers turned towards his palm. The princess came and bent low to hear his weak voice. Shuddhodan looked at Gautama who helped his father and together they placed the crown on her head.

Yashodhara was shaken up. So was everyone else. Shakyas so far had never had a lady to rule the republic. Not that it never happened in the ancient past. Yashodhara stood there and touched the crown with her hand, overwhelmed. Relieved, Shuddhodan closed his eyes for some moments and then opened them again. He spoke with effort and looked at Siddhartha, "Son please teach her, how to form an ideal republic on the pattern of monarchy, so that my people can live peacefully under her rule. She is an expert in marshal arts and can lead our warriors under the capable guidance of our commander-in-chief and the chief-minister Mahanaam!" He then turned to Queen Mahaprajapati and asked for water. His head was lifted up by Siddhartha after announcing Yashodhara, the Queen. Everyone bowed to her while some water was poured on his lips with a small spouted tumbler.

Then the king spoke for the last time. He looked at Praja, "My dear you were always so dedicated to me and I hardly showed any appreciation. I am indebted to you for everything." His head abruptly tumbled towards her.

Seeing this his queen gently shut his vacant eyes and took off her bangles and handed over to her maid. She wiped the red spot from her forehead, signifying her marital status, and rubbed her forehead on her husband's feet for the last time, with a queenly composure. Her unseen tears were her only companion for now.

The queens of Siddhartha started crying under control but the seraglio women outside started wailing and beating their breasts. Siddhartha got up and pulled the sheet over his father's face. Yashodhara placed the crown on the tall table again and asked her maid to get the holy lamp. The king's body was lifted up by his brothers and sons and placed on a mat on the floor. A lighted lamp was placed towards his head on top of a small mound of kneaded dough. Everyone sat on the floor and chanted Gayatri Mantra softly, guided by the court priest. Men got busy to make arrangements for the funeral when the king's body would move through the streets of Kapilvastu for the people to see the face of their king for the last time before his cremation.

Buddha before the final ritual announced, "King Shuddhodan in his last breath, had placed his foot into the river of Nirvana, and would get a chance to gain a full entrance into its waters, in his next lifetime."*

Siddhartha and Nand together lit the pyre. The older son went around with an earthen pot full of water, in which a hole had been made by the priest, while he circled around the burning flames and then dropped it to the ground breaking it into smithereens.

*****

* Based on Lotus Suttra.

Chapter - 17

Ruling Queen Yashodhara

THE KING BEFORE HIS DEATH
HAD PROCLAIMED YASHODHARA HIS HEIR.
SHE FELT 'A SNAKE AROUND HER NECK',
YET HONOURED THE KING'S LAST REQUEST.

Siddharth stayed in Kapilvastu for forty five days to take care of all the rituals his parents believed in and then took leave of his mother Prajapati, Yashodhara, and his uncles, aunts and cousins. While he had stayed at the Nigrodh Van there were preachings going on every day. Attended by men and women alike.

After the thirteenth day, till when the soul is suppose to stay around the place of its bodily death, a lunch was organised for the Brahamans, relatives and the council members.

Next day a meeting of the council took place in the 'Sansthagrih' hall to discuss Yashodhara's coronation. Gautama was requested to attend as an honourable guest but he declined and invited everyone for the evening discourse at the Nigrodh Park instead.

The meeting was convened by Mahanaam on a serious note. Mahaprajapati along with other lady-members sat in the sidelines, facing Rajans. An oral voting was the usual norm and was done. Mahanaam Senapati, the army commander, Dhrotodan and many others along with the ladies were in favour. Those who were indecisive didn't matter because they were less than half of the total number. Prajapati stood up and folded her hands in front of the assembly.

"Honourable members! I am grateful to you all for respecting the last wish of your Chief Shuddhodan."

A priest came forward and marked a red 'tilak' on Yashodhara's forehead and announced, "The auspicious day for her royal 'abhishek' and coronation is after thirty two days."

The meeting was over without much fan-fare.

On the appointed day, the crowning ceremony was simpler, than what it might have been for a prince. The hallway of Sansthagrih was decorated with tinsels and flowers as the members entered one by one in their dazzling clothes and ornamented turbans. The ladies sat in their side galleries; many of them wearing white saris. When all were seated, Mahaprajapati entered from the main entrance after the crier announced that the two honourable Queens are about to enter the court. The members, all stood up with folded hands. They both walked the length of the multi-coloured carpet and took their seats, slightly lower than the king's empty throne.

After all were seated Mahanaam who was still standing, addresses the members, "I hope we all are proud to have a queen as a ruler." And paused to look at everyone. A few faces looked the other way. The chief minister continued, "It'll be a good precedence to show the other republics that we are pioneers in giving equal rights to our women. There was a half-hearted applause from the men but the women cheered."

Then he addressed Prajapati, "Please O' Honourable Queen assist the court priest with the inauguration."

Yashodhara was dressed as a nun with a brown bandana on her forehead and was wrapped in an ochre cotton sari. Her bosom was covered with a broad cloth tied at her back and further covered by a royal, yellow silk stole with gold border. While she stood on the pedestal dignified, flanked by Queen Prajapati in a white attire and the royal chaplain, a red mark of 'kumkum' was placed by the priest between her brows and auspicious rice and flower petals were sprinkled on her, along with holy water of the Ganga. Her beautiful face glistened with melancholic excitement. Chant of Sanskrit shlokas was sanctifying her thoughts and the ceremony. She was beginning to be imbued with a heavy sense of responsibility. Queen Prajapati placed Shuddhodan's crown on her bald head, while everyone applauded. Yashodhara stood as if carved in bronze.

The chief-minister requested the newly anointed queen, "As our chief, your highness, please say a few words before we start the administrative proceedings."

Queen Yashodhara started in an authoritative tone, "Our late king had made a proclamation when The Buddha visited Kapilvastu last time, now to give respect to both the dignitaries I need your support."

A silence followed and she looked at the disinterested faces of the members and continued. "I would like to base my policies on the advice given in the Vedas and to some extent in Gautam Muni's preachings. Hence to begin with, I would like to ban animal sacrifices at once."

Before members could react Mahanaam requested, "Those in favour please stand up."

First of all Amritodan stood up and questioned, "Are we all suppose to give up non-vegetarian food your highness?"

Some heads nodded in agreement to the question.

The queen replied, "Although our religion does not believe in killing of any living being except in self defence, I do not expect you to constrict your choice of diet. At the same time I would like to ban religious animal sacrifices. Especially the 'Ashvamedha' ritual. Nowhere in our scriptures animal or human sacrifice is advised. People have twisted the language of the Vedas and abused them. The sacrifices were meant to be of lentils, rice from our fields and sweetmeats prepared at home, along with purified butter and 'Soma'* the divine juice of a certain plant. The bloody and ostentatious events fill up the pockets of the priests and glorify the power of kings rather than that of gods. And the public gets something to talk about, for long. However, since the non-vegetarian food is staple diet of warriors, especially horse meat makes them strong. They may indulge in it in moderation but there is no need to make a spectacle out of it."

"What if the Gods become angry and destroy us?"

"If we are his children, He won't. I am sure! A political system with a sound and logical ideology avoiding extremes, is all in line. I agree that a kingdom can not be run without violence but we can try and avoid it as far as possible. Why do we fear God more than our enemies? The amount of money spent on sacrificial rituals can be put to better use, benefiting our poor public and wounded soldiers or their widowed wives; as well as some money could go to the homes of those prisoners who have left behind small children with their defenceless mothers. Don't you agree Pradyuman? You are the financial adviser, you should know."

"That should work out My Lady."

The court priest was shocked. "Forgive me Queen, you are trying to abolish centuries old traditional ideas. Your revolutionary decision can destroy the clan."

"Sorry Sir, to contradict you. If our republic is to be destroyed, it would be due to the result of our foolish, past mistakes, which I won't repeat at present! In Mahabharata it is clearly mentioned that brahamans should not perform or preside over violent acts."

"Though Bhishma Pitamah advised Yudhishtra, the king, "Be the king, win heaven, protect the virtuous, (yet) kill the wicked." A reasonable punishment was not considered violence."

She continued, looking at the high priest, "You must have heard Mundak Upanishad, it says—

'The fools that delight in (the) sacrificial ritual as the highest spiritual good go again and again through the cycle of old age and death.

Abiding in the midst of ignorance, wise only according to their own estimate, thinking themselves to be learned, but really obtuse, these fools go round in circle like blind men led by one who is himself blind.

Regarding sacrifice and merit as most important the deluded ones do not know of any other higher spiritual good…'"

The compromising attitude of king Shuddhodan was replaced by a firm leader.

The stunned oligarchy members twisted and turned in their seats, aghast and were trying to absorb the implications. The lights from the 'mashal' torches were flickering on their humiliated pale faces while a fierce autumn wind was building up outside. The wind of change. Their expectations of turning the Queen into a puppet became dubious.

Mahanaam rose from his seat and spoke in a cool tone, "Maybe most of you need to ponder over this question in privacy. We can have half an hour break and then resume with the voting."

He clapped and the girls came in with drinks and snacks while the ladies retired indoors.

That day the resolution was passed yet the ripples of discontent were visible on many of the faces especially those of the Brahamans.

When Gautama heard the news at Vaishali he was glad to know that as he had set the eight-spoked wheel of Dharma in motion at Isipatana, Yashodhara had set the wheel of politico-social change, in motion at Kapilvastu. Little did he know that the powerful priestly class of Brahmans would not let the power slip through their hands so easily. Siddharth and Yashodhara were in for a fight with the orthodoxy.

During the interlude the ladies were enjoying their soft drinks and fragrant juices in another private chamber. They were excitedly chatting about the new rule proposed. Mahaprajapati was talking to Yashodhara, "You did great as a chief. Just keep up your confidence and follow

Gautama's suggestions regarding politics. Which should reduce the big gap between rich and poor, as he always desired."

Queen Utpalvarna added, "Our Mother Queen is right. Equal opportunities for all! This is the age of growth due to the benefits of iron technologies. Our harvests are bountiful, making the traders and kings richer yet the needy are still where they were."

Mangala who was sitting on the other side of Yashodhara joined the conversation, "I too agree with Mahaprajapati ji. Keep it up daughter! Form a society which believes in fare-share"

"But I feel as if a snake is coiled around my neck, 'Chachi' Aunt! It is like swimming against the current."

Just then a girl entered to announce that the meeting would resume soon. The ladies got up from the upholstered divan with velvety bolsters and moved towards the two galleries.

After the voting the results were announced. Fifty-one to forty-nine percent. The resolution was passed.

A few more administrative issues were addressed. And an allowance was setup for the wounded and maimed in the war and the war-widows, from money that would be saved by abolishing 'Bali' or animal sacrifices.

There was an uproar in the priestly class who would be loosing a good income coming from sacrifices after the proclamation was made formal through a drummer.

A committee was formed to see to it that the new rules were implemented properly. The hill-people were not the type to be intimidated by the wrath of Brahmans who considered themselves divine middle-men between the communities and the gods. However other religious exercises were left untouched to pacify them. So the corporate style of government now also gave importance to Buddhist monastic orders which provided a model for the clan-based republican states.

The Brahmanical forces were now challenging the new emerging civilisation in a subdued manner. A social revolution was underway. The impoverished were happy. Trying to please gods had been an expensive affair and the Buddhist philosophy was simpler to follow.

Yashodhara in the meantime was facing the thrust of a storm valiantly. Many dissatisfied members of the republic were strategising against her.

*****

---

* Soma – a drink made from the juice of 'Asclepias acida', a climbing plant which thrives in the mountains. It was first used in ancient Persia. Hindu mythology (Rg. Veda) believed it to he a drink of gods. It is similar to the greek drink, ambrosia. It can cause hallucinations.

By the next meeting of the council, things became murky and almost rebellious. Buddha's ideologies were followed due to respect for him, but the general public was instigated by the brahmans to revolt against the new laws, or be prepared to be cursed by their priestly class, if they ignored the early Vedic values.

Whereas in truth, Buddha had often spoken that, "I am not really against the Vedic norms. My new concepts are not a belief system, nor a rival faith to the Vedic cults and practices which prevail under the influence of the priestly class. I simply want people to self-discipline their minds and bodies so that they could make logically correct decisions in life and become the masters of their own destinies. They need to forget blind faith in the Vedas which they do not understand anyway. And come out of the shadow of fear, in connection to god. This would give them a great sense of mental freedom and self reliance. This gratification which comes after following the right path could lead to self realisation and happiness.

The sufferings of life; sickness, old-age and death do not disappear but the mind and heart learn to cope with the miseries, reasonably and calmly. I never asserted to be extraordinary. I never claimed to have any divine revelation. I simply wanted to do the job of a shepherd guiding his mistaken sheep on the right path home."

His approach was practical and psychological, having a deep insight into things, which could help everyone to make the right choices that would lead to successful results. 'Buddha was born a Hindu and he died a Hindu.'

*****

Yashodhara while speaking to council members in the next assembly tried to placate them. "Respected members, I am not trying to make people follow Gautam Muni, I am only asking you all to take benefit from a wise enlightened soul who has some valid points to make while advising us to choose a middle way between a monarchy and a republican state. Where the final decision would be the Chief's but an advisory committee would guide him from time to time."

An uproar rose among the members. The chief of Pithoragarh got up and spoke bitterly, "This is getting too far. New ideas are good but should be applied in practice gradually. Such cataclysmic changes could spoil the balance of administration."

Mahanaam intervened, "Please Sir, calm down. So far only one resolution has been passed for the welfare of lowest section of society. No one is trying to put the brahmans or us down. This way the brahmans can choose some other profession as well and we must learn to be more flexible towards our modern society. That's all!"

"That's not all dear Sir! That's not all. You shall see!" and he plopped into his cushioned chair with a red face.

Another member got up and expressed his view curtly, "With due respect I think the inexperienced queen should go back to her preachings and social work rather than trying to shake up the entire Shakya kingdom. As it is, our young warriors are disappearing from the army, following The Buddha. Some monarchs are even conniving to kill our former prince. Who, they think is teaching his bhikshus a life of indolence and non-violence. In today's strife ridden society who can survive without wars. Our economy too will suffer if we don't fill our treasury with warfare. Then who will support the non-profitable section of bhikkhus and other ascetics?"

A pregnant silence! The Queen then announced, "Honourable members I quite understand your fear of a new social order. So I comply with your decision. However I am not going anywhere before Late King's first 'barsi' (annual prayer day, for the departed soul). So, please bear with me for that long!"

The queen composed herself gracefully, before addressing the congregation once again."I am grateful to the intelligentsia for accepting my last resolution atleast so far. Discussions are healthy. I don't mind them." Unobtrusive snickering went unnoticed. Then she turned towards Mahanaam, "Please request the Chief of Mahamatras to evaluate our military footings. And any other matter our honourable members might want to discuss."

Next morning Yashodhara after her prayer with the royal priest attended to various responsibilities as the Chief of her Republic. In the end when everyone left a skinny bhikhuni entered in dirty saffron clothes. Sat down on the floor near the Queen and whispered in a hushed tone.

'I was in the town of Pithoragarh. At first I spent the night at the resting stopover of Lateshar Shrine where pilgrims bound for Kailash Mansarovar were given shelter and food. I was all ears to hear any gossip that floated in the air to leak any secret about Chief Tapodan. Nothing. I begged around the fort, in the narrow lanes and the market places for any clue. No luck again. I even frequented the Nakuleeshvar temple dedicated to King Pandu's son Nakul, and the Chandika Ghat Mandir.

In the end I trudged towards the foothills on a stony track. After climbing throughout the pine forests uphill, I was breathless when out of the bushes emerged a leopard. I ran for my life when I fell, the beast was on top of me. I was squeezed under its weight when a powerful tribal appeared holding a bow and pushed the bleeding animal aside. The sharp arrow sticking from its dead body.

"Why are you here sister in this wilderness? This is not a safe place for you."

"Thanks for saving my life young man. I just wanted some peaceful place to meditate."

"Better go now. Leave!" He commanded in a stern tone.

"Leopards usually stay in high altitudes. He must not have found a prey so might have ventured down."

"Sorry." I meekly ran down the hill till he couldn't see me.

"Cut the story short my dear." The Queen admonished gently.

"When the fog started setting in I sneaked up again and found…"

The Queen offered her some water to ease her parched throat and she continued. "… a huge clearing surrounded by ghostly tall trees, faintly visible from the 'mashal' torches burning at the openings of many caves. A few hefty, wild tribals were moving around with bows, arrows and axes."

"I found a small empty cave outside their arena and hid behind my blanket shivering till morning."

"At dawn I heard some voices and crawled out, enveloped in my cover to find the tribals standing in rows, behind a thick layer of mist, all dressed up in military uniforms and ready with their weapons. A Mahamatra officer started to train them in war tactics. The drill continued and I strode down the hill covered with a thin film of snow, reaching the valley. I was lucky to find a bullock-cart, coming in our direction."

"Thanks Shikha you are turning into a good spy but next time be more concise," and she placed a few silver coin in her hand.

Shikha left the room blessing the guard at the door, "Our Queen is so generous to us bkkhus!"

After breakfast The Chief sent for the army commander and the prime minister to come to her in a private chamber.

The three sat and discussed the situation at Pithoragarh. After listening to Yashodhara the commander commented, "It is obvious that Chief Tapodan is secretly increasing his military strength. But for what we do not know yet."

Mahanaam who was in deep thought reminded them that an invitation from the Governor of Pithoragarh is awaiting a reply. He is planning to perform a 'yajna' to satisfy the Goddess beforehand so that no drought appears when the crops are thirsty for water.

The Queen answered at length. "Let's accept the royal invitation and see for ourselves what's in store for us!"

The 'senapati' commander suggested, "Let's add an extra platoon of fifty soldiers, as a precaution."

"Good strategy. But the information about wild brutal tribes being trained, should stay among three of us." And the meeting was adjourned.

Queen Mangala was excited to hear the news that after all her brother has reconciled to the idea not to break his link with King Shuddhodan's family.

The procession of royal chariots surrounded by soldiers was led by the bards.

After having many breaks with tents erected for food and rest the party reached the ancient historical town of Pithoragarh mentioned in the 'Puranas.' The 'yajna' for better crop was performed with pomp and show the next day on 'puranmasi' (full moon).

The festival was organised in a verdant park surrounded by pine trees. There were rows and rows of small, square 'havan kunds'(vessels) around each sat two couples to perform individually with the chants of 'swaha' (Manyanti goddess of sacrifices in the Vedas), at the end of each Mantra. A group of young priests was reciting the mantras in unison so that all the dignitaries could hear it loud and clear.

The fires were lit at the same time in all the vessels and the fragrant holy smoke was pervading the ten directions, as the 'samagri' mixed with rice, lentils, camphor, oily sesame seeds along with 'ghee' (purified butter) were offered reverently to the holy fire.

Queen Yashodhara sat with her girl companions, Renu, Ganga, Rohini and Surma. She whispered before the 'puja'(prayer) started, 'Yajana' is supposed to purify one's mind, body and the environment, yet I am not sure of the effect it'll have on our Governor."

Renu replied, "Maybe he keeps Dharma (religion) and politics in separate boxes."

After a sumptuous dinner, Yashodhara was talking to Tapodan while the poor were being fed outside the huge hall.

"Brother, our duty calls us at home so we intend to leave tomorrow morning before the crack of dawn."

Tapodan answered rather testily, "I am sure kings and queens have serious responsibilities. But let my sister stay for some more days with me."

Chapter - 18

The Nuns

THE COOLING SHADE OF BUDDHA'S BLESSINGS
SAVES US FROM THE SCORCHING SUN,
AND THORNS AND ROCKS AND BLISTERING FEET.'

At first, the Buddha was reluctant to admit women to his Sangha because it was a huge responsibility to keep them safe from corrupt men, mostly outsiders. When he had visited his hometown at the death of his father Mahaprajapati wanted to become a nun. But he had answered, "I am sorry mother the time is not right yet, wait a little longer please." But she and Yashodhara decided to follow literally on the Buddha's footsteps, after he was gone.

In Kapilvastu and Giriviraj, as the Buddha's popularity increased young men were joining his Sangha in large numbers. With husbands, fathers, brothers and sons gone the widowed women were left to fend for themselves and their families. Buddha however never suggested anything about fatherless children although women could become lay disciples. Some scholars blamed Shakya Muni for this error. Whereas men with many children to take care of, could have chosen to be lay followers and still get the benefits of his practice. In any case it appeared that Buddha was targeting the youth.

When Shuddhodan was gone his faithful women did not want to live in the seraglio. But Buddha told them, "The time is not ripe yet."

With Mahaprajapati the leader and Yashodhara the follower, most of them, one fine day after Shuddhodan's first death anniversary marched towards east. It was as if they still held their loyalty to their prince. These women who had lived almost all their lives together were like one family. They wanted to be together under whatever circumstances. Their reason to become nuns was hardly the practice of Buddha's philosophy. Relationships were more important to them. Mrigi also joined the group, along with Gopa, Utpalvarna and Siddharth's other queens, if there were any. Mrigi was attached to her son as well as Siddhartha so she thought that this way at-least she would be able to see them. Yashodhara felt the same way with Rahul gone, along with Anand. Both being the youngest disciples. Many of the dancing girls and maids also joined the toughest path for their lives. Thus in total about five hundred women dressed in ocher saris with heads shaved and barefooted, undertook the long walk of twenty five yojana from Hamsavati palace of Kapilvastu, towards Vaishali where Buddha was residing at that time.

It was a long and arduous journey for the ones who were delicately brought up at the palace. As the group of royal ladies walked the paths, the people of Kapilvastu were gawking at them in awe. Many of them came forward and presented them with gifts especially to Mahaprajapati and Yashodhara. Which they kept along with their alms bowl in their make-do bags made out of a piece of rectangular cotton cloth, knotted at the two ends and slung over their shoulders. Those who had children they left them in the care of the elderly or other ladies of the seraglio who still had many servant girls working there as slaves.

They walked and walked on the rough road strewn with thorns and sometimes pointed stones. Bathed in the rivers, naked because they did not have an extra set of clothes. Small hamlets on the way filled their alms' bowls with food. They had never seen such a large group of Bhikshunis, most of whom were beautiful and dignified in their bearing. Many of them developed fever or other problems en route due to fatigue. Then they would take rest in some forest park; weary of lecherous hounds, more than the real ones. The few eunuchs and women-warriors had also come along to go to Buddha's refuge and had guarded the ladies with staffs and piled up stones. The warriors still had their lances and arrows to shoot.

Bye and bye they reached their destination. Filthy, and exhausted with bleeding, blistered feet and painful expressions. They could barely stand on their feet. But a monk at the entrance of the grove would not let them in because women were not allowed in the 'all-male cloister'. They all were highly disappointed and just collapsed on the sides of the bamboo doorway. Mahaprajapati was weeping but Yashodhara sat resolutely next to her sister-in-law Nand Sundari.

When Anand saw their miserable condition, covered with dust and half dead, his breast was full of sorrow and his eyes filled with tears, and he asked Queen Gautami, "Why have you come? For what reason have you endured such hardships? Have the Shakyas been driven from their city by the enemy? Why does the mother (of Buddha) remain in such a place?"

He goes to the Buddha, with a heavy heart while a monk comes to offer boiled and strained-water to relieve their parched throats. They all sat or lay down under the cool shade of a mango trees and waited for Anand to come back with news from Tathagat.

Buddha outside his straw and wattle hut, was watching his breath, sitting on a Bamboo stool, when Anand, his son and attendant approached him. He talked about the request from his mother and wife along with other ladies. Buddha refused. He replied,

"Be careful Anand of the going forth of women."

Anand beseeched him again and he repeated,

"Anand seek not to have females admitted to the profession."

Since Buddha was slightly biased towards Anand, Kaludayin and Chandak unlike his other disciples; so when Anand insists, "My lord, it is right that women should be admitted to the profession; when you delivered the Budhvamsa discourse you made known that this was one of the institutions of the twenty-four Buddhas[1] who have preceded you." They had women members, earlier," then Buddha smiled, "Okay I agree but they would need to be very careful about protecting themselves from other men."

Anand still stood in front of the Buddha hesitantly, "What more?" he was asked. "Lord, they have a few eunuchs with them from the palace!"

Buddha became thoughtful. He couldn't condemn the transgenders, for they were made by nature or the men of power, that way. Monks may not easily accept them; even if they do it could lead to some cases of sexual misconduct. Whereas women were use to living with them. Besides they may be helpful in the women's quarters. He believed that all men have some feminine qualities in them and all women have some masculine ones. Besides all creatures have a right to Buddhahood.

However, after Buddha's demise, queers were not allowed in the Sangha.

At length Buddha made his decision, "Okay let them join the women's sections of the Sangha and dress and behave like other Bhikshunies."

1. During the two eons (Glorious and Virtuous) many Buddhas existed. In the Glorious Eon there were 1000 of them. Vipasyin was 998th. Gautam was the 4th in the Virtuous and Kashyapa was the 3rd, who transmitted the Dharma to Shakyamuni.

Anand bowed at his feet and elated he went to his grandmother to give the good news.

The first night of women from Samsavati was spent in Amrapali's mango grove. Next day they were moved to a nearby forest, not too far from the Ganga with the king's permission. And started building their own huts with help from Chandak, Kaludayin and Anand along with the strong eunuchs. Mahaprajapati was asked to rest while others worked. She sat under a tree and watched her breath with closed eyes. Many shanties were erected in the forest, near the city. Utpalvarna refused to share her cottage, which she had built herself, alone. Mahaprajapati was appointed the 'chief of all the nuns'. However, in reality Yashodhara was the one who took charge of the women's hermitage, as she had earlier organised her seraglio. Everyone felt at home with the thought of their prince's presence. Their life seemed to have come back to near normalcy. The only difference was the palace was transformed into a cloister. Their king and family was with them.

According to a Sinhalese account the Buddha says,

"Are the (Buddha) born in this world only for the sake of men? Assuredly it is for the benefit of females, as well. When I delivered the 'Tirokudha-Sutra', many women entered the paths, as did also many (goddesses) when I delivered the Abhidharmma in (Tryastrimsha heaven). Have not (Vishakha) and many other (laywomen), entered the paths? The entrance is open for women as well as men.

*****

Coming back to Vishakha, her family had moved from Vaishali to Sarasvati, before her marriage. Her father, Dhananjaya a wealthy treasurer of the court, also had lands and other businesses in the city. Where an unusual custom was practiced. On an annual public holiday, high born maidens of marriageable age would go on foot to bathe in the river accompanied by their attendants. Young men from good families would stand on the roadside to look at them with garlands in their hands. If any of them fell for a pretty girl he would throw the garland in her neck, to show his choice. Now it would be for the parents to decide whether the particular boy is suitable for her. The girls coming from overprotective families were not bold enough to negotiate the marriage proposal themselves. Eight brahmans were seen standing alongside the young men, as representatives of another wealthy man, Migara of the same city to find a suitable match for his son, Punnavaddana Kumara. A girl who possesses the 'five beauties.' 'Beautiful bones, hair, flesh, skin and youth.'

All of a sudden there was a flash rain and everyone ran for shelter except Vishakha who did not alter her pace though getting drenched. She was being watched with curiosity. When she reached the shelter, one of the brahmans standing there asks her, "Why didn't you run like others?" she answered demurely, "Our parents take great care of us as we are growing up because one day they would marry us in another good family. If I had run on the slippery road and had fallen resulting in some damage to my body or broken limb I wouldn't be able to get married and become a burden on my parents."

The eight Brahmans talked to her a little more and concluded that she 'possessed wisdom and her intelligence was as keen as the edge of a diamond…'

When during their interaction with the sixteen year old beauty they learned about her worthy family and wealthy father, they threw the garland of flowers over her head.

Now Vishakha discussed with them about the family of their client wisely and concluded that it would be a perfect match for her. She sent a message to her father, through one of her attendants, 'Please father, send a chariot for me as I have chosen my suitor. As you know, after being garlanded the girl is not supposed to walk on the road.' *

Her wedding, was honoured by the presence of King Prasenjit along with his entire family.

Considering the wise and bold step taken by her during those conservative times puts Vishakha in a class of her own. Her wisdom was much trusted by the Buddha. She was always ready to share with Buddha, the huge burden of managing the Sangha. Just like so many other experienced and faithful disciples.

Vishakha once sold her jewels to build a monastery known as Pubbarma or Eastern monastery. Some of the ornaments, no one could afford to buy, she bought back herself. She had helped Buddha in many other ways as well.

*****

When a nun became pregnant in the sequestered nuns' residences, at Sarasvati everyone wondered. The novice nun was crying and saying, "Maybe I was pregnant when I came here after my husband's death."

---

* Jataka Tales.

Devdatta wanted her kicked out but Vishakha took charge, after taking permission from the Buddha. She went to her hut and behind a makeshift curtain checked her condition. She discussed the situation with Gautama and they both decided to let her have her child in her hut. Vishakha provided medical assistance during her delivery. After a few months the baby was adopted by King Prasenjit himself.

Those were however very unsafe times for unprotected women. According to Vinaya Pitaka, in Pali literature, crime was rampant in those times. Most common, were robberies and sexual assaults on helpless women under exposed circumstances.

Once a young nun was coming back home through the forest, a ruffian barred her way. He said to her, "You are young and beautiful come with me. I'll provide you with all the comforts, clothes and jewels."

Fear rose from her belly like a snake but she bravely took charge of the situation and confronted him.

"Really! What is it you like about me?"

"Your eyes are beautiful."

She flashed out her razor and shouted with indignant fury pointing the blade at her eyes, "If I destroy my eyes, would you still want me?"

The rogue got scared with her defiance and as he saw a king's patrolman coming their way, he absconded.

The nun told her story to other nuns and through monks it reached the Buddha. Who looked at Anand, "See for yourself son, the heavy responsibilities which come from admitting the women to the Sangha. However the king has announced severe punishment for those who trouble the Buddhists."

Anand looked at his feet and apologised, "But they were hoping to be safe under your umbrella!"

"I am afraid so! I'll ask King Prasenjit to do something about it."

Before Gautama got a chance to do so, another misfortune happened from within the Sangha.

*****

The women from the ministry would start from their huts together for collecting alms and later, they would spread out in different areas. On reaching home, Utpalvarna went to her lone hut after sharing the meal with other nuns. And lay down on her straw bed after meditation. It had started drizzling outside. She covered herself with her spare sari which Vishakha had provided every nun with, so that they did not have to bathe naked in the rivers sometimes in company of prostitutes who laughed at them.

She had snuffed the flame out of her tiny lamp when from the dark, emerged a muscular hand and clamped her mouth. Despite her struggle she was brutally raped.

As the debauch man was leaving, Gautama's ex-queen called out on an impulse, "Devdatta!" The cruel face turned and looked at her. She could discern his sensuous lips and glittery snake-like eyes in the dark.

Next day when the Buddha came to know that the filthy louse who raped Utpalvarna had come slithering in the dark as she lay on her bed before she came in to sleep, he decided to meet Prasenjit urgently.

"Your majesty our women live in the forest, where you have kindly allowed them to. Yet they are not safe from … evil-minded men inflamed by lust may conduct towards them with disrespect and arrogance, do them violence and bring their religious life to naught…"

Prasenjit who had great respect for The Buddha understood his problem and a monastery for alms-woman was built within the city.

A new rule was passed by Gautama. Women would not go alone in dangerous places and no nun would sleep all by herself.

Prajapati and Yashodhara were heart-broken to hear about Utpalvarna's tragedy. Senior nuns consoled her and Gopa became her companion.

*****

Ajatshattru, side tracked Devdatta after the successful coup d'état, and forcing his father Bimbisar in prison to starve him to death. Devdatta was bitter about his deceit even after becoming a monk. But again he decided to make the jackass, his father in the time of need. In order to break the harmony of the Sangha he decided to go to the King for help.

First he started sowing the seeds of dissension amongst the bhikshus at the Bamboo forest.

Then he suggested to Buddha, "Don't you think Tathagat that we monks have an easy life. The rules should be made stricter."

Buddha disagreed. "I do not think so. I don't believe that one has to torture oneself in order to understand the moral aspect of Dharma."

"Well, your ideas clash with mine"

"It appears so." Buddha answered calmly.

"I think I'll discuss the issue with the ruling king Ajatshattru who has recently been blessed with a son."

"Go ahead spit-licker. Do what you like. You are a lazy bum who does not want to work to achieve anything. Be it a crown or the Sangha! "

Anand who was standing unobtrusively to one side asked later, "Master, I've never heard you use such harsh language to anyone."

"He is like a sick child who needs a bitter pill to cure him of his delusions. I hope it helps, though his decease has become chronic."

*****

"Hail O Majesty!" Devdatta came to his court, to congratulate him. Ajatshattru invited him to wait in his private chamber. After a few hours he came. Devdatta instead of meditating during the wait was planning how best he could destroy Buddha's reputation.

Devdatta got up and folded his hands instead of the other way round. "Congratulations your Majesty for the arrival of your future heir."

"Thank you Dev. Please sit."

Taking a higher chair of ivory the king sat a little distance from him.

"You would be surprised to know that when I held my first-born in my arms for the first time, I found out, what a father's love is all about. And I was truly ashamed of myself for my cruelty against my own father, I wish you had advised me better. My father who had turned a Buddhist was ready to willingly transfer his power to me. But I was afraid that if he lived his loyal subjects and army might revolt. Now I know that Buddha's teachings can dispel the fear of death in one's mind. My father had forgiven me before he died. I now feel regret from the depth of my heart for my actions."

"I can understand your pain. He was your father after all. By the way I came to also ask for a favour."

"What?"

"I want to bifurcate Siddhartha's Sangha. His many disciples are on my side."

"Why?"

"We have difference of opinion."

"What can I do, to atone my neglecting you in the past?"

"Provide me a park or someplace to have my own Sangha."

"I'll do that but somehow I feel that Buddha's dharma is good for people. I wonder how differently you would teach!"

"I wish you knew him better, Your Majesty!"

"However, when I decide on a place, I'll send a messenger to you."

Thanking him with a bow, Devdatta left without being offered any food. He soon founded his own monastery. And Buddha's clever disciples Shariputra and Maudgalyana came and also joined his group of hundreds of monks. The treacherous monk was pleased with himself that now he had two of the top-most disciples of the Buddha. Under their guidance the new Sangha flourished. But when they both explained Buddha's true word, the monks realised that they had been misled by their new master. And one fine day, behind his back most of his monks except one Kokalita and some others left him, and rejoined the Buddha at the Bamboo grove.

Devdatta's frustrations were increasing day after day like a snowball rolling down the hill.

Tathagat, apart from his Dharma Talks, stayed in a cave at the Vulture Peak provided with a staircase for him to climb up. After Bimbisar's death at the age of sixty-seven his son from Amrapali Jivak, who had studied medicine and surgery at Takshakshila left the court where he had been the royal physician and joined the Sangha.

Ambitious Magadhan king Ajatshattru now wanted to expand his empire towards east. Kashi was already under him which came as a dowry to his mother Kaushalan Devi. She was the sister of Prasenjit whose daughter Padmavati was married to Ajatshattru. Both the families were powerful. The news of Bimbisar's death was kept a secret. But slowly and gradually the truth leaked out to the public. At the same time they also learnt that three attempts of killing the Buddha have already been made. The two sad events combined moved the people of Giriviraj. They had believed that The Buddha sitting at the vulture peak would become their protection and strength. They forgot that real strength lies within one's own self.

After Bimbisar's death his son Abhayaraja from another queen also became a bhikshu, to live a life of no anxieties.

King Prasenjit annoyed with Ajatshattru revoked the land of Kashi given to Bimbisar as his sister's dowry. It was reclaimed by Kaushal jurisdiction. Ajatshattru resented losing the money-paying rich district. To win it back he crossed the Ganga and captured Kashi, defeating the army of his uncle Prasenjit. At Sarasvati the expert and experienced general Bandhul had strong defence system to safeguard the city. The war lasted for six months and in the end Ajatshattru lost and was captured. On Buddha's advice, Prasenjit not only freed his nephew but also advised him to change his advisory committee for better. Ajatshattru could see the affection his maternal uncle, who was also his father-in-law, had in his heart for him and he developed respect for him and the Buddha, whose suggestions Prasenjit had followed. Kashi too was returned to Magadh.

When Prasenjit's beloved queen Mallika died he came to Buddha for solace. Who said, "This is what I mean that attachments have the seeds of suffering."

He advised him. "Instead of mourning for your loss do things for others. Feel their sorrow to forget yours. If you can improve your judicial system and economy, you can help most of your subjects. Healthy economy can reduce crime in any kingdom. Fertilisers and seeds for farmers; loans to small businessmen; retirement funds for those who cannot work. the people below the poverty line should not be taxed. Get cheap accommodations available for the homeless and 'homes' for the widows where they are well-protected."

Prasenjit found a new purpose in life, at Jetavan. While his son from the Shakya queen, named Virudhaka was growing up to be more and more vengeful and impudent in the wrong company of Bandhul's ambitious nephew Digha Karayan.

*****

By the time Prajapati and Yashodhara became elderly nuns giving guidance and care to other nuns, their number of followers had become five hundred at Vaishali under Prajapati and forty-six thousand at Giriviraj, under Yashodhara, respectively.

When Yashodhara had first become nun at Vaishali, people use to give her expensive gifts because she was Buddha's wife. She did not care for popularity so she had moved away to the capital of Magadh.

At the age of hundred and twenty, Mahaprajapati was still in good health mentally and physically, both. One day she thought, 'It seems my son would not last long. He is almost eighty and frail of health. I wouldn't want to live beyond him.' So she told her nuns after the morning discourse,

"My dear friends, companions and nuns, I have made my choice to enter Nirvana. Tathagat would select another leader to guide you the same way I had.

There was a lull before the verbal storm. After listening to a few, Prajapati announced, "Those who want to join me keep sitting the rest can stand up."

*****

After one day given to them to change their minds if they wanted to,

Prajapati visited the Buddha with her five hundred nuns who wanted to follow her into Nirvana.

When Buddha's mother and her close following had faced him in Kutagrahashala grove, she spoke to him with tenderness, "Son, I have come to ask your permission to enter Nirvana. You have paid me in a way that no son can assist his parent. I have sheltered you from sun and the storm and you have protected me from the perils of existence…It is time for me to get away from the bondage."

The Enlightened One replied with great respect, "Mother, you have understood the Dharma well so if that is your desire, so be it but why is your following with you?"

"These are the companions I lived with, all my life. They share my thoughts. None of us wants to outlive their Buddha."

The solemn day was selected by a priest when the sun was in the Uttarayan Phase. The sun at that time was travelling from Capricorn to Gemini and would stay in the northern hemisphere for six months. The period is auspicious because the sun throws its maximum energy towards the Southern Hemisphere where it is summer.

The nuns sat together and calmly held their breaths. Their lungs were ready to burst. Some of them gave up. But the 'Arahants' continued till they lost touch with reality and their bodily functions stopped. Tathagat watched them stone-faced. As many watching them had watery eyes.

Five hundred bamboo 'arthies' carrying the bodies of bhikshunies were being led on the strong shoulders of young monks turn by turn… Flames from pyres could be seen burning till late at night; with ghee and fragrances poured over the bodies covered by sandalwood logs at the cremation ground. The sky turned ochre. Nand and Rahul couldn't stop crying.

For many days good happenings were observed. There was good rainfall and crops were the best that year.

*****

Buddha now preferred staying at the Vulture peak, whenever at Giriviraj. Thankfully availing the steps built by late king Bimbisar for him. Small bridges over tumbling waters and crystal clear springs, added further to the charms of the holy peak. Only a few huts existed around his cave, of his senior-most disciples. Shariputra, Uruvela Kashyap, Maudgalyana, Devdatta, Anand and Upali who use to be the barber at Hamsavati palace and still shaved the Buddha; and above all, Jeevak the son of Bimbisar and Amrapali. He still owned his mango grove but lived in a hut at the base of the Vulture peek during Buddha's sojourn. He was his physician as well as surgeon. Sometimes he would go up to check on the Buddha and then he also enjoyed the beautiful sunset from the sacred top of the mountain.

*****

Chapter - 19

The Fatal Attraction

To fetch clear water out of the (well)
The little maid (Savitri) ran,
'From the (sink-hole) to the palace wing
It was but a bowshot span;
On the sedgy brink where the (Kalpavriksha stood)
Lay a (wounded knight) pallid and wan.[1]

According to the Jain tradition – Once Queen Padmavati, chief wife of Ajatshattru saw from her mezzanine that his two half-brothers with their queens were going past the palace on a special elephant known as Sechanak.[2] One of the ladies was wearing a priceless eighteen layered gold necklace which glittered on her bosom with every swing of the 'howdah.' Padmavati got jealous of her proud expression.

The same night, when Ajatshattru was in an amorous mood, beautiful Padmavati denied his advances, and stood up from their bed.

"What's wrong dear?" He asked, baffled.

"First promise to get me two things."

"Anything you say my love!"

"Procure for me the eighteen-layered gold necklace and the gorgeous elephant, Sechanak!"

The husband had to give in. He sent a request to his half-brothers Halkumar and Vihalkumar to hand over those items to him as gifts. They refused because the two novelties were gifted to them by their father, late

---

1. Gordon's Poems.
2. Sechanak was a rare white elephant. Its skin soft reddish-brown, turning a light pink when wet. It had fair eyelashes and toenails. Such elephants were considered auspicious. Bimbisar had captured this bull when it was in his 'masth' period. He use to water the plants on his own without being given any training.

Bimbisar. At the same time knowing Ajatshattru's temperament they, with their wives secretly absconded to their maternal uncle, Chetak at Vaishali who was the father of Chellana, one of Bimbisar's wives and their mother.

*****

Raving mad Ajatshattru attacked Vaishali with his forces. Amrapali as usual was encouraging her people to join the army so that the enemy at the door could be driven away.

Despite Ajatshatru's two war-inventions, the 'rathamusala' (scythed chariot) and the 'mahashilakantaka' (engine to eject big stones) the victory was slipping out of his hands. In the mayhem, he got cutoff from his unit and was wounded in a hand to hand combat with a gallant Vajjian soldier on foot. After killing him, he exchanged his uniform for his. He started walking away from the remote clump of trees, where he was trapped. Unknown to him, that his army had succeeded in defeating the enemy.

Ajatshattru was trying to sneak out of the gates of Vaishali but King Chetak who seeing his defeat imminent, withdrew within the city walls and closed the gigantic gates with thick pointed nails studded all over. In the confusion Ajatshattru dressed as a Vaishali soldier couldn't escape and was trapped inside. Not knowing the ways he strayed, lost his consciousness and fell in front of a magnificent palace of white marble, outside the city. Before his eyes closed he could hear the soft flip-flopping sounds of waves of the Ganga.

Amrapali had been helping the wounded soldiers with her care and money all day. When she returned home, tired, in the evening, she found another wounded Vrijjian[1] fighter in front of her house. She asked her men to take him up in a bedroom. "I'll have to nurse him at my house, since he is in no condition to be moved. After all he was hurt while fending my Vaishali."

Ajatshattru gained consciousness after a few days of nursing and care. The arrow from his shoulder had been removed and a salve applied. When he opened his eyes he heard the most melodious female voice talking to her pet parrot in a golden cage. Her back, which was turned toward him was most provocatively sensual. In a well-fitted black lower garment with silver spirals going up her shapely long legs. She turned and stunned him in her black, silk 'patta', thrown carelessly over her voluptuous blossom. He couldn't blink his eyes. Her dark brows were arched like bows; her eyes were like cups full of wine and her lips, were pouting and of the coral colour like the Bimba fruit.

When she saw him awake her face lit up like the shiny full moon, and

1. Vijjian is a soldier of Vaishali.

the bimba fruit split open into a dazzling smile. She came near him gliding like a swan and touched his forehead. "Well your fever is gone soldier. Are you hungry?"

He was thinking, 'Yes! I am really hungry… for you.'

Amrapali clapped for her maid and told her, "Please get some light food for our patient and call Malu to come and play some healing symphony."

When Malu came, she saw her friend helping the soldier with his tumbler of turmeric milk with honey. She saw a look in her eyes, she had never seen before. Malu played the strings of lute ever so gently. There was romance in the eloquence of the resonance which was easing his aching limbs.

"What is your name young man?"

"Aman" Ajatshatru answered briefly, charmed by her beauty.

Both their hearts were full of longing when she left for her chamber for the night so that he could heal in peace. Amrapali had felt passion and lust before but never a true love which touched her heart to the core. When Aman gradually came back to his normal self she asked him, "Ready to go home now, your people would be happy to see you."

"There is no one waiting for me. I am an orphan. May I stay a few days longer?" He beseeched her.

"You can't afford me."

"Yes I can!" And he offered her his gold bracelet.

She wore it and spoke softly, "I'll keep it as a token of love from you, 'O' Handsome."'

They both spent the happiest days of their lives together when one day a spy of king Manudev saw the Magadhan Monarch at her balcony and reported to the king. Ajatshattru's sharp eyes quickly discerned the snooper and felt alarmed. Amrapali was not home. So he left a ring with a huge diamond studded in it on her bed and was gone. Borrowing a steed from her stables.

When Amrapali came home she was perplexed with his sudden disappearance and found his ring on the bed. She was fiddling with it, with a frown when suddenly her house was swarming with the king's soldiers. Before she could react her hands were tied and she was taken to the court like a criminal. Her ring being confiscated.

"What have I done? What have I done?"

"Don't ask us. Talk to the Chief". And she was presented to the court. On seeing her, King Manu shouted, "Traitor!"

The beauty queen stood transfixed looking at him with large innocent eyes; not understanding what was going on. She then spoke in a hurt tone,

"Is this the way to treat someone who has nursed a dying Vrijjian soldier back to health?"

Ignoring her the king threw the Magadhan ring in front of her and demanded, "What is this?"

The Royal Courtesan bent to pick it up and turning it over replied, "I don't know why the soldier who disappeared suddenly forgot it on my bed?"

"He was no ordinary warrior. He was Ajatshattru, our greatest enemy."

"I didn't know your majesty, honest! When he was found, you may ask my staff, he was in our Army's uniform."

"This ring has his royal insignia at the bottom."

"I didn't notice."

For the moment she was ruthlessly thrown in the prison till it was found out to what extent she betrayed her own country, towards which she had always professed loyalty.

King Ajatshattru after crossing the Ganga reached Magadh safely. When he came to know that his beloved has been imprisoned he turned into a lunatic. But his ministers suggested, "Your Majesty if you want to plan another attack on the Vrijjian republic be fully prepared. They are not easy to win. The King thought it over. He now had two reasons to attack Vaishali, the capital of Vrijji. One was that Magadhans and the Vrijjians had shared the produce of a diamond mine between their kingdoms. Once he forgot to collect his share so the Vrijjians took it. Second reason was to free his beloved, the most desirable woman of the world at that time and more precious than the diamonds. He sent one of his ministers Vassakara of foreign affairs to the Buddha with a message.

"Tell him, that Ajatshattru, the king of Magadh, has resolved, 'These, Vajjis powerful and glorious as they are, I shall annihilate them, I shall make them perish, I shall utterly destroy them.'"[1]

The brahman messenger was told to listen to his answer carefully and repeat it word by word on return to the king.

When Vassakara reached the Buddha and gave him king Ajatshattru's message he replied, "You have come in time, O messenger, I am about to give my evening discourse to my bhikshus. You are welcomed to attend it and you might find your answer."

---

1. PDF Academia: pp. 6,7. By Ven. Nguyen Linh, 2014, Kelaniga, Sri Lanka; Digha Nikaya, Maha- Parinibbana Suttra, trans. By Maurice Wales. p. 231; Wisdom Publications Boston, 1995.

As the bhikshus gathered at the grove in circles to listen to the Dharma Talks against the backdrop of Eagle Peak, Ajatshattru's foreign minister also joined them. Buddha sat on a bamboo platform and started. Then he asked Ananda, "Please tell the bhikkhus about the seven conditions leading to the welfare of a republican country."

Venerable Ananda answered, "'The (republicans like) Vajjis have frequent gatherings, and their meetings are well attended; they assemble and disperse peacefully and attend to their affairs in concord; they neither enact new decrees nor abolish the old ones, but proceed in accordance to their ancient constitutions; they show respect, honour, esteem, and veneration towards their elders and think it worthwhile to listen to them; the Vajjis refrain from abducting women and maidens of good families and detaining them; they show honour, respect,...towards their shrines...'"[1]

"Bhikkhus," spoke the blessed one, "If we too follow these seven conditions and value equal rights for all, our Sangha would flourish for ever as a democratic republican society. If you all stay many in body yet one in mind; if there is no dissension among all of you nobody can defeat you in your purpose. This is the technique of survival. For you and for everyone else."

Vassakara thought that he meant to say, 'the Lichcchavis of Vaishali were too strong to win.' But when he repeated Buddha's sermon to king Ajatshattru word by word he understood the underlying meaning of his talk.

Soon a competent spy, Balbhadrasen along with a few men was sent to Vaishali to misguide and disrupt the harmony of the members of that republic, and incite them to break their altars of faith. The secret agent succeeded to some extent before being found out. And was executed.

His responsibility shifted over to Vassakara. At Vaishali he mingled with ordinary folks as well as the politicians, to sow the seeds of discord. Which sprouted soon. And the rock of Lichcchavi solidarity developed cracks in it. Ajatshattru seeing the iron hot ready to be pounded, attacked the first ever republic of the ancients; with his powerful army of elephants, cavalry, chariots and infantry men numbering in tens of thousands.

The Magadhan archers on foot, were equipped with quilted cotton jackets and coiled turbans, secured with scarfs tied below the chin and bands of cloth tied across their waist and chests as a protective armour. The lower garment was a loose cloth. One end of which was drawn between the legs and tucked at the back of their waist. However, the elites commanding

1. Digha Nikaya, Maha- Parinibbana Suttra, palicanon trans. by Maurice Wales. Wisdom Publications Boston, 99. 231-232.

the army wore metal armours. At times they also wore Vedic and Epic period, chainmail armour.

Well armoured they jumped into the battlefield with vengeance. There was strong resistance and the battle stretched beyond expectations for the Magadhan Army. Sometimes lady bad-luck sneaked into the camp of their adversaries.

For instance due to lack of wisdom on the part of the Lichcchavis once, a considerable part of their army was swept away in a flash flood, while the unaware soldiers were sleeping safe and sound in the dried bed of a tributary of the Ganga. The horrendous sound of the sudden, crashing waves was heard by the distant enemy.

*****

During the war, Ajatshattru secretly sent a message to Amrapali,

"Be ready to be my Queen sweetheart, I shall rescue you as soon as I destroy the Vrijjian Lords.

Waiting to have you in my arms, once again. Your true love Ajat."

Amrapali's heart sank when she realised that her beauty which was earlier used for the benefit of Vaishali was now becoming a reason for its destruction. She had been released on bail from the prison. She immediately called Mahanaman and asked him to help her dress up in an armour. And she rode a horse and flashing a sword entered the fray. Malu came running and looked at him questioningly. He recited,

'The warrior's look is like thunderous rain-cloud's when,

Armed with mail, (s)he seek the lap of battle. Be thy victorious with unwounded Body: so let the thickness of thy mail protect thee…thy vital parts I cover with thine, armour: with immortality…clothe thee…*

Slaughtering the enemy on her left and right Amrapali proceeded to protect King Manudev, forgetting her hatred for him. As she moved forward tearing the onslaughts and screaming, she saw Vrijjian soldiers falling or fleeing. Their army was routed and the king had fallen from his horse and was being dragged by Ajatshattru. She moved like lightening and cut the rope with which he was being pulled. Manudev stared at her with stony eyes. His body was bruised and battered and wrapped in blood; his royal garments were tattered like that of a beggar's exposing his pink flesh, a would've delight for the vultures if she left him there. She stood aghast. Her dead mother's enraged and helpless face loomed large in front of her eyes.

---

* Lines by Gordon.

"I cuss him with all my heart, he will roll in dust and have a miserable death."

A smile of bitter satisfaction lit up her face for a moment. But was soon replaced by a frown reminding her of duty for her King. She got hold of some escaping infantrymen and got off her horse to help them carry the body to safety. She turned to focus on the situation around her, still holding her bloody sword when she saw Ajatshattru standing next to his chariot, looking at her with longing. She had fire in her eyes as she returned his gaze. She mounted her horse in one jump and kicked him hard and disappeared in a cloud of dust. While the victorious flag of Magadh was waving high in the evening haze.

Sechanaka the elephant died after falling in a pit of vertical, pointed iron rods and blazing fire started by Magadhan Soldiers.

*****

Disturbed by the war, Buddha with his bhikshus had left Giriviraj.[1] They reached the last village of the Magadhan Empire on the bank of River Ganga named Pataligram. He was surprised to see that a new fortress was being built there by Ajatshattru.

As the Buddha and his companions passed the city gate, two officials Sunidha and Vassakara welcomed him and asked, "May we with your permission, call the entrance to the city as the 'Gautama Gate?'"

Buddha complied, "Yes you may."

After spending a night at Patali Buddha wanted to cross the Ganga to go to Vaishali. Sunidha and Vassakara again requested Gautama,

"Allow us to escort you to the 'ghat' for ferry-landing Tathagat and could we please name it 'Gautama Ferry Landing'?"

He agreed again. "I don't object to that."

Five rafts carried the Buddha and his followers to the northern shore of Vaishali, where he spent the night at the Kutagrahshala grove donated to him by Manudev.

Next morning, when Buddha was leaving for alms-collection, Anand requested, "You look tired my lord why don't you rest while we bhikshus would go to receive food from the citizens."

"I know you would Anand. Actually, I want to see the beautiful shrines of Vaishali, for the last time. Udena, Gotamaka, and the shrine of seven mangoes, shrine of many sons, and the Sarandada shrine."

---

1. Girivraj was the ancient name of Rajgrih the Capital of Magadh.

"You forgot the Chapal shrine."

"That too" and he smiled at his own recent forgetfulness.

In the evening discourse he informed his disciples about his future lifespan. 'Today my disciples are instructed, formed and intelligent; they will be able to refute all their adversaries, and pure conduct I have taught is wide-spread throughout the world. Three months from today I shall take Nirvana.'

Having said this, he threw off his vital forces.[1]

'Ayushankhram Khiyanti.'*

*****

The very next day Amrapali reached Kutagrah Park as the bhikshus were about to leave for alms collection. Seeing her disheveled and in painful condition Buddha postponed his outing and let Anand leave with the monks. He told him, "Please ask Shariputra and Maudgalyana to stay with me."

Amrapali related Tathagat the whole story with tearful eyes. She then requested to be ordained as a nun. Her request was attended to right away.

She then resided in the monastery for nuns at Vaishali. Her palatial home had already been confiscated by Vrijjian government. Her faithful friend Malu and lifelong companion, her dance teacher Mahanaman too joined her in the refuse to Buddha.

---

1. Digha Nikaya II.
2. The Vrijji or Vajji, was a confederacy of many clans of which the Lichcchavis were predominant. The capital was at Vaishali and it was governed by an oligarchy composed of a governing body of 7707 members, called The kings. They were the rulers of different Janapada or the 'Clan's Feet'. All these dignitaries and Amrapali were contemporaries of the Buddha and interacted with him.
3. Sculptures made in the Mauryan Period, like those present at the Sanchi Stupa, show the true nature of Magadhan armour of those times. Different terminologies were used to denote coverings for different body parts. Head covering=shiratrana was a turban or a helmet; for protection of neck=kanthatrana; a coat extending till the knees=kanchuka made from various animal skins; hastagana=arm guard, worn on the left arm to avoid friction of bow strings. It was made of leather; for legs greaves, anklets and shoes.
   —Rig Veda, tr. By Ralph T.H. Griffith, (1896), HYMN LXXV.
   Weapons of War.
4. Rig Veda, tr. Ralph T.H. Griffith.

* 'Ayushankhram Khiyanti': waning of the life force.

******

Chapter - 20

End of Yashodhara's Journey

How the great spirit had passed in the moment last
There was little trace to reveal;
On the still calm face no imprint ghast,
Save the angels solemn seal…*

"Almost five months had passed since Mahaprajapati's Nirvana." Yashodhara was telling her companion at the cottage site of bhikshunies at Giriviraj, in Magadha Empire, "Even my work, is all done Krisha Gautami." Then she gave a sheepish grin. "I am sorry I still call you by your original name."

"I don't mind anything you say friend. You never made me feel that I am a boorish simpleton who had lost her only child as an infant. Our Master showed me sense and you spoke to me tender words to make me forget my loss after I had gone from house to house for the so called magical 'mustard seeds,' to bring my son back to life."

"I know and I am so glad that you are way past that state of mind. This time when Tathagat visits Giriviraj I shall ask for his permission to enter Nirvana. I am seventy eight and I've had enough of everything. "

Shocked Krisha stared at her in disbelief. Then, with a creased forehead and a firm expression answered her, "So would I."

Buddha was at the Vulture Peak when Anand conveyed to him Yashodhara's request. "She says, 'O'Venerable One,…the time is mature for me to leave my physical plane. Please allow me to perform voluntary Nirvana. Many of my nuns too want to follow me. We await your answer.'"

He agreed and told Anand, "Please invite them to come to Bamboo Grove, and show the monks, what they have achieved!

The night before they were to face the monks was the night of introspection for Yashodhara. She couldn't sleep, so she came out in the courtyard. The moon felt balmy to her distraught mind, and the stars held a promise of eternal peace. Nothing mattered to her anymore yet she could feel the faint prick of a thorn embedded deep in her subconscious somewhere. She wanted to leave the world with a tranquil consciousness. But a shard of love for Siddharth and remorse for his leaving her in the past; the contradictory emotions, still clung to her like a never ending trail.

In a secret desire, she still felt like thrashing the past with him. 'She had to do something.' She got up still pondering. Walked around with determination to face the emotional struggle in her entire being.

'Have I really forgiven my husband for giving me a life of loneliness of fifty years? I always thought that after imbibing his teachings, I had! But now at the crucial moment of self confrontation, the realisation has hit me that I haven't! The Enlightened one had told us that a realised soul neither holds grudges nor attachments for anyone. But it is not true in my case. Is it?'

A sense of guilt was beginning to cloud her thinking. She immediately chided herself and thought, 'I have come far in religious maturity, I can't be defeated by a negative emotion at the last moment. I need to understand that love is like the twinkling glimmers of the fire-flies. It does not give a continuous light and fades away like the morning dew when the sun-rays dissolve the misty yearning and the stark naked truth glares us in the mind's eye. The brightness of love gives fleeting joy like the koel's cooings are heard only in the mating season yet it does help us ride with hope above the grinds of life. The two emotions of pain and pleasure have played havoc with my feelings. It's time that I quit playing this game of duality and suspend my mind into 'shunya' to become a true 'Arahat', to cross the bridge to Buddhahood.

I'll sit down and meditate till all malice has evaporated from my consciousness. If any doubt would still persist I shall get the opportunity to let my steam out in front of the assembly of the monks. And be free of all misgivings, before the final departure.'

Thinking thus Yashodhara was up meditating all night watching he breath. When pink of dawn tinted the outline of the mountain range she felt the regrets oozing out of her 'self' which had dissolved into nothingness.

*****

1. Gordon's Poems'—Sciences Morales et Politique.

By that time King Shuddhodan, Queen Mahaprajapati, her son Nanda and Yashodhara's own son Rahul had all passed away. Although she was the same age as Gautama, but she wanted to die before him so that he would perform her last rites.

She sent messages to those bhikshunis who had grasped the Dharma well and were teaching in different cities. She encouraged them to keep up the good work even after she was gone. These were sisters, Khema, who had been King Bimbisar's wife, Utpalvarna, Patacara, Dharmadina, and Bhikshuni Bhadra Kapilani.

When she and her nuns settled down in a separate group next to the monks, she noticed the Blessed One sitting in the open surrounded by Bhikku Sangha, ready to convene the Pavarana.

He was speaking in a deep and serene voice. "As per tradition, after the past fortnight now you need to select your new Sansghathera or president for the coming period. That being done, we would need to select two speakers to speak on 'Vinaya' and 'Dhamma' respectively. Since Mahakashyap is busy elsewhere I'll let Modgalyana handle the responsibility.

The meeting went on in complete silence. Yashodhara was totally focused without any thoughts about her chosen self annihilation.

Buddha gently applauded and at times corrected the speakers. Question-answer session followed. There was a small break and the proceedings began once again.

"Honourable gentlemen, let the Order listen to me (and then the bhikkhunies). Today is an Invitation day, Pavarana. If it seems right to the Order, … I may invite you all to answer my query. Is there any deed of mine, either bodily or verbal, which you would censor?"*

Then Shariputra rose from his seat, arranged his Sandgati over one shoulder and answered him with folded hands in courtesy, "None whatsoever Blessed One, according to me". However, "Is there any deed of mine, either bodily or verbal, which the Blessed One would censor?"*

The Buddha responded, "There is no deed of yours, Sariputta,…I censor…"*

After the monks were done Tathagat faced the nuns' group. He posed the same question to the female gathering. In the end he addressed Yashodhara, "Have I in any way bhikkhuni, verbally or bodily, disturbed you in any manner?"*

Yashodhara got up with folded hands, and downcast eyes but said nothing. A wave of murmurs rose and fell. He encouraged her to speak.

"Speak up Yashodhara, in the Sangha everybody can freely argue about anything going on in the Sangha. That is why we have debates.* I know that you are one of the most virtuous and humble women who has reached the stage of Arahat and would attain tranquil nirvana while passing away but I want this fact to be known by other monks as well, for future. So please talk to the bhikkus' Uposatha assembly today and tell them what you have achieved."

Yashodhara faced the male assembly at Buddha's encouragement, she enumerated her various sacrifices as a wife to serve the Buddha to the utmost:

"Waiting upon him, cooking for him, dressing and undressing for him, gave up everything for him including money, treasure, villages, small towns, fields, sons, daughters, elephants, horses, cows, slaves, slave girls, and all the wealth he gave (me) to acquire merit, during (my) many past lives."**

She resumed, "The waters of the ocean 84,000 leagues deep, would not be sufficient for dissolving the salt I used for the gruel I prepared. So it was with water, molasses, oil and lemon that I used ..."**

'I did all this during the many lives, I was espoused to him. In return, he too made many sacrifice to make me happy.' "'I am proud that he like a good husband,' usually supported me. Yet I grieved when he left me, in my present life. But if I and his parents hadn't allowed him to go forth, where would he be today? So when you feel gratitude for him feel for us too. That's all I say."**

Soon after finishing this dialogue she felt a mild cloud of gloom lift off her chest. She felt light and one with the entire cosmos; pervading the whole universe. Her new 'no-self' seemed to have generated in her, immense spiritual powers. She rose up in the sky and gave a discourse on seven kind of wives.

Thus, she proved that the Buddha-hood of Gautama was the result of their joint efforts and the merits were equally shared by them. Then she addressed the nuns who were from Siddhartha's past 'ranivas' and were ready to attain nirvana with her, "Dear friends the fact is that we all had a role to play in Buddha's achievements. If all of you as his consorts hadn't given him satiety in lust earlier, how could he have known the futility of satisfaction of sense organs? Along with Buddha you all too were able to snuff out your own fires of passion."

The elderly nuns were happy that they followed a parallel journey with the Buddha though apart from him, physically.They all died together as Buddha's wives.

---

* Samyukta Nikaya I, Bhikkhus Bodhi, "Vangisasamyuttam", Wisdom Publication, Boston, 1981, pp. 286, 287.

** Source: Buddhist Studies Review 4,2(1987):105-18.

When Buddha had asked them to say something about their merits they all had recited in unison, "We are all Yashodharas!" Their voices echoed in serene environment of the forest. "We are all many in body yet one in mind! Whatever we wanted to say has been expressed by our group leader. We all want to undergo nirvana with her."

Thus, spoke the Enlightened One:

'If a monk (or nun), with deliberate intent, takes with his own hands the life of a human being…or himself gives him a weapon and encourages him to kill himself; or praises death…that monk (nun) should be excluded from the Community.'***

"I prohibit an instigation to suicide, but I also leave each person free to end his own days. For them morality only rules their behaviour in relation to others, but does not impose any duty with regard to themselves."***

'According to my Discipline, suicide is not murder. 'Paap' and 'punya' or fault and merit result respectively from a wrong done to others or a good done to others. It is not by caring for one's own body or killing one's own body that one acquires merit or commits a misdeed.'***

"Suicide is a normal matter in the case of the Noble Ones who having completed their work, sever their last link with the world. Such Arahats or Pratyekabuddhas, who have annihilated all desires and understood the phenomenon and impermanence, they do not get demerits for their actions."****

Yashodhara and her following were listening with great concentration. Buddha's tone had become more pensive. Skinny Krisha Gautami was sitting next to Master's ex-wife. In her last moments she was reminiscing her dead infant son and the episode of the mustard seeds.***** She pushed the disturbing thoughts away and focused.

*****

***Buddha's ideology according to Pali Canon, presented by Etienne Lamont's— 'Religious Suicide in Early Buddhism.' Trans. By Sara Boin-Webb, titled 'Le Suicide religious dans lebouddhisme ancien' in the 'bulletin de l 'Academie Royale de Belgique-Sciences Morales et Politiques, 5 serie, Ll, 1965 – 5, pp. 156–68.

****Nagarjuna's trans.

Pratyekabuddhas are lesser than Buddhas. Although they understand the mechanism of cause and effect but they do not like to spend their energies uselessly in teaching. Arahat is a stage just before Buddha-hood.

*****Krisha Gautami was a farm labourer. When she lost her only child she came to Buddha to revive him. The Enlightened One asked her to get a handful of mustard seeds from a house where no death occurred. When she failed to do so she realised her folly and allowed her husband to bury her dead baby. She joined the order.

On the auspicious day hundreds of bhikshunies were gathered on the ground of grove where they had lived. Those who were determined to leave the transient world, were sitting in a semi-circle on the grass. Krisha had a sharp knife by her side because she knew that only the Noble Ones, who have curtailed all their desires and who strongly feel that their mission in this world is complete, can attain Tranquil Nirvana by gradually diminishing their life force at will, as taught by great Acharyas. The rest could use other means if they chose.

Yashodhara and some others were experiencing various stages of dying. Yashodhara felt herself suspended into nothingness. Her body became stiff and motionless; her feelings and consciousness was gone. She appeared dead yet she wasn't. From the last lucid state she gradually entered Nirvana,* while Buddha, Anand, Sage Kashyap, Kaludayin and others watched from a short distance. It was like a flame extinguishing itself when the oil is consumed.

Yashodhara and several Arahat women passed away peacefully. Krisha and some others 'took to knife' and ended their lives. One elderly bhikshuni was found hanging with a rope around her neck from a sturdy branch of a Neem Tree; many, simply walked to the river to drown themselves.** Two, took the drastic step of cremating themselves alive; a group was calmly sitting or lying in their huts to starve themselves unto death.

Many of the women who weren't able to annihilate themselves were spoken to by the Buddha, " Get up and resume your practice more diligently if you want to control your moment of death, like Bhishma Pitamah of 'Mahabharat.' At this juncture, decide whether you want Nirvana or to stay!"

That month of Uttarayana*** phase was overcrowded with burning pyres. Throngs of people clustered around the ghats, amazed and saddened. They were being reminded of voluntary death of Rama and then the five Pandva brothers of Mahabharat Epic. In the Saryu River of Ayodhya, capital of Saket. The ones who were gone, had lived their lives to the hilt.

Buddha and the bhikshus closest to him sat through the sacred silence in meditation. An era of courageous and worthy women was slipping away. They had enhanced the status of women during the times when they were considered inferior to men by their society.

Their ashes were immersed in the river, on the fourth day. Nice and slow, from innumerable earthen pots. To everyone's amazement, a cloud of dark gray ashes hovered over the surface for a considerable length of time as if bidding 'farewell.' Buddha explained,

"'Do you see O Monks, that dark cloud which is drifting in all directions ...? It is Mara the Malign One who is seeking the whereabouts of consciousness of all those women. But their consciousness is nowhere, because their Nirvana is complete.'

Hence only the Noble Ones who have triumphed over delusion and eliminated passion can, once their task is done, speed the hour of deliverance by voluntarily taking their lives."

With Yashodhara's dissolution into oblivion, Gautama too was passing through the last facet of his lifespan. However, for Yashodhara, duties for the family always came before a desire for enlightenment. If one doesn't leave home yet learns and follows the four Arya or noble truths and the eight-fold path one can become an arahat even as a householder. She was the first one; even before the monks of Gandhara, to sow the seeds for Mahayana Buddhism. But she never received recognition for it.

When she had married Siddhartha she had vowed to be a true companion to her husband, under all circumstance and a true friend to all his relatives. When she married him, she got related to his entire clan in one relationship or another. She achieved her wisdom and spiritual awakening through her compassion and gradual insight into the true nature of things…often through living deeply with others. Yashodhara believed that 'the vehicle of awakening is in the relationship itself, and everyone who is part of it is changed thus. Wrestling through solitude Buddha achieved enlightenment and going through communion, Yashodhara did'.

*****

Chapter - 21

Destruction of Kapilvastu

MARSHY SOIL WHERE BRISTLES CLUSTER,
SCATTERED SEED-PODS, SOWN.
SEEK NOT MANGOES WHERE THORNS MUSTER,
PLANTED BABOOLS ARE GROWN.

'Jatitthaddho dhanatthaddho, gottatthaddha yo naro;

Sannatimanneti, tam parabhavato mukham'[1]

If any man out of pride of his birth clan and wealth despises his own relatives – that is the cause of his downfall. (Trans. dhamma.org/publication)

Since about last two hundred years the Shakyas had ardently guarded the purity of their clan. There were no marriage alliances outside their tribe even when it might have been the politically correct thing to follow.

In the past when they had refused to give a Shakyan maiden in marriage to the powerful kingdom of Panchal a war followed which led to bloodshed and subjugation. Similarly when king Prasenjit, wanted to marry a Shakyan girl, the federation opted to deceive him by sending a slave girl in marriage whose father was a Shakyan but mother, a slave. Her mother's 'gotra' being unknown.

Gautama had warned his council that truth would sooner or later emerge, "You are playing with fire!" Now the time did come when their unwise actions were ripe to bear a bitter fruit.

King Prasenjit's son, from his Shakyan queen Vishabhakshatriya, was named Virudhabha. As he was growing up he was keen to visit his maternal

* This saying in India denotes the Karma Theory: i.e. if one sows the thorny babool, he shouldn't expect to reap sweet mangoes.

relatives, he had heard so much about. At the age of thirteen he was allowed to do so. On reaching Kapilvastu with his band of soldiers and a minister, he was astounded by the ethereal beauty of its surroundings. Tinted with pink evening sun rays, the lumps of clouds were floating around the mountain tops. As the fowl of varied hues glided down towards the sal trees.

He was further impressed by the lavish treatment of a very important person he was given. After enjoying sumptuous meals and taking the tour of the entire palace as well, he was planning to go back.

Laden with expensive gifts he bade farewell to the gathering of his relatives and his grandfather king Mahanaam, after breakfast. They were also given packed lunch for his entourage and himself before they commenced their journey back home.

They had barely left the city when Prince Virudhabha exclaimed touching his waist, "Please Mr. Minister wait! I forgot my sword there."

"Do not worry Prince, I'll send one of the reliable soldier."

The soldier galloped fast and reached the Town Hall where his prince was entertained in the end. There was no one there except a few servant girls who were cleaning up the place. The maid scrubbing the ivory-chair was grumbling, "That low-caste son of a slave polluted our furniture and we have extra work of cleaning them with raw milk." The other, who was scrubbing the marble slab of the table-top on which he ate agreed, "She herself is living like a queen though King Mahanaam had begotten her from his slave-servant."

The soldier was shocked to hear their conversation and was dumbfound when the girls noticed him, "Now what?" They asked, irritably.

"Our Prince forgot his sword."

"Take it. Its lying on the side table!" and they got busy again.

The soldier returned as fast as he could and whispered his secret to the minister.

Prince Virudhabha was busy putting the sword back in it's place.

After reaching Sarasvati the minister went straight to the king, though it was late.

"How was everything?"

"Very good except for one thing.. " "What?" the short tempered king asked.

The minister told him the whole story and advised him to wait till the next morning to take any action. The furious King Prasenjit ordered his chief queen and the prince to be imprisoned the very next day. They were made to wear coarse cloth meant for slaves and were stripped of all their other luxuries. The teenager son was greatly humiliated and the flames of revenge were burning his entire being.

Highly disturbed the king went up on the top terrace of his palace and walked thoughtfully. He could see his wealthy city sprawled out around his palace. His eyes went over the roof tops of mud houses and beyond to the broad sweep of the Akiravati River and yonder stood the mountains and forests. Many orange – robed bhikshus were in and out of the Jeta grove. The king needed a wise friend's counsel at that moment. He had lost his best friend Bandhul due to his own impulsiveness and the only one he could trust now was Gautama. Prasenjit was not spiritual and had hardly changed due to the Master's teachings, although he had reduced his food intake to loose extra seers following Buddha's advice.

King left for Jeta grove on his highly adorned elephant, to meet the 'physician,' Buddha whom he expected to give him a prescription for his suffering. More than anger it was humiliation which was torturing him and the thought that his crown prince is not his legitimate heir but a slave at best.

Heavy with all the turmoil going on in his head the king reached Jetavan and left his elephant outside. Entering the magnificent gate he walked towards Buddha's hut called Sugandhi, meaning fragrance. In this case, of sandalwood. As the Buddha was informed by Anand of his presence he came outside and welcomed the king who had left his sword, turban, fan, parasol and sandals on his vehicle with an attendant. He was offered a bamboo chair while the Buddha sat down opposite to him. Gautama waited for the king to gather his painful thoughts before starting. "Lord I have been betrayed by the Shakyas, my vassals. Did you know?"

"I am afraid I do. Because the Council Members did not listen to me when I had advised them against it. That was one of the reasons why I left the palace. Respect and trust is important in a relationship. Your father and I were on good terms."

"I know! I loved my wife and son but now I've thrown them in prison as traitors."

"Please, your Majesty don't be hasty as you were in the case of Bandhul and later regretted your mistake. Did your chief queen ever give you a reason to complain?"

"No! Never."

"And your son?"

"He had been obedient so far. But now I see a rebellious hatred in his eyes, probably for the entire Shakya tribe."

"That's understandable. He is still young. Give him time. Besides in fact, in our patriarchal society gotra cast is decided by the father. So Vrishabhakshattriya, your chief queen is no doubt a Shakyan maiden. There is no sense in punishing them for no fault of theirs. At the same time stop punishing yourself. Keep it a well-guarded secret from your people, as far as you can."

Buddha's calm voice and friendly advice kept on ringing in the king's ears. He realised that at this stage avenging the Shakyan tribe would not be a wise choice. So much wastage of money, lives and peace just for a false ego. Influenced by Buddha's wisdom, mellowed down Prasenjit decided to bring back his wife and son to their former glory.

Virudhabha unfortunately was constantly living with his fury and humiliation. He started despising his loving father for taking the step of throwing them in the jail, at an impulse. Above all he practiced hard, at marshal arts so that someday he could capture King Mahanaam and torture him to death. The angry lad heard about the techniques his tyrant father, had used to punish his opponents. Who bound his adversaries in chains and tied rebels to the stakes to be tortured with a pointed post piercing through the body.

*****

For Buddha, on the other hand another issue needed to be resolved. He heard that due to less rainfall that year there were chances of drought at Kapilvastu and Devdah. It was the month of Vaishak-Jyeshtha (April/May). Although a dam had been built across the River Rohini by the two cities yet there wasn't enough water to irrigate the crops on both sides.

The farm labourers of both the sides got together to reach at an amicable solution, good for both the sub-tribes. When they couldn't come to a conclusion they hurled verbal onslaughts on each other.

Since endogamy was practiced among the Shakyas, the Koliyans, who too were although originally from the same stock, however tried to demean them by saying-

"The Kapilvastu clan you depend upon behave like common dogs, jackals of the forest, cohabiting with their own sisters. What harm can their elephants, horses and armours do to us?"*

The Kapilvastu farmers retorted in the same belligerent tone-

"You threatened us by relying on your lepers inflicted by horrible leprosy. The Koliya descendants in a miserable plight were banished from the city and lived like animals in the hollow of Kola Trees. What harm can their elephants, horses and armours can do to us."*

The same night Koliya farmers stealthily dug up a canal with their hands to divert the course of Rohini waters towards their own crops. When the news reached the Shakyas, they got ready to take army action. The Buddha too heard about it, at his sojourn at Jetavan and quickly reached the sore shore of Rohini River. He could see its both flanks lined with warriors from both sides. Ready to break into armed hostilities. On seeing the Tathagat, both the armies laid down their weapons as was the custom, and paid homage to the Buddha. A spot at the bank was cleared for him to sit.

Buddha explained to them the importance of unity.

"You are both weak republics, under the dominion of powerful Kaushals to whom you pay regular fealty and salutations. If you be disunited, Kaushals could even take away whatever autonomy both the kingdoms have."

He emphasised, "Blood has more value than water. Both states can irrigate farms on one side. Work together on it and then share the produce. On next such dire situation you can reverse the process." Thus, a war was averted.

*****

Virudhabha had come of age. Prasenjit had grown old like his friend and well-wisher Gautama, who depended on the king to a great extent for the survival of a large part of his monk-community. He would even look the other way if he disagreed with the King's actions at times. Virudhabha also respected the Buddha since childhood but he hadn't forgotten the revenge he had harboured in his heart for the Shakyas.

King Prasenjit found great solace in Gautama's company. On his advice he had also made the life of Late General Bandhul's widow as comfortable as possible. Her name too was Mallika, like that of his late, first wife. Prasenjit had become infatuated by her when once he had seen her sneakily, having a bath. Due to some intrigue of the courtiers as well as his own weakness of the flesh, the king got misled and he got General Bandhul and his son killed by trickery. To make amends on Buddha's suggestion he appointed Bandhul's nephew Karayan to the post of General, the new Commander of his Army.

*****

* A page from 'Maha-Buddha-Vamsa' (The Great Chronicle of Buddhas) by Mingun Sayadaw.

From Jetavan, the Buddha travelled towards Medalumpa, a town in Shakyan territory. It just so happened that King Prasenjit was also in the vicinity with Prince Virudhabha and General Karayana. So he decided to pay the Buddha a visit at the place he was, since it took only half a day's journey, to reach there. Four chariots followed each other along with the King, the Prince and the General in one and rest were vacant.

After reaching the spot where Buddha with his close favourites was residing, the King left his royal insignia in his chariot and moved towards Buddha's hut. Two slaves were carrying some gifts and fruits for the Enlightened One. The King had several things on his mind he wanted to talk about, to his old friend. He was greeted by Anand and Shariputra and led to the wise-one's hut. Gautam was happy to receive him but was concerned with the worried expression on his face. He asked the king, when he settled down, "Why don't you look contented with your life? We are both seventy-eight. We may have some more years to live, so why not perform our duties pleasantly till the end!"

"I understand what you are implying my friend but I have a strange feeling that something is amiss in my life. I sense, something sinister is coming my way."

"Please your majesty, do not lose heart!"

"I'll follow your advice as I always did but my purpose of coming was to spend some peaceful moments in your pure presence. And also …"

"Yes your highness, go on with whatever is weighing upon your mind."

"If we don't meet again I want you to know that I am very grateful to you for all the care and wisdom you had always bestowed upon me."

"The gratitude is reciprocal my friend, may you be guided by thine own light."

The king walked back to his carriage, which was the only one parked there, and did not hold the Royal Paraphernalia. The attendant told Prasenjit –

"Your Majesty, after you left the general took away your crown and everything and ordered the other three carriages to leave with him and the Prince." Your son was not willing to deceive you at first, but the General told him, "The King is too old and weak. It is time, he retired from active duty. If you won't usurp his throne, I will!" "General Karayan and the Prince have left for Sarasvati, so that during your absence, they could announce Prince Virudhabha as the presiding king."

Prasenjit knew it won't be safe to go back home, forthwith. So he ordered his charioteer, "Forget about them and move fast towards Giriviraj instead."

The man did as told. After girthing his sash tight, around his slim waist he took the reins of his four yoked horses. Realising the urgency to reach the gates of Ajatshattru's fort before nightfall. He clucked and urged the horses and spoke to them, "Gallop! Gallop my friends, I'll feed you butter in the end."

Heartbroken Prasenjit reclined in his seat thinking of getting help from his nephew and son-in-law Ajatshattru. By the time he reached his palace, the gates were closed for the night, it was too late. The king and his attendant checked in an inn.

All through the journey Prasenjit had not eaten anything. Dejected, he lay in bed, and fell in a delirious sleep. He woke up seeing Digha Karayana bent upon his prostrate form with a glinting dagger. He screamed, "Help! Help! Some one help me." His attendant came running. Seeing him burning with fever, requested the inn manager to arrange for a doctor. At night he fell seriously ill shivering with cold. Before a physician could be located he died in the arms of his attendants, gasping for breath. In the morning when King Ajatshattru heard of his unfortunate demise, he was extremely sad. He gave his uncle a state funeral, that he deserved.

Vimala Kondana who was previously known as Jivika, son of Amrapali was the physician who came to the palace to confirm King Prasenjit's death. Ajatshattru was planning to send an army to teach Virudhabha a lesson but Jivika advised him against it. He said, "It doesn't matter how he claimed the throne but now he is the rightful king."

Virudhabha after ascending the throne, with the support of Digha Karayana, advanced towards Kapilvastu to equate his insult. He vowed to wash the seat which was washed with raw milk, with the blood of proud Shakyan Princes.

Buddha on learning about the impending attack went and sat under a dried up tree at the border of Shakya kingdom. Virudhabha had been grateful to the Buddha for convincing his father late Prasenjit not to punish him and his mother and give them back their formal rank and privileges, instead. Due to deep veneration for him, Virudhabha asked the Buddha, "How is it that the Exalted One is sitting under this bare tree, all alone? May the exalted one sit under this shady banyan tree within our boundary?"

The Buddha replied, "Great king, the shelter by the kinsmen is cooler."

---

* Prabhava Sutra

The Kaushal king understood that the sage was sitting there to protect the Shakyas. He withdrew his army out of respect for him and went back.

After a few days Virudhabha before advancing again sent a letter to King Mahanaam.

'The clemency we extended to thee and thine we recall;
And the treaty 'twixt us is ended—
We are to storm the wall.
Now tear your parchment to tatters,
Thou shalt make no further use
Of our safeguard; the wind that scatters
The scroll shall shatter the truce.'*

Next he told his soldiers, 'Now saddle your horses and girth them tight,
And see that your weapons are sharp and bright,
Come, lads, get ready as fast as you can.'*

Virudhabha came to attack the city a second time with his forces and after seeing the Buddha sitting there, again returned.

Buddha then left with his group of followers towards Kushinara. And let Kapilvatsu bear the consequences of its own karmas.

After leaving Kapilvastu for good, Buddha walked with small steps due to his old age while Anand and another disciple supported him. They sat down under a shade to rest outside the city of Sarasvati. Wondering when Virudhabha would move to attack, finally the Capital City of the proud Shakyan tribe. Anand looked at the old man squatting under the tree. His shoulders huddled together clasping his both hands in regret. He was ill via a headache to imagine the horrendous fate awaiting the small republic. He then straightened up and closed his eyes as Anand approached him and sat behind, gently pressing his curved aching back.

King Virudhabha in the meantime called one of assassins in the middle of the moonless night. Outside an unusual dust storm rose swallowing everything in sight. The man who had come in dark clothes, hiding half his face with the edge of his black turban stood still. The stony eyed king handed him a pouch of gold coins and whispered, "Take this Jarasandh and find Tathagat to help him attain 'nirvana.'"

* Gordon's Poems.

He disappeared like a ghost unseen by anyone. Through a long secret tunnel.

*****

Protected by a wall of war elephant the files of knights stood erect as a result of their training and discipline; in special uniforms of dyed flax cloth and fastened by munja grass girdle adorned with bits of iron. The cavalrymen wore quilted cotton jackets instead of metal or leather armour due to the heat. Their thickly coiled turbans were tied below the chins with scarves. And the lower garment was a loose cloth worn as a kilt or in the drawer style; one end of the garment drawn between the legs and tucked in the waist at the back. They were waiting for command by their General, Karayan. Who was dressed in a Vedic period style metal and chain mail armour.*

'One line of smart profile, and bearded lips dressing...

One streak of blue sword-blades, one row of red nostrils;

That (exhaled) battle fumes.'** Came charging on an amnesty day.

To avenge the proud Shakyans and innocents too were killed.

The battle from the very beginning was uneven. The archers did not carry the hide shields. Infantrymen with arrows in their hands (sarahattha) were helping them.The big fish was ready to swallow, small. The war conches bellowed, fifes, war drums, cymbals, horns were resounding in the ten directions, and the troops headed by the field marshal and instructed by the king beforehand marched to destroy, the militarily weak republicans.

The royal standard of Shakyas was shivering with fear, backed by a tight row of elephants to provide shelter to the front line of foot soldiers; archers and swordsmen. The horses plunged into the battlefield, drunk on wine fed to them, earlier. The two wheeled war chariots and the thudding hooves overcast the sky with dust and war-cries. As per the war laws the battle stopped at sunset, to be resumed next morning. Nobody counted the days it took to get defeated by the Kaushalas.***

The streets were full of streaming blood with vultures hovering, high above.

---

* 'Why was the Shakya Republic destroyed?' An article by S.N.Goenka. Tr. From Hindi by Vipassana Research Institute (2003).

** Gordon's Poems.

***Battle scene based on 'Ancient India': Auboyer.

Flapping wings, ready to dip through smoky dust, to devour warm flesh.

The jackals prowled, smelling gore, inching slowly towards the dead,

Many a pyres were burnt around, of the slain according to caste.

Digha Karayan, devastated the small republic while Shakyas from many parts of the kingdom fled to safety, of other dominions.****

Those who fled to Piplival were later known as Mauryas. Only king Mahanaam and his family were spared. Virudhabha had special punishment in store for them. All his women, including the queen were enslaved; the treasury was confiscated and the Kaushalan flag flapped proudly on the Kapilvastu fort.

The day after the next, the residents of the palace were chained as captives and dragged to Sarasvati. On the way they camped near a lake to have breakfast.

Virudhabha eager to crush the caste pride of the Shakyans asked king Mahanaam to eat from his plate. Mahanaam requested for permission, to have a bath in the lake before partaking of his first meal of the day. He was allowed.

His second request was to let his people escape as long as he could stay under water. Since he could not escape from under the water Virudhabha agreed to that as well.

The captive king dipped in water, while the soldiers stood, on guard.

The proud head plopped downstream deep, never again, came up.

Which let his beloved countrymen escape, to various kingdoms afar,

Raving mad, forgetting the drowned, Virudhabha moved onto his next, stop.

By evening the exhausted warriors had a stopover at a creek and sat down to eat before sleeping.

The destiny stark, naked, aghast rolled the clouds with thunder,

The night turned dark, the warriors slept, under its blanket; limp.

A downpour ensued and a flash-flood cast, engulfing in its jaws,

Virudhabha and his marauding troops.

Commander Senapati Digha Karayana, happy to get rid of Virudhabha proceeded to Sarasvati with his surviving army and slaves, leaving behind more than seventy-seven thousand corpses.

On reaching Sarasvati Palace the five hundred Shakyani maidens refused to be turned into concubine. They mocked and ridiculed the late king Virudhabha and were ordered by the new king to have their hands and feet cut off along the banks of a pond. They died a terribly painful death but their self-pride stayed with them.

These were the same kind of dancing girls who had repulsed Siddhartha before his 'great departure.' The people of Sarasvati praised their valour.

Karayana did not care. He needed to harness his newly gained power and consolidate his monarchical regime.

The bloody pond came to be known as 'The pool of severed hands.'

*****

Ajatshattru who may have been a Jain or a Buddhist but he had great regards for the Buddha. So when he heard about the destruction of Kapilvastu he found an excuse to attack Kaushal Kingdom. He burnt Karayana alive along with his minister Ambarisha and annexed both Kaushal and Kapilvastu to his dominion. Thus, Magadh became the most powerful kingdom of that period.

Ajatshattru as a prince had been made the Governor of Anga** East Bengal in the past, by his father Bimbisar after winning it in a war. He had stationed his Naval Forces there and overseas trading was brisk.

History repeated itself. Ajatshattru's son, Udayabhadra shifted his capital from Giriviraj to Pataliputtra. After brutally murdering his father for his greed.

*****

When the Buddha arrived in Pava a metalsmith's son named Chunda invited him and his monks to a meal. Before serving he told the Buddha proudly that he had cooked a special dish for them of boar's meat called 'sukramaddava.' For some reason Tathagat asked Chunda not to serve it to the monks. "Serve me only the boar's delight which you so much want me to relish and bury the rest in a deep hole in the ground."

"So be it my master."

After the meal, Buddha thanked Chunda and his wife, "The loving hospitality is appreciated. The food has given me strength after the journey." Then he sat down and taught Dharma to his devotees.

Buddha, whose digestion had already gone weak due to age, developed dysentery after leaving Pava. Yet he asked his Bhikshus to move

* 'Gordon's Poems'.

** Anga, an important city of ancient India is mentioned in Atharva Veda.

forward. "Kushavati* is only about three 'kose' away, we'll reach there by evening." "Whatever you say Lord." But Anand was worried about his condition.

*****

One of the disciple asked Anand, "Does it appear that the great teacher had been poisoned? The brahmans, jealous of his popularity can not be trusted."

"Chunda is not a brahman and he adores the Buddha. I could be wrong though. Due to his Practice our Master's senses have become sharp and he could make out that some thing was wrong with the boar's meat, before anyone else could. Besides he suffered from dysentery the same evening he consumed the meat. Poison should take longer than that to effect his stomach."

"Some poisons work fast. I have a bad feeling about King Virudhabha, because Tathagat came in his way when twice he came to attack Kapilvastu."

"It doesn't matter now, we just need to take care of him.

Before they reached the town, there was a small forested area of sal trees.

Buddha took his bath in the Kakutta River and asked Anand feebly, "Anand please make a couch ready for me with its head to the north between the two sal trees. I am tired and would like to lie down." He then asked him, "Please get some water for me from the river, to drink." Anand went and found the murky water unclean. He wanted to boil some when Tathagat said, "Go again and get clean water."

This time the river water was crystal clear.

When Tathagat lay down everyone noticed that the trees were blossoming earlier than their season and were showering their flowers on the Buddha. Anand turned his face and sobbed like a child. He heard a faint voice telling him, "Now send some monks to Kushavati and tell all the people that tonight, in the last watch of the night, the Buddha will pass away into Nirvana."

'He lay down on his right side and entered the first absorption, and from there to the next, till he reached the ninth absorption. The monks around him thought him to be dead, as in this absorption his sensations

---

* Kushavati, is mentioned in Ramayana Epic as the city established by Kush, Rama's son. It was an insignificant village in the Malla kingdom, to which his and Prasenjit's friend Bandhula too belonged. It was a site where Jainism, Vaishvanism and Shaivism were practiced.

became suspended, muscles and posture became rigid and he lost contact with the environment. In this state he was devoid of consciousness and perfect lucidity. From there he passed into Nirvana.'* The never-ending silent night stood still in its holiness. At the very instance, Kapilvastu's soul was crushed to its very core, by Virudhabha.

Men, women and children came to bid last farewell to the Buddha.

The Buddha's body was carried from its forest grove through the north gate of the city, and from there to a well known cremation ground. He had left instructions that his body be wrapped in linen and cotton encased in an iron vessel and burnt on a pyre. The bones were then divided among the representatives of eight states. The capsule itself was given to Drona who had divided the relics.**

Buddha's body was honoured by the Mallians everyday with fresh flowers scents and music while they sat around it waiting for the eminent follower Mahakashyap to come and pay homage to him before its cremation.

At the time of cremation Buddha's two surviving wives were present, Utpalvarna and Mrigi. 'Bandhula's frail old widow, Mallika unfurled her most precious jewelled cloak over the corpse.'***

*****

Maudgalyana who always spoke the truth, sometimes rather too blatantly, was murdered, due to his resolute belief in Buddha's ideals. Shakyamuni considered Shariputra to be his wisest disciples also died as he too, did not want to outlive the Buddha and was gone of his own choice. The stanza dedicated to him is:

I do not yearn for death,
I do not yearn for life;
I only wait for the hour to come,
Conscious and with mind alert.****

Devdatta ill on his deathbed had been brought to the Buddha by his disciples in Jetavan, Sarasvati. His last wish was to apologise and hear Dharma talk from the Master. Whereas actually he had dipped his nails in a deadly poison to scratch Buddha's ankle, as he would pretend to touch his feet in reverence. But Tathagat moved backwards. And the bent body

---

* Mahaparibbana Sutta.

** Digha II 156 ff. Tr. Etienne Lamotte.

*** Pali Texts. Kushavati was ancient name for Kushinagra.

**** 'Confessions of a Buddhist Atheist' by Stephen Bachelor.

of weak Devdatta toppled from his litter... He rolled from his stretcher and lay on the ground. His frustrations and failures made him feel as if he was burning in flames. His last memory was of great physical and mental agony.*

*****

Buddha had once told Anand, "My success as a teacher was the result of Yashodhara's sacrifices and constant encouragement in subtle ways. I remember her last words, 'Lord, just as the water reaches the sea does not flow back into the river and as the water that goes into the mouth of a... sea-monster does not come out again. I would be gone forever. Never to come back.'"

"But Anand, 'Sun and rain and dew from heaven, light and shade and air.** As long as these exists, Yashodhara's memory would be there."

The Buddhists believe, an envelop of Divine spiritual energy still remains where Yashodhara took her last breath.

*****

* Pali Text Society editions. 'Theragatha', v. 1003.

** Hiuen Tsang, tr. Watters, 1, p. 390.

Chapter - 22

Journey Back to China

Shi Banto put down his pen in the ink-pot and heaved a sigh of melancholic relief. At last he had finished his book based on Yashodhara's life. Who was as beautiful as Urvashi* yet as pious as Sita.* He had written it in Chinese and intended to translate it in Sanskrit for Shilabhadra, and the posterity on his trip to see, the rest of the north Hind.

One day in 642 C.E. when Hieun Tsang and Banto were planning their route back home after the prayer assembly, Shilabhadra came and showed him the invitation from King Harshavardhan of Kanyakubja. "I am suppose to select one scholar for a national debate on Mahayana Buddhism." After catching his breath he went on, "According to me you are the only worthy candidate for this honour. You are allowed one companion."

It was an eighteen day event with three thousand Buddhists, and same number of Brahmins as well as Jains. While the King of Kamarupa (Assam) and those of eighteen vassal kingdoms attended. Hiuen Tsiang in his presentation proved Mahayana was greater than Hinayana and Santana Dharma.** The furious Brahman class connived to kill the Chinese scholars. As a result Harsha made an announcement, "Anyone dared to harm the participants would be beheaded and whoever insulted them, would have his tongue cut out."

After winning over everyone else, the great scholar from China was honoured. Along with exotic gifts, he was to lead a procession, on the royal elephant through the city with people thronging on both side of the road, cheering and waving.

Hiuen Tsiang only accepted one gift, a coat made of buffalo-hide to keep him warm along his journey back home. He also thanked the King

---

* Urvashi was the most beautiful and accomplished dancer of Heaven and Sita was the most pious queen on earth.

** Sanatan Dharma is the actual name for Hinduism.

for the silver and gold coins he had accepted to be used on the way. The elephant was useful for his last lap of journey within 'Yindu' Land to carry his invaluable Bauddha Dharma* documents. Nalanda Vihara which was loosing its lusters day by day received a last boost to its image, due to his visit.

A few centuries thereafter Islamic Invasions destroyed Nalanda as well as hundreds of monasteries. Nine million books were burned by Turkish Muslim invaders called Mamelukes under Bakhtiyar Khilji.

*****

After staying at Kanyakubja for three months, Hiuen Tsiang and Banto were invited by King Harsha to visit the Kumbh Mela at the confluence, Triveni, of three rivers-Ganga, Yamuna and Sarasvati at Prayag. They witnessed the fine line dividing the waters of Rivers Ganga and Yamuna. One being light in colour and shallow and the other, dark and ten times deeper than the Holy One. The largest religious festival of the world was mystifying and spiritual. Millions took a dip in the water to wash away their sins.

Leaving the king, Hiuen Tsiang and Banto travelled around northern part of Hind.

They visited Kausambi, Banarasi, and Vishakha.

The pilgrims had already travelled around 'Dravida Land' of Yindu,' as Hiuen Tsiang pronounced it. He had visited Andhradesa, Amravati and Kanchi before coming to Nalanda and had studied there.

*****

The two travellers finally reached the Sindhu River, along with King Harsha's borrowed elephant and a few mules. He and his followers stayed the night at a small hamlet and reached the river bank early next morning. The previous night had been rather windy. The morning wind, however did not seem threatening enough to postpone their departure.

The crowd was thin on the embankment dotted by men in varied dresses and head gears. Local traders, tall and hefty Afghans, Persians, Mongols, Chinese and a few pilgrims of varied nationalities. By now Hiuen Tsiang and Shi Banto were able to communicate in local languages. Their body language and gesticulations helped. They boarded a large ferry with no roof. The elephant and the mules which needed to be taken across

---

* Bauddha Dharma =Buddhism.

the river were placed in the centre, for balance. The cargo was still tied to their backs. The people mostly stood on the raft, while the boatmen were at the ports ready with their oars. Banto kept on reminding the loaders, "Be gentle with our cargo, it's priceless."

Finally he calmed down after paying the boatswain. Hiuen Tsiang was holding his ornamental religious staff which tinkled due to its rings. His back pack with a tiny umbrella was still intact resting on his back. He turned to Banto, "Well Monkey, are you ready to risk your life again on the Silk Road?"

"I sure am, Master! The trip had been so knowledgeable and exciting. But after spending sixteen years in the Hindu-Buddhist country I felt that Bharatvarsha should have become all Buddhist."

"And why so?"

"For one thing, you have proved, how Mahayana is superior to Hinduism, which might be outdated for present needs of Hindu society. Besides it could politically be beneficial for the country. All around this great country are Buddhist empires and dynasties, like Lanka, Mranna Pran, Tibet, land of the Pashtuns, Tang Dynasty, Kingdom of Agni and many other strongholds of Buddhism in south east and Central Asia. The wave of Islam has started throwing its weight around in the land of the Pashtuns and might even crush Buddhism there, just like Persia is converting the Zoroastrians into Muslims. Now I feel, unless the powerful ruler Harshavardhan, who has converted to Buddhism and whose empire extends till the northwest frontiers does something about it, the cultured Hind might have to bear the brunt of rough and tough Pashtuns. If entire Hind becomes Buddhist then so many Buddhist countries around it could be backing it up to resist their advent. Besides one religion binds a country stronger together."

The Mentor, who had been listening attentively so far, answered.

"I admire your observation son, but that can only happen if all the rulers are aware, united and ready to listen to a central authority. As Tathagat had taught fourteen hundred years ago. That for achievement of unity, all representatives of various states should attend regular meetings for mutually beneficial dialogues."

"You are so right Master. But this kind of harmony cannot be achieved without spilling blood."

"When a child is born, despite all the blood that flows, the end result is gratifying."

I agree. But the defeat and treaty between Pulakeshin II and King

Harsha at the Narmada River made Harshavardhana subdued. He could not extend his power towards south. He also has no heir. If he dies in some war, his kingdom could disintegrate to pieces. Finding the north weak, the greedy Muslim invaders would miss no chance to enter Hind."

"Yes. But I can't forget how bravely he had led his army into the battlefield at Narmada and fought to the utmost. I even admire his gesture of sending a diplomatic mission more than a year back to Emperor Taizong, to China. He is a great fighter and a compassionate man."

Banto nodded, "He is a man of culture and finesse."

Hieun Tsiang was quiet as he heard a distant murmur, while Banto walked up the centre of the boat to check on the animals. When he came back and looked at the sky, a frown creased his forehead. The Master raised his eyebrows and chin at him questioningly. "The sun seems to be slipping behind the darkening clouds and the wind appears erratic, without any direction."

"I won't worry Monkey the boatswain should know his job. Besides we are in the middle of our journey already."

Banto's fears were coming true. A strong blast of air rocked the raft and all were shook up. The Mentor prayed calmly.

Banto went and stood near his precious consignment. He started thinking about Yashodhara and the ups and downs of her life, to keep his mind off the eventuality which might happen.

*****

The few travellers aboard watching the cloudscape, had an anxious look on their taut faces. Yet no one spoke lest it spread panic. The sun playing hide and seek with the clouds had vanished. This time the glaciers in the Himalayas seem to have started melting during the edge of the spring instead of waiting for summer. The water was gushing forth from north to south. The waves became restless and so did the passengers, as the boat lurched and swayed. The rowers were straining their muscles to keep up. While the animals whined, grunted, and shuffled. Master and disciple stood near the animals to sooth them down by patting. An inevitable thunder boomed dangerously and big drops of rain tapped all over, converting to downpour. The angst was replaced by dread. Whimpering and shitting mules started pulling at their binds. Chaos was near, laden with fear!

The panicked elephant tried pulling his chains which tied it's feet to thick iron rings on the raft. It succeeded in walking away and went down the tilted boat followed by the rest, in freezing waters.

There was hue and cry as the rest of the passengers clung to the upturned boat. Since the opposite bank was already in sight some youths started swimming to the shore. The books and the Buddha statues, wrapped in makeshift waterproof material went down. So did Banto, trying to retrieve those. His dripping head popped up while he held the strong cable tied to the larger parcel carried by the elephant. Petrified Hiuen Tsiang who was clinging to the capsized ferry for his life, got hold of the rope and with help pulled the heavy freight up on the bottom of the barge.

Banto went down again for the smaller package with the diving manuscript of Yashodhara and fifty other books. There were also seeds of exotic plants which Hiuen Tsiang had lovingly collected. The remaining crowd pulled each other to the safety of the hull. The rowers who lost their paddles managed to get hold of some poles and tried steering the upside-down ferry towards shallow waters as the mules swam alongside. The elephant reached the shore on its own.

Desperate Banto was left behind almost in the middle of the river. One of the ferrymen who still had a rope coiled around his shoulder had thrown it towards the drowning man, with a firm thick knot tied at the end while shouting over the din, "Hold fast to the knot, a whirlpool is heading your way." Retracting the last bundle he tried swimming back towards the cable with one hand. Unpredictably the current became rapid and he was being pulled down the stream. He chose to let go of his lifeline but kept on holding the package containing, 'Yasodhara,' with one arm. Struggling to swim backwards with the other. A murderous pull of the choppier waves aided the deadly vortex which sucked him with vengeance. His shocked mind became numb and he sunk into the tides of eternity, along with his idol Yashodhara. Once again a great queen like Sita and a kind soul like Banto were lost into oblivion.

Apart from two sad casualties the rest of the survivors reached the shore along with some cargo and the mules. Shaken and soaked they all thanked their individual gods for saving their lives. Hiuen Tsiang was heart broken to lose his faithful companion along with his precious Yashodhara. Some guards escorting him from Kanyakubja, helped him organise things till he was ready to travel again. His sedate look was beguiling to his companions, his heart was still leaping up and down-falling with the turbulent waves which took away an innocent Buddhist, whom so many daring young men tried to save, yet lost the battle.

The east bound pilgrim started his journey with a heavy heart and crossed the rugged mountainous terrain of 'Land of The Pashtuns, to reach the Khyber Pass, the Gateway of Bharatvarsha.* The gorge looked as if God had cleaved the mountains with his giant axe in the middle.

It took him seven days to reach Hindukush Maintains. The mules and the horses found it hard to walk on the craggy terrain and at times, lose rocks. So everyone got off their backs and walked with the help of sticks. The distant summits had scanty growth of trees. The ones on the Plateau had their trunks covered with lichens and moss. The velvety mountains were scattered with shrubs here and there. But there was no sign of springs or hamlets. Their guide a local, warned them, "Try and descend, as fast as you can to the first community dwelling you can find. People living in dire conditions are honest and helpful. Otherwise, the life threatening cold would bury us alive in the snow, despite it being springtime."

They rode their horses at times when the going was smooth. Hiuen Tsiang always felt the sound of an extra pair of boots by his side. When he would look over his shoulder there would be no one. Once he heard a soft whisper through the swishing wind, "Master, be careful!" He looked around at others who were following him but their faces were blank.

Some porters arranged enough water to relax their parched throats. As the group started their descent, the mists started climbing up the mountains to turn into clouds. It was still after noon and their side of the mount was well lighted while its back had gone dark. Going through the dense fog, squealing winds and rumbling clouds made them feel that they were on some other planet. Their fears dissolved in the vapours when they witnessed random patches of white aromatic, scented flowers. The melting glaciers were spiraling their water downwards to make passageways for travellers; lined on the two sides by red and blue blossoms.The approaching evening converted the monotonous thudding sound of the hooves into distant booms of life saving village drums. The huffing and puffing slowed down with a breath of fresh hope and soon they found shelter in a hospitable hamlet. The hut they occupied was made of piled up stones and thatched roof. But the local warm food felt like 'mana dew' out of heaven. It had started raining outside as they ate. It continued all night accompanied by the echoes of roaring thunder in the hills.

After a distracted sleep they woke up to the welcoming sun which had torn the dark clouds to shreds. After hot spiced tea, 'kahava' with dry snacks followed by yak's milk they were ready with their well fed animals. Hiuen Tsiang offered the host two blankets and some cash payment in silver coins. Outside, the chief of the guards from Kanyakubja, started talking to the renowned Buddhist Scholar and his four followers from Nalanda. He smiled and spoke, "We part here Master. Have a safe journey! Beyond this mountain lies the road to the eastern regions." And he bent slightly, folded his hands in a Namaskaram and bade his goodbye.

"Zaijian my friends!"

"Xie xie!" Thanked Hiuen Tsiang.

The master heard his own words being echoed in monkey's voice as well. He developed goosebumps on his arms. Bewildered he marched forward on the Silk Road after seventeen years.

*****

On their way back, the Buddhist monks first stopped at Dunhuang, a thriving Silk Road oasis. Here they met many Sogdian Merchants (Zoroastrian or Parsi) who were coming from Queshqer on camels with bales of silk, heading west to their royal customers of Persia and the Mediterranean. These were skilled traders of Central Asia and acted as the middlemen in the Silk Road trade. Hieun Tsiang was glad to hear that they educated their boys soon after they turned five and started teaching them business early.

The two parties exchanged news. When Hiuen Tsiang was told by one of the Sogdian trader with a sharp nose, "Sorry friends the king Ch'u Wen-tai has expired, and the new king has bad relations with Tang Dynasty," Hieun Tsiang changed his route around the Taklamakan Desert. He selected the shorter, southern road for onward journey with a sad heart.

Qushqer was situated at an intersection of the Silk Road on a fertile land.

It was also the converging point of northern and southern routes around Taklamakan desert and roads coming from the valley of the Oxus, Afrasiab (Samarkand in Uzbekistan), Yutian (modern Khotan,) and from Hind. This is where the crops of corn, rice, wheat and cotton were nurtured by the Qushqer River in Tarim Basin.

The five monks stayed at the vibrant city for two days. They dined on wheat- bread and goat meat and relished the fruits being sold by vendors, in huge baskets. They rambled through the wooden stalls where dried vegetables hung in strings. A young monk couldn't stop himself and admired the luscious grapes and melons. He evaluated the merchandise before consulting his mentor.

People of various cultures abounded there, in colourful flowing garments. Chinese, Mongols and Tibetans. A few Christian Priests were walking towards their churches. Some Turkish men sat cross legged outside a caravan Sarai where famished bellies were entering to satisfy their hunger.

"Did you notice my friends," Hiuen Tsiang asked his followers, "that the people here have flattened their babies' heads, tattooed their bodies and they have green eyes?"

"Right Master, I find it bizarre and also, that all kind of slaves of different nationalities are being sold in today's special bazaar."

The youngest monk informed the others, "I just saw a Chinese walk away with almost an eleven year old girl. He had been haggling for the price and ended up paying forty silk bolts for the underage girl he just purchased."

"How shocking! One of the monks exclaimed, "But when did you notice all that?"

"When you had gone to enquire for a place to stay the night."

"Good observation young man," replied the Master. "The price of a camel here is mere forty bolts of silk. At least she is considered more valuable than an animal, although she may be treated like one."

Since Hiuen Tsiang had the spiritual charisma his following kept on increasing. The coins gifted by the king of Kanyakubja were a big help in bearing their upkeep. They walked past the shabby awnings where several people were bargaining for silks, terracotta or glazed ceramic figurines of warriors or merchants; rugs, furs or potteries. The coins used were gold, silver or copper. From different territories, with strange faces on them.

By evening the merry-making drinkers crowded the makeshift pubs. Their carousel made the Bhikkhus walk away faster towards a monastery for the night. Along with the burdened mules.

The monks left the monastery early next morning. One of the Hindu bhikshus exclaimed, "I never expected the whether to be so pleasant!" And looked at his companions for approval."

"Just let the sun rise!"

*****

Hiuen Tsiang was riding his horse, followed by the mules. While his entourage was hitch hiking on camels. They had entered an endless bubble of yellow haze. The heat waves thrashed their faces and the sand tried to pierce their scrunched up eyes. In some low lying landscapes, trees were visible at the fringes.

Yutian was the next oasis city. A long distance away. An outpost of Indian culture. Their path at times was strewn with, human skeletons

---

* According to religious/historical texts Puranas of 5th CE, King Bharat had conquered the entire Jambudwipa or India which included seven countries of today. Nepal, Bhutan, Pakistan, Bangladesh, Burma, Maldives, and Srilanka. India was named Bharatvarsh after him.

Sharp nose—characteristic of Sogdian Men.

scattered in the sand. The bleached-out bones were reminders of the dangers that stalked the world's most important trade route for commerce and ideas. 'Sword wielding bandits, preyed on caravans,' for their cargo of silk, tea, and ceramics, going westwards or horses, gold, gems, oils musk and expensive spices from Hind, coming eastwards.

In 643 AD, Hieun Tsang reached Yutian within Chinese Territory with his followers and mules laden with 657 Sanskrit Texts on Buddhism. His special interest being Yogachar or 'Consciousness-Only.' Exhausted from their fearsome journey they rested for a couple of days before planning further.

People of this oasis worshipped mice because some time in the past, during a battle, mice saved the kingdom. The place was also known for its jade, silk and hand woven carpets.

The Buddhist master with his disciples had taken shelter in an inn. After evening prayers and free dinner he sat on a fur-hide in a pensive mood, pondering. Tibetan bhikshu Kumarjiva asked, "Master, why are you so thoughtful?"

"I had a dream last night, my son and it made me think about the history of this land."

"Tell us all about it my mentor. Please enlighten your followers."

All the bhikshus sat in a circle around a flaming-stove, courtesy the owner of the Caravanserai.

Hieun Tsiang, who sat on a higher cushion started. "One fierce night, deep into the faded past, their were rumblings and thunderings, which the Buddha heard far away in his cave at Vulture Peak in Yinduland. He sat meditating while Shariputra and Kondlana, his disciples watched. I dreamt that the Buddha has flown here with a large entourage. Blessing the creatures of a huge lake surrounded by Gashringa Mountains he requested Shariputra and divine Yaksha King Vaishravana, 'Please use your super powers to drain this lake so that a fertile land could be created for people of this desert. Which would be known as Tarim Basin.' The earth quivered as the earthquake rose in velocity and flash rain poured down with intensity. With an ear-deafening echo the mountain split opened at one point and the water gushed forth through the gorge towards River Gyisho (probably River Karakax).

The light from the flames made weird shadows on the stone-wall as the young men held their breath while the wind outside was whooshing and whizzing past the narrow window. The master continued.

"I had read this prophecy in the sutra-'Questions of Vimalaprabha',one of the daughters of King Prasenjit. It says...The bodhisattvas accompanying the Buddha were seated on floating lotuses in the lake, each above particular underwater locations where the stupas and monasteries of future land appeared. Canonical Tibetan scriptures also prove this."

After resting well Hieun Tsiang sent a letter of apology to Emperor Taizong of Tang Dynasty the very next day. In which he requested to be allowed to enter Changan, capital of his kingdom.

He was not only forgiven but applauded. Two white horses were sent for him and a companion. The master missed Banto acutely but allowed one of the senior monks to ride it. But the animal whimpered, whined and stood on its hind legs to shake off the rider. He refused to let anyone mount its back. Hiuen Tsiang whispered ever so softly, "Is that you Banto?"

"Yes Master! And I also was able to retrieve my script of Yashodhara."

The master took a deep breath and kicked his horse. He had worn his new shoes, a gift from King Harsha which Banto so admired. They were made up of a replica of and embroidered with rainbow-coloured silk threads, clouds.

Hieun Tsiang galloped through the Yumenguan Pass, and waited at the square castle for his followers to reach him. He could see the brilliant rays coming from the large, black-green luminous jade inlaid on top of the building, to be used as a beacon for the tinkling bells of lost caravans, in the desert at night.

The procession then moved towards the waiting and cheering crowds of the capital.

It was the first time China and Hind exchanged diplomatic convoys. Both countries learnt from each other and cultural exchange took place for more than half a century.

*****

Source: Brook Larmer, National Geographic, June 2010, as well as Travelogue of Hiuen Tsiang.

Note: Hiuen Tsiang's translations of Sanskrit scriptures were done in a cumbersome style. Earlier translations by Kumarjiva are much easier to understand. Yet what Hiuen Tsiang produced was "the fruit of seven centuries of Indian Buddhist thought."—Grousset, the founder of Mahayana idealism.

*****

Post Historical Events

After the destruction of Kapilvastu by Virudhabha some of King Mahanam's family members under the cloak of dark were able to escape, towards south. Travelling under hardships they took a long trip to reach Vadisagiri. They became merchants and later the daughter of one of the descendants, Shakyakumari Vadisadevi became the first wife of Ashoka, before he became the emperor.

Among other Shakyans who escaped was Pandu, who crossed the River Ganga and on the opposite bank founded a city. His daughter was Bhadracanchan who later married Pandudev, King of Lanka and founded many community villages there. Those who had escaped towards Himalayas and were called Mauryas had built a city known as Moriyanagar because the spot echoed with the screams of peacocks. Ashoka belonged to this dynasty, eight hundred years after the Buddha. Thus, was his kin, and grandson of Chandragupta Maurya. He brought to reality the vision of the Buddha of ideal political administration. He also encouraged his people to pursue Buddha's moral ethics. He used two means to do that legislation and persuasion. He followed the two most important precepts of the Buddha – non-violence and generosity or sharing with the society.[1]

However, he had exiled his son Kunala who was adopted by king of China. He later became founding ruler of Khotan, where people of India and China are said to be the original settlers. Khotan influenced Tibetan culture in the future.

By medieval period Islam spread its tentacles towards Central Asia and the Buddhist culture in Khotan became a thing of forgotten past. The famous trade route lost its significance under the marauding Mongols and became disrupted and non functional, till Tamerlane revived the oasis belt.

---

1. 'Ashoka The Great ' : Originally written in Dutch Tr. By J.E.Steur; author: Wytze Keuning. (2011) Roopa Publication.

Afterword

Beautiful Queen Yashodhara suffered the fate of Queen Sita, King Rama's wife, one of her ancestors. They both were accused of being unfaithful to their husbands. Although their husbands knew better. They both had sons they lovingly nurtured till they could. Princess had a happy childhood, passionate love life which barely lasted a decade. Then, pain, loneliness and humiliation of an abandoned wife like that of Sita.

In the end Sita disappeared in the womb of Mother Earth and Yashodhara undertook voluntary nirvana.

History of Buddhism would be incomplete unless Yashodhara's contribution is accounted for. Information about her is scanty but reading between the lines could give us a fairly near true picture of the role she played in advancing Buddhism, especially among the women of the era.

I as a female Buddhist practitioner of twenty years, am grateful to her. Because she was the first one to approach The Buddha for women's participation in the Sangha.

Bibliography

1. Buddha Charita – Trans. By Beal Samuel – Life of Buddha in Sans. by Ashvaghosha.
2. Stars at Dawn – Wendy Garling.
3. Mahavastu (Sans.) Trans – by J. J. Jones (London).
4. The Buddha's wife – Janet Surrey & Samuel Sam.
5. Romantic legends of Shakya Buddha (Sans.) Trans. By Samuel Beal.
6. Life of Princess Yashodhara – Suneety Devee, Bhuben M. Mukarji.
7. Nidankatha – Tr. – Rhys Davis.
8. Old Path White Clouds – Thich Nhat Hanh.
9. Glimpses of world religions – Jawahar Lal Nehru.
10. Kamasutra – Vatsyayana – Trans. – A. N. D. Haksar (New York – Penguine Books).
11. Lolitavistara Sutra – Trs. By Dharmchakra Trans. Committee from Tibet.
12. The Buddha – (Poem) – Krishna Srinivas.
13. The Lotus Sutra – Trans. By Burton Watson.
14. Yashodhara – The wife of Bodhisattva – Rajani – Obeysekere (Sri Lanka) Trans – from Palm Leaf manuscripts – London.
15. "Life of Buddha, Early Buddhism and Indian society" – A thesis by Mahendraatta Jaidy – Thailand. (I. B. College).
16. Mahayan Buddhism of Nichiren Daishonin (1300 CE Japan) Dissertation by Kusum Kapoor – Dayalbagh Institute a Deemed University.
17. Manu Samhita: Hindi Trans.
18. Buddha's Times – John Keay – 'The Epic Age' (900 – 520 BC).
19. Daily Life in Ancient India – Jeanine Auboyer.
20. Confessions of a Buddhist Atheist – Stephen Bachelor.

21. The Buddha – Trevor Ling.
22. Abhinishkramana Sutra – Trans. Samuel Beal – Publish. Motilal Benarsidas.
23. Gordon's Poems – 1894 – Melbourne – A. H. Messina & Co. Printers and Publishers. By —Adam Lindsay Gorden.
24. The Legend of Amrapali _ Anurag Anand.
25. Si-Yu-Ki: Buddhist Records of the Western World—Trans., Samuel Beal.
26. The Silk Road Journey With Zuanzang. (Penguin)—Wriggin, Sally.
27. Yashodhara And The Buddha : A novel by Vanessa R. Sasson. (Bloomsbury.)
28. Religious Suicide in Early Buddhism: Etienne Lamotte. *Source:* Buddhist Studies Review.
29. Bride of the Buddha: Barbara Mc Hugh
30. 'Baudh Dunt Kathaen': (Jataka Tales) Hindi by C.B. Varma
31. The Bhagvad Gita (Hindi).
32. Research paper by Dr. G.R. Krishnamurti and Dr. Chandrasekhar Mujumdar.
33. Tulsidas' Ramcharitmanas : in vernacular Awadhi and Hindi.
34. Mahabharat Epic: composed by Rishi Ved Vyas. Sanskrit, translated in Hindi.
35. Articles from 'Acadmia': (1) 'Women in Buddhist Literature with particular reference to Jataka.' By Panyadeepa Mog, PhD, Gautama Buddha University, Greater Noida, U.P. (2) Non-dualism: Fabian Volker: Encyclopaedia of Philosophy and Religion, (2021) (3) 'The Buddha favoured Monarchism or Republicanism?'
36. T. N. Nguyen Linh (N.T.N. Bich), 2014, Kelaniya Sri Lanka. (4) Sacrificial Sutras: Natalie D. Bummer.
37. Saha star Tal Trek.-Tarun Musafir.
38. National Geographic, June 2010-Brook Larmer.
39. The Ancient Past: Burjor Avari.
40. Buddha: Enlightened Warrior – History-net.
41. Magadha Kingdom- Paper by Anindita Basu.
42. The Art of War in Ancient India—P.C. Cakravarti.
43. Political Violence in Ancient India. By U. Singh.
44. Paper by Dr. Awantika Lal. Specialising in military operations.
45. R.C. Majumdar: History and Culture of the Indian People, II Vol.